MISSING MAN

MISSING MAN

The American Spy
Who Vanished in Iran

BARRY MEIER

Farrar, Straus and Giroux   New York

Farrar, Straus and Giroux
18 West 18th Street, New York 10011

Library of Congress Cataloging-in-Publication Data
Names: Meier, Barry.
Title: Missing man : the American spy who vanished in Iran / Barry Meier.
Description: First edition. | New York : Farrar, Straus and Giroux, 2016. | Includes
  bibliographical references and index.
Identifiers: LCCN 2015037598 | ISBN 9780374210458 (hardcover) | ISBN 9780374712792 (e-book)
Subjects: LCSH: Levinson, Robert A. (Robert Alan), 1948– | Spies—United States—Biography. |
  Missing persons—Iran—Biography. | Hostages—Iran—Biography. | United States. Central
  Intelligence Agency—Officials and employees—Biography. | Rescues—Iran—History—
  21st century. | United States—Foreign relations—Iran. | Iran—Foreign relations—
  United States. | United States—Foreign relations—1989– | BISAC: BIOGRAPHY &
  AUTOBIOGRAPHY / Political. | POLITICAL SCIENCE / Political Freedom & Security /
  Intelligence. | TRUE CRIME / Espionage.
Classification: LCC E901.1.L48 M45 2016 | DDC 327.12092—dc23
LC record available at http://lccn.loc.gov/201503759

Designed by Jo Anne Metsch

Our books may be purchased in bulk for promotional, educational, or business
use. Please contact your local bookseller or the Macmillan Corporate and
Premium Sales Department at 1-800-221-7945, extension 5442, or by e-mail at
MacmillanSpecialMarkets@macmillan.com.

www.fsgbooks.com
www.twitter.com/fsgbooks • www.facebook.com/fsgbooks

10 9 8 7 6 5 4 3 2 1

FOR ELLEN AND LILY

Contents

MISSING MAN

Prologue

Rain splattered against the windshield of her silver-gray BMW as Sonya Dobbs pulled up to a security gate blocking the street. It wasn't much of a gate, at least by Florida standards, just a long, rolling fence stretching across a road. She punched a code into the gate's keypad. After two unsuccessful tries, she used her cell phone to call her boss, David McGee, who opened the gate from inside his house. It slid back and Sonya drove through, a laptop resting on the passenger seat.

Sonya's Saturday night had started very differently. She had planned to spend it sorting through photographs. Sonya worked as Dave's paralegal at a large law firm called Beggs & Lane located in Pensacola, a city at the western end of Florida's Panhandle, the narrow, two-hundred-mile-long coastal strip tucked between the Gulf of Mexico and the states of Alabama and Georgia. Sonya wanted to carve out a second career as a photographer, and she had been on a chase boat the previous day in Pensacola Bay, snapping pictures of a new oceangoing tugboat, christened *Freedom*, as it went through test maneuvers. The photos showed the big black and gray tug slicing through the foamy water under a blue sky filled with white, puffy clouds. A maker of some of the boat's parts had ordered pictures, and Sonya was happily spending her Saturday evening playing with different ways to crop the images.

Then the phone rang, and she heard a familiar voice on the other end of the line. Over the past three years, she had spoken to Ira Silverman hundreds of times, if she had to guess. Most days, the retired television newsman phoned Dave at least once. Their conversations were always about a mutual friend, Robert Levinson, a former agent with the Federal Bureau of Investigation turned private investigator. Sonya had never met him, though she felt as if she had.

Bob disappeared in 2007 while on a trip to Iran. Dave and Ira, who had both known Bob for years, were trying to help his desperate family find him. Months after the investigator went missing, Dave convinced Bob's wife, Christine, to ship his work files to Beggs & Lane. Sonya had read through them and organized the reports. She was a natural snoop, at ease with computers. Before long, she had tracked down Bob's email accounts and figured out the passwords. As she walked through the record of his life, she learned a secret that Dave, Ira, and Chris already knew: the explanation that U.S. government officials were giving out publicly to explain Bob's reason for visiting Iran wasn't true, at least not the part that really mattered.

Since the investigator's disappearance, there had been reported sightings of him in Tehran's Evin Prison, the notorious jail where political dissidents are tortured or killed. Some tipsters had come forward to claim that the Revolutionary Guards, the elite military force aligned with Iran's Islamic religious leaders, were holding him at a secret detention center. His family had made public pleas for information about him, and the FBI had assigned agents to the search. But the hunt for the missing man had gone nowhere.

Ira's call was about an email he had gotten earlier that Saturday containing a message that read like a ransom note. He had received similar emails before and had passed them on to the FBI. But this one wasn't like the others. This email had a file attached to it. Ira told

Sonya he couldn't figure out how to open the attachment and was forwarding it to her to see if she could. The email read:

This is a serious message

Until this time we have prepared a good situation for Bob and he is in good health. we announce for the last ultimatum that his life is based on and related to you

You should pay 3000000$ (in cash) and release our friends: Salem Mohamad Ahmad Ghasem, Ahmad Ali Alarzagh, Ebrahim Ali Ahmad.

We are waiting for your positive answer without any preconditions. We would announce our way to receive the money.

Sonya clicked on the email's attachment, but nothing happened. She didn't recognize the file's extension, the three-letter code that tells a computer which program is needed to open a file. She suspected the extension—.flv—signified it was a video file, and she hunted around on the Internet for information about a recommended player. Finding one, she downloaded the software and clicked again on the attachment. This time, the file launched and a man's gaunt face appeared, seemingly staring out at her. He had closely shorn gray hair, a moustache, and sunken cheeks covered by stubble. He started speaking in a deep, raspy voice. Strange music played in the background, rhythmic instruments accompanied by a singer's droning call. After a few seconds, the camera pulled back and Sonya could see that the man was sitting in front of a gray stone wall in what appeared to be a stark prison cell. The polo shirt he wore looked threadbare and hung on his frame as though it was several sizes too big for him. Part of the shirt's right sleeve was gone. There was nothing immediately threatening about the video. Masked jihadists weren't standing over the man brandishing guns or swords, and there wasn't a black political banner hanging behind him. Still, the video was disquieting. The man's arms didn't move as he spoke, suggesting that his hands, which couldn't be seen in the video, might be lying manacled in his lap. He struggled to stay calm and to keep his words measured. Occasionally, his voice came close to breaking and he would briefly close his eyes, pause, or gesture by turning his head. He said:

> *For my beau— my beautiful, my loving, my loyal wife, Christine . . . and my children . . . and my grandson . . . and also for the United States government . . . I have been held here for three and a half years . . . I am not in very good health . . . I am running . . . very quickly out of diabetes medicine . . . I have been treated . . . well . . . but I need the help of the United States government to answer the requests of the group that has held me for three and a half years . . . And please help me . . . get home . . . Thirty-three years of service to the United States deserves something . . . Please help me.*

Dave McGee opened his front door and ushered Sonya out of the rain. They went into the kitchen, where the lawyer's wife, Joyce, was waiting. Sonya put her laptop on the table, opened it, and launched the video. Dave wasn't positive that Bob was the man on the tape. The last time he had seen the former FBI agent, he resembled a big, overweight teddy bear with a mop of hair. The man on the tape was so thin that the skin on his throat sagged. Dave realized that the only way to know for sure was to call Christine. Sonya dialed her number, and when Chris answered, she put her cell phone next to the computer and clicked on the video. A few moments passed.

"That's Bob's voice," Chris said. "That's Bob."

1

The House on Ninety-Second Street

When they were teenagers, Bob Levinson's oldest sons thought the greatest way to spend a Sunday afternoon was to sprawl out on the living room couch with a bag of Famous Amos cookies and watch Mafia movies. Dan and Dave were big fans of *Goodfellas*, and Dave had memorized nearly every line spoken by Ray Liotta, who portrayed Henry Hill, a mobster in the federal witness protection program. The boys would crack up as Dave reeled off dialogue. Their father liked to sit nearby, at the kitchen table reading a book. But sooner or later, he would get up and walk over to his sons with a disapproving look. "I used to put guys like this away for a living," he would remark, and tell them again he thought movies like *Goodfellas* romanticized thugs. Dan and Dave knew it came with the turf when your father was an FBI agent. "That's cool, Dad," they responded before going back to the movie.

Bob and Chris had seven children. The three oldest were girls, Susan, Stephanie, and Sarah, followed by Dan and Dave, then Samantha, and finally, Douglas. Their children had been born over sixteen years and they were all brought up to revere the FBI; they liked having an agent for a father. As kids, they would race to the front door when they heard it open in the evening because the first one to greet him got to pull off his shoes. He always came back from FBI trips with presents. One time, he handed out tee shirts decorated with pictures of pineapples, a reference to "Old Pineapple Face," the name coined by Panamanians for Manuel Noriega, their pockmark-faced president who was arrested by the United States on drug trafficking charges. The kids helped him keep his files organized by stapling his expense receipts into them. None of them realized some of the receipts were records of cash that their father had paid to criminals and other sources for information.

For Bob and Chris, raising a big family on a $90,000 FBI salary wasn't easy. The couple's first home in Coral Springs, Florida, where they moved in 1984 after Bob transferred to the bureau's office in Miami from New York, was tiny. The three oldest girls shared a bedroom outfitted with bunk beds and a trundle underneath that was pulled out at night. When a new baby arrived, Bob created a nursery by cordoning off part of the dining room with a curtain. Chris never went food shopping without filling her purse with coupons, and a big family night out meant going to McDonald's on days when two hamburgers were on sale for the price of one. No one minded and the kids were happy and thriving.

By the late 1990s, the family needed more money. Susan, Stephanie, and Sarah were in college or about to start, and soon there would be four more college tuitions to pay. Bob also wanted Chris to have a bigger home and a more comfortable life. During their long marriage they had never gone away alone together for a weekend. In 1998, when he was fifty, Bob decided to leave the FBI, seven years before mandatory retirement age. After three decades as a federal agent, he joined the exodus of graying government detectives into the private sector, where he could triple his salary. But leaving the FBI behind would prove far harder than he imagined.

When Bob started in law enforcement in the 1970s, private investigators were regarded as sleazy snoops hired to catch cheating spouses or find runaway teenagers. By the 1990s a new corporate investigations industry was feeding a growing demand for information from companies, Wall Street firms, lawyers, and others. Manufacturers making pharmaceuticals, cigarettes, and high-fashion handbags needed investigators to track down criminals producing counterfeit versions of their products. Hedge funds and private equity firms were hungry for secrets about investment targets. American companies and banks doing deals with businessmen in Russia and Eastern Europe wanted to know if they were corrupt or had criminal ties.

The big investigative firms were staffed by former prosecutors, retired agents from the FBI and other agencies, and ex–newspaper reporters. They adopted the veneer of law firms and charged clients similar rates. One of the largest, Kroll Associates, employed dozens of investigators and had offices throughout the United States, Europe, and Asia. It was a highly competitive industry in which firms won contracts by convincing clients they had the connections to deliver valuable "strategic" information. Often, they produced high-priced smoke—reports that blended fact, rumor, and speculation. Their tactics could also be as bare-knuckled as those of the old-time private eyes who spied on love nests. In the late 1990s, one major new source of work for corporate investigative firms came from Russian oligarchs, financial and industrial magnates who had gained astronomical wealth after the fall of the Soviet Union. The oligarchs liked to depict themselves as a new breed of Russian entrepreneurs, Western-style capitalists who succeeded through shrewd dealings and risk-taking, rather than payoffs and political corruption. That often wasn't the case, and some oligarchs hired investigative firms to dig up dirt that could be used to blackmail a critic into silence, a technique known in the trade as a "hard shoulder."

Bob preferred to keep his nose clean. His first job was with a firm called DSFX, in its Miami office. Construction was then under way on the American Airlines Arena, the indoor stadium that became home to the Miami Heat basketball team, and DSFX was hired to help local officials monitor possible fraud on the project. Bob also began to work with Philip Morris, the maker of Marlboro cigarettes, trying to locate pirate factories producing counterfeits of its famous brand. At the time, drug gangs in Latin America were also doing a brisk business in kidnapping American executives and demanding large ransoms for their release, and companies used Bob to negotiate those deals. "If you do this right, it's not like in the movies," Bob told a reporter then writing an article about corporate kidnappings. "You don't hear music in the background, only the sound of pens on paper."

With more money, Bob and Chris, like most people, found ways to spend it. They bought a big new home in a gated community in Coral Springs and two new cars. While their three older daughters had gone to Florida State University, their two older sons wanted to go to more expensive private colleges outside the state and Bob and Chris agreed to send them.

When DSFX was sold in 2001, Bob started his own one-man shop, R. A. Levinson & Associates, which he ran out of his home. He had never operated a business before and it proved a constant hustle. He had to scramble for work, cater to clients, pay bills, collect on accounts, and make sure more money was coming in than going out. As a lone wolf, he took what he could get. His assignments were a hodgepodge, running from background investigations into Russian businessmen to counterfeit product cases. In a typical month, he might take three or four trips, including travel abroad to cities like London, Kiev, and Managua. He would book a hotel room to meet with a source and, in the evening, go to a different hotel to sleep. Before turning in, he would order room service and spend hours typing up reports to clients, responding to emails, and sending out feelers to drum up new work. The constant travel and bad eating habits took a toll. At six feet four, Bob had always been a very big man, but he soon weighed 240 pounds and had diabetes and high blood pressure.

In 2004, another large investigations firm, SafirRosetti, hired him to open an office in Boca Raton, Florida. With a steady salary, he didn't constantly have to scramble for clients and could provide his family financial security. But there was a problem—his head and his heart weren't in the work. Chasing product counterfeiters didn't compare to the thrill of an FBI agent hunting criminals for Uncle Sam. After he worked hard to investigate a case, a company's executives might decide not to alert law enforcement officials to his findings, fearing that the resulting publicity might damage their reputation or give a competitor a leg up. He would tell friends he was working for the "rich people's police," and even some of his kids could see that he wasn't happy. He tried to strike a balance by taking on assignments for public interest groups. One organization, the Center for Justice and Accountability, used investigators like Bob to track down people who had committed human rights abuses in their native countries and had since moved to the United States, often under an assumed name. When Bob met one of the group's lawyers at a Miami café, he beamed and said, "I love what you guys do." He couldn't imagine saying that to a corporate executive.

When he traveled on jobs, he fed information he picked up back to friends at the FBI and other federal agencies. Every ex-cop turned private investigator does that in order to keep doors open when they need help. Bob, however, wanted more. He still wanted to be part of the action. Every few months, he traveled to FBI field offices in cities like Memphis, Kansas City, and Seattle to teach seminars for young agents on techniques for identifying and recruiting informants.

From the very start of his career, Bob was a collector of information, intelligence, and people. He cast himself as the proverbial "good cop," a big, friendly guy who liked everybody and who wanted everybody to like him. It wasn't an act or even a stretch. By nature, he was gregarious and possessed an instinct for knowing how people wanted to be treated and what they wanted to hear. Ten minutes after sitting down in a restaurant, he would be on a first-name basis with the waiter or waitress serving him, and he would leave a big tip behind to make sure they remembered him. He loved handing out nicknames; everybody got one, family members, friends, and new acquaintances. The names were usually corny—stuff like "Professor" or "Doctor"—but people walked away charmed, thinking that Bob had coined the name just for them. He even varied how he introduced himself, depending on the impression he wanted to create.

Some people knew him as Bob. Others called him Bobby. He liked to use "Bobby" at times, he explained to one of his sons, because its boyish sound made his large stature and status as an agent seem less threatening.

Once Bob got people talking, they often kept talking. If they were criminals, they might hope he would cut them a break. Other people might cooperate to get cash or because they wanted him to solve an immigration problem. Whatever the specifics, his relationships involved the give-and-take that binds together a cop and an informant. From the start of his law enforcement career, Bob believed he could make more cases from informants than he could from working the street. Once he ran into a Drug Enforcement Administration agent he knew outside a Manhattan courthouse. The DEA agent, who did undercover buys, was dressed for the part in jeans, a battered leather jacket, and a bulletproof vest. Bob, who worked for the DEA before joining the FBI, had on his own uniform—a suit, a white shirt, and a rep tie. He looked at his friend and pulled a pen out of his jacket pocket. "I'm going to put more people in jail with this than you are with all that armor," he told him.

During his seminars for young FBI agents, he talked about his experiences and showed PowerPoint slides. He discussed the types of personality traits found in people willing to become informants. They tended to be independent thinkers, he said, rather than rule followers and were often empathetic, imaginative, and social. A variety of motives might cause them to open up; some even saw cooperation with the cops as a way to eliminate or take revenge against a rival. Other informants were thrill seekers or wannabe cops. Bob sprinkled his presentation with references to espionage and true crime books, quoting passages from authors such as David Ignatius, a journalist who wrote spy thrillers, and Robert Baer, a former agent for the Central Intelligence Agency who chronicled his experiences as an operative in the Middle East. " 'Soon recruiting agents became as natural as ordering a pizza over the telephone. It's all a matter of listening to what people are really saying,' " read one of Bob's slides quoting Baer. He warned agents about the pitfalls of dealings with informants and urged them not to get too close to a source or consider one a friend. Another slide read:

> When you are trying to recruit a member of a criminal organization or terrorist group, remember one thing—you are, in effect
> - Selling suicide
> - If that person is discovered cooperating with the FBI or law enforcement, the penalty is usually death

■ ■ ■

Bob knew from the age of eight what he wanted to be. His inspiration came from a movie called *The House on 92nd Street*, released in 1945, three years before he was born. The film was a B-grade thriller about a college student who goes undercover for the FBI during World War II to infiltrate a Nazi spy ring trying to steal secrets about the atomic bomb. The FBI officially sanctioned the movie, and it contained a brief introduction by Director J. Edgar Hoover extolling the agency's mission. After Bob saw it, he was all law-and-order. While other teenagers played sports, he hung out with friends in the attic of his parents' home in New Hyde Park, a Long Island suburb, acting out courtroom dramas. For dialogue they used transcripts from real trials that his mother typed up for lawyers to make extra money. He attended the City College of New York and worked during summers as an aide in the New York City Department of Investigations, an agency that ferrets out municipal corruption. When he graduated from college in 1970 with Phi Beta Kappa honors, he didn't attend the ceremony because he was training to be a DEA agent. The FBI required five years of law enforcement experience to qualify for a job and the DEA was the place where he would cut his teeth.

One evening two years later, he went to TGI Friday's, then a popular singles bar on Manhattan's Upper East Side. An attractive twenty-two-year-old office worker, Christine Gorman, was there with a girlfriend. Chris, who was short and had dark hair, was convinced that Bob was interested in her friend. He was interested in her. Before leaving the bar, he got Chris's phone number, and they soon began seeing each other. The only obstacle to their romance was his parents. Chris, who had grown up on Long Island in a large Catholic family, wanted to raise her children Catholic. Bob couldn't have cared less about religion, but his family was Jewish, and when he and Chris got married in 1973, Bob's father cut him off and sat shiva, the Jewish mourning ritual for the dead.

The DEA transferred Bob to Denver, and it was there in 1976 that he got the call he had been waiting for—the FBI wanted to hire him. He went to the bureau's training facility in Quantico, Virginia, and was assigned to its office in Los Angeles. It was a short-lived posting. Chris, who had already given birth to the couple's first child, was again pregnant and wanted to return to the East Coast to be close to her family. In 1978, she and Bob got their wish; he was offered a plum assignment in New York working on organized crime cases.

In the early 1980s, one of those Mafia cases captured the country's attention. It involved President Ronald Reagan's choice for secretary of labor, Raymond Donovan, and allegations that his New Jersey construction company had Mafia ties. Donovan, a top executive of Schiavone Construction, denied the rumors, and FBI officials testified during his Senate confirmation hearings that a bureau investigation had found nothing to suggest connections between Donovan's company and the mob. But after the new secretary of labor assumed his post, *Time* magazine published a bombshell—during an investigation in the late 1970s, the FBI had secretly recorded members of the Genovese crime family discussing Donovan, Schiavone, and a scheme to use minority-owned firms as fronts to win public construction contracts. To Bob, the revelation wasn't news. He had headed the investigation that produced those recordings, and a bitter dispute within the bureau over his handling of the informant in the case had nearly destroyed his young FBI career.

That informant, Michael Orlando, was a onetime schoolteacher who had turned to theft and armed robbery. Another FBI agent, Larry Sweeney, initially recruited Orlando as a source, and after he learned Orlando was close to Genovese family members, he introduced him to Bob. Orlando, who was being paid $500 a week by the FBI to be a top, or "high-echelon," informant, told Bob he was willing to infiltrate a Bronx meatpacking warehouse, run by a Genovese lieutenant named William Masselli, that served as a drop-off point for hijacked trucks and other criminal activities. In return, Bob reiterated Larry Sweeney's earlier promise to Orlando not to disclose his identity as a bureau source even to other FBI agents working on the case, for fear it might leak out and get him killed.

In 1978, Bob wrote a fourteen-page memo to FBI headquarters based on information picked up by bureau listening devices planted inside the Bronx warehouse. In it, he said the material being gathered had "excellent prosecutive potential" for cases of political corruption, fraud, labor racketeering, police corruption, and narcotics trafficking. But the inquiry ran into trouble when other bureau agents, unaware of Orlando's role as an informant, started reporting that he was taking part in truck hijackings and other crimes. When Bob and Sweeney confronted Orlando, he offered the informant's perfect excuse—fellow gangsters would quickly finger him as a stoolie, he said, if he walked away whenever a crime was going down. He promised to behave, but some FBI managers viewed Orlando as an informant run amok, and before long it wasn't clear who was playing whom. In addition, William Masselli was heard on an FBI bug telling a fellow gangster that Orlando had carried out multiple contract killings for the mob. "This kid Mike . . . When I say he's a bad kid . . . Forget about it . . . He knows it," Masselli said. "This guy's got about ten under his belt already."

Bob and Sweeney hadn't seen any evidence connecting Orlando to mob hits, and they argued that arresting him for truck hijackings would prematurely end the Bronx investigation, expose him as an informant, and violate their pledge to him. Supervisors overruled them, and when Orlando was arrested, Sweeney filed a complaint with FBI headquarters. A subsequent internal FBI review largely supported how Bob and Sweeney had handled Orlando, but by then the episode had resulted in too much bad blood inside the bureau's New York office. Bob's supervisors took him off organized crime and assigned him to foreign counterintelligence, an effective demotion. When a job opened in the FBI's Miami office in 1984, he jumped at it, eager to make a fresh start.

Bob's arrival in South Florida was perfectly timed. In the mid-1980s, the world of organized crime was undergoing a sea change. It was the era of *Miami Vice*, as Colombian drug cartels smuggled tons of cocaine into the United States by the plane- and shipload. Bob, who spoke some Spanish, jumped right in and soon found a new informant, a Colombian-born fashion photographer, Baruch Vega, who shot assignments with top models such as Lauren Hutton and Christie Brinkley. During those years, it was almost impossible for law enforcement agencies to get information about the cartels because arrested gang members knew they would be killed if they squealed. So Bob and Vega concocted an off-the-wall strategy to try to trick cartel leaders into letting their subordinates cooperate.

The plan revolved around a fictional character they created—a corrupt FBI agent named "Bob Roberts" who was willing, if paid off, to get arrested gang members out of jail by telling his bureau bosses they had agreed to become informants. Vega told cartel leaders, with whom he hobnobbed while on photo assignments in Central and South America, about Roberts and how gang members only needed to pretend they were cooperating to be freed. Cartel heads liked the deal, so they gave Vega bribes meant for Roberts and told underlings about him. After Vega pocketed the cash, Bob or another agent, pretending to be "Bob Roberts," visited a gang member and said they could get out of jail but only by sharing real information about drug running.

By the early 1990s, Bob became one of the bureau's resident experts on another ethnic crime wave—the flood of mobsters, thugs, and financial con men who, following the collapse of the Soviet Union, arrived in the United States from Russia and other parts of Eastern Europe. Many of the gangs set up shop in Brooklyn and Miami, and Bob was sitting in his office in 1994 when a terrified-looking man walked in. The man, Alexander Volkov, had fled to

Florida from New York after learning that a feared Russian enforcer was looking for him.

Volkov was hardly an innocent. He and a partner had operated a Wall Street investment firm called Summit International that was really a Ponzi scheme. When the scheme collapsed, a Russian bank that had invested with Summit hired a gangster named Vyacheslav Ivankov, who headed a gang based in Brighton Beach that specialized in blackmail, loan-sharking, and murder. Volkov initially hid out at the Miami home of a friend named Leonid Venjik, who convinced him that his best hope for staying alive rested with the FBI. Soon afterward, Volkov, his Summit partner, and Venjik agreed to become part of a bureau operation aimed at Ivankov. The three men told the Russian gangster they were coming to New York to strike a deal to repay the bank's money. After Ivankov listened to their proposal, he responded with death threats, which were captured on hidden FBI video cameras. He was indicted and convicted on extortion charges, a case that marked the first successful prosecution in the United States of a major Russian criminal.

By then, Bob's connections in the world of intelligence gathering were deepening. He worked closely with CIA operatives on Colombian cocaine cases and traveled to Europe to represent the FBI at international law enforcement meetings about Russian organized crime. In 1992, at a conference in New Mexico about Russian crime put on by the Justice Department for FBI agents, prosecutors, and others, he met a CIA analyst named Anne Jablonski. They clicked immediately. She was a walking encyclopedia of information about Russian gangs. He entertained her with stories about the Russian mobsters he was chasing in Miami. He soon gave her a nickname. He called her "Toots."

■ ■ ■

When SafirRosetti hired Bob in 2004, the firm was eager to build its product counterfeiting business. Bob brought an old client, Philip

Morris, to the firm along with one of his informants, Leonid Venjik, the Russian émigré in Miami who had worked with him on the Ivankov case. Venjik had a network of sources in Eastern Europe, and Bob used him on product counterfeiting investigations. Soon, Venjik started sending in reports warning that Philip Morris had a mole within its ranks.

The informant said his sources had spotted an executive from the company's Richmond, Virginia, headquarters selling technical expertise and equipment to cigarette counterfeiters in Bosnia. That information included Philip Morris's most closely guarded secret, the "recipe" of tobacco varieties and additives used to produce a Marlboro's distinctive taste. As a result, the counterfeiters were flooding the market with fake Marlboros that looked and tasted like real ones. In a SafirRosetti report to the cigarette maker, Bob provided a description of the mole, who was called "David."

> From conversations overheard by the source, "David" is employed by Philip Morris in a very responsible position, but not in a sales capacity—rather he is involved primarily in "technical operations" and he displays a familiarity with the equipment and machinery involved in the manufacturing of tobacco products; he also shows a technical expertise in the areas of tobacco filters and paper, along with how "production lines" are operated.
>
> "David" mentioned that he was going to be attending some type of "seminar" which Philip Morris was holding in the United States at the beginning of July 2004.

While at SafirRosetti, Bob continued to hear from other old informants. In 2004, one sought his help on behalf of the president of Kazakhstan, Nursultan Nazarbayev. The Kazakh president was then at the center of the biggest foreign corruption case ever brought by U.S. prosecutors. In the previous year, an American oil industry consultant, James Giffen, had been arrested and charged with paying millions in bribes to Nazarbayev and other officials in the former Soviet republic to win oil exploration contracts. Federal prosecutors froze Nazarbayev's Swiss bank account, alleging it contained $70 million in kickbacks paid him by Giffen.

Bob's source said that he and one of Nazarbayev's closest associates had been secretly meeting for months with FBI agents in New York in an attempt to cut a deal on behalf of the Kazakh president. In exchange for unfreezing his Swiss bank account, Nazarbayev was willing to help the United States track down Al Qaeda terrorists and identify traffickers in chemical and biological weapons. They hadn't made any headway, so Bob's informant asked him to contact his government sources. Bob drafted a memo and apparently sent it to several agencies, including the CIA. He wrote that the Kazakh president was willing to help the U.S. government by:

1. Identifying and locating leadership, membership and associates of Al Qaeda, utilizing the full cooperation and resources of the Kazakhstan government's special services, including the country's intelligence organization.
2. Identifying and locating traffickers in weapons of mass destruction (WMD) such as chemical, biological and nuclear devices or materials.
3. Any and all counter-terrorism targets as identified by the USG.

In the memo, Bob suggested setting up a meeting between a top U.S. official and an emissary of the Kazakh president. "This may, in fact, be the last opportunity to engage in dialogue along these lines as credibility has been lost because of the time and effort already invested" by representatives of Nazarbayev, he wrote.

Right around that time, two Miami-based FBI agents visited Bob at his SafirRosetti office. For months, he had been passing along to the bureau information Leonid Venjik was giving him about counterfeiters selling fake Marlboros. As was his practice, Bob hadn't revealed Venjik's identity in the memos, referring to him simply as his "source." The FBI agents told Bob they were interested in the information and were hoping he might give them his source's name or set up a meeting with him. Bob smiled. He replied that he had never given up an informant during all the years he spent in their shoes and he wasn't about to start.

The visit hadn't been a friendly call. It was a test and Bob had failed. The DEA already knew that Leonid Venjik was Bob's informant because the drug agency, along with police officials in Austria, were investigating him for trafficking in counterfeit Marlboros and cocaine. Venjik had even bragged to an undercover DEA agent that he was playing Bob by feeding him dribs of information in order to use his role as an informant to collect money from SafirRosetti and shield his crimes. Bob had been totally in the dark, and if he had given up Venjik's name to the FBI, the episode might have ended there. But by refusing to do so, he heightened the suspicions of some DEA and Austrian investigators that he had known about Venjik's activities. He then dug himself a deeper hole. After Venjik's arrest in Austria, Bob flew there in December 2004 to visit him in prison and gave Austrian authorities a sworn affidavit attesting to his honesty. He was doing exactly what he warned young agents not to do for an informant, and, with each well-meaning step, he made things worse for himself.

In early 2005, he learned that a federal prosecutor in Miami was asking questions about him, a sign that he might soon face charges. Chris urged him not to worry; everyone knew he was honest, she said, and they would come to their senses. But as the months passed, the federal prosecutor handling the inquiry, Joseph Cooley, let Bob twist in the wind. When Bob tried contacting Cooley, his calls weren't returned. It was a tactic he had seen prosecutors use when they wanted to make a target sweat.

Bob became so gripped by anxiety that he called David McGee, the lawyer in Pensacola. Dave had spent twenty years as a federal prosecutor before going into private practice, and he knew Bob from his days as an FBI agent. Bob asked Dave to represent him as his lawyer. "I'm going to get eaten alive by the knowledge that my life, my livelihood, my reputation will be in ruins by the time that people find out this is a big mistake," Bob said in a note. "I did not spend a lifetime in law enforcement and investigations . . . to go over to the other side."

On that same day, Bob sent a letter to Joseph Cooley from Panama, where he was working on a case for the Center for Justice and Accountability, the human rights organization.

I am writing this letter from Panama City, Panama where I am trying to locate and bring about the apprehension of an international fugitive wanted by the Government of Spain for torture and human rights violations. I believe that I'm getting close to getting this guy, utilizing 35 years of experience in this business and the assistance of sources I recruited and directed.

A horrible tragedy is about to happen to me and it is in your power to do something about it. A miscarriage of justice and colossal error is about to take place, in effect ruining my life, my reputation, in effect, all that I have built over a career spanning more than thirty-five years.

It is very tough to be able to concentrate my efforts on catching bad guys when you hear the kinds of things that I am now hearing.

I have not done anything wrong.

I have not conspired to violate any law.

I have lived a life dedicated to law enforcement, even after I retired from the FBI helping practically every federal agency, foreign law enforcement agencies, INTERPOL and the U.S. intelligence community.

I strongly urge you to hear my side of whatever story is being put to you and your investigators, and that this be done as quickly as possible.

Cooley's response was more silence, and Chris's faith began to waver. Bob told Dave McGee she had started to ask him what they were going to tell their children if their father was indicted. Bob had alerted his bosses at SafirRosetti about Venjik's arrest, and the firm scrambled to stop payment on a $50,000 check it had sent him. Explaining to Philip Morris that its money had been going to a trafficker in counterfeit Marlboros wasn't going to be easy. SafirRosetti executives told Bob they were closing his office in Boca Raton. He was a talented investigator, they said, and offered to send him free-lance jobs, but they had come to realize something about Bob that he probably already knew: he didn't have the polish, the patience, or the interest to make it in the corporate world.

That spring, while on a trip to Washington, Bob visited Ira Silver-man, the retired television journalist, at his home in Falls Church, Virginia, a D.C. suburb. The men had been close friends since the 1970s, when Bob was a young DEA agent and Ira was digging up crime stories for NBC in New York. They both loved chasing crooks, and Ira would show up unexpectedly at Chris's apartment when she and Bob were dating to buttonhole him and talk about cases. Ira became such a regular presence in the lives of the Levinson kids that they grew up thinking of him as an uncle.

On the day of Bob's visit, the weather was pleasant and Ira sug-gested that they sit in the backyard. Bob said nothing to him about his troubles at SafirRosetti or Joseph Cooley's inquiry in Miami. Still, Ira sensed something was very wrong. Bob had always been happy and upbeat. That day, he seemed defeated, almost suicidal. Out of the blue, he told Ira that he felt that his life had been shit and that he should have spent it doing something of value. Instead, it had all been a waste. When Bob left, Ira was worried about him.

In the end, Cooley dropped his inquiry after finding the evidence didn't implicate Bob. The investigator was relieved, but he was back out on his own and needed to find work fast. He grabbed one of the first cases he was offered even though its financial terms weren't ap-pealing. Typically, private investigators get their fees and expenses paid as they work on a case. But they can also enter into contingency-style arrangements, forgoing part of their payment until the conclu-sion of a case. Most investigators steer away from the arrangement, which is known as a "success fee," but Bob apparently agreed to work on that basis for a New York law firm, Reed Smith. It was defending the Bank of Cyprus in a lawsuit brought by a group of investors who claimed that the bank had laundered Russian crime funds. Bob spent three months on the case. When the judge hearing the lawsuit delayed issuing a decision, his bill to the law firm, which exceeded $100,000, was left hanging.

He faced a big financial shortfall and realized he couldn't keep on living from case to case. He needed steady income. One possible job was a full-time position with a group that investigated auto theft. He also applied for a job as a part-time instructor at the CIA's training center, where new operatives learn skills such as how to interview sources. Then Anne Jablonski, the CIA Russian crime analyst, told him she thought she could get him a part-time consulting contract with the spy agency. Bob and Anne had stayed close since their meeting in the early 1990s, regularly swapping information about cases. Anne was now working in an analytical unit called the Illicit Finance Group, which specialized in gathering information about international crime, foreign government corruption, and money laundering. The intelligence was summarized in briefs sent to top government officials at the White House and elsewhere.

To Bob, it sounded like a dream job. He would get to work with an old friend on big, heady assignments. But getting his contract written and approved seemed to take forever. Every month, Anne told him about a hang-up, budgetary constraint, or technical snafu. Several times, the contract's language had to be reworked to make certain that it would be awarded to Bob rather than being put up for competitive bid. Numerous CIA officials, including ones from the agency's spy side, had to review the contract and sign off on it. He tried to stir the pot by sending Anne notes about the hot leads he could pursue once he was on board and proposals for areas to investigate. He kept his notes friendly, but there was also an insistence in their tone. "I strongly believe that I will be able to pull this one off," he wrote her, about a possible Russian crime investigation. "If so, we would be right in the proverbial center of the action."

In early 2006, Anne brought him to CIA headquarters in Langley, Virginia, to meet with the head of the Illicit Finance Group, Timothy Sampson, and other analysts who worked in the unit. He jotted down their names and specialties: Anne, Sarah, and George covered Russian organized crime and business in Eastern Europe; Kristin followed corruption in the Middle East; Katy's area of expertise was Venezuela and international bribery; Eric followed the global trade in narcotics; other analysts were responsible for countries such as Iran or North Korea or oversaw broad subject areas like money laundering. Soon after he returned home, he went through his files, pulling old reports and sending them to Anne to distribute to her colleagues. "Attached is another paper I promised your staff when I was up there earlier in the week," he wrote.

Finally, in June 2006, his CIA contract was approved. When Anne notified him about it, Bob quickly replied. He was thrilled to be back in the game.

Today is my thirty-second wedding anniversary and aside from celebrating those years with Christine, I'm going to (prematurely) celebrate this. It seems like something too good to be true. I really look forward to working with you and trying to make a contribution. Yeah, you really made my day, Toots.

2

Toots

The lights inside the three-bedroom white Colonial on South June Street went on early, usually around 5:00 a.m. Anne Jablonski liked the still hours before sunrise. It was her time to meditate and practice yoga. She also fed Duke, the cat. As a kitten, Duke had suffered from severe diarrhea. When a series of veterinarians failed to cure him, Anne decided to approach the study of feline digestive problems with the same intensity she applied to the monitoring of Russian organized crime. She read everything she could find on the subject, textbooks, articles, and medical journal reports. She spoke to experts in the field. After a lengthy investigation, she concluded that Duke's problem was a basic one. In the wild, feral cats hunted birds and rabbits, eating their entire prey—organs and eyes included. Some of these nutrients were not found in commercial cat foods, even "natural" brands, and Duke, along with many other cats, was suffering as a result.

To test her theory, Anne began buying whole rabbit carcasses from local butchers and, with her husband's help, processed them at home using a commercial meat grinder. Duke recovered, but Anne didn't stop there. She wrote a letter to schools of veterinary medicine nationwide in which she detailed her experiment and its successful results, including with it a list of recommended reading materials for the institutions to distribute to students. For fellow cat lovers, she created a website called Cat Nutrition, on which she described her beloved "Dukie-boy's" return to health. "Meow . . . And welcome," its homepage read.

Around dawn, Anne, slightly built, with dirty-blond hair and a toothy grin, made the short drive from her home in Arlington, Virginia, to CIA headquarters in nearby Langley, arriving there ahead of fellow analysts. By the summer of 2006, she had passed her twentieth anniversary at the agency, and had worked long enough to collect a federal pension when she was ready. She had begun thinking more about what she wanted to do next, and a second career as a yoga instructor was high on the list of possibilities. Anne had started at the agency in the mid-1980s, a decade after graduating from the University of Wisconsin fluent in Russian. The CIA's analytical division, or the Directorate of Intelligence, as it is formally known, was an ideal fit for her, a place that appreciated her quirkiness and sense of humor and rewarded her obsessiveness and attention. Many of her Langley colleagues resembled graying graduate students, brilliant misfits absorbed in obscure studies while buffered from everyday pressures.

Anne first worked alongside other Soviet analysts collecting data on economic and military issues. Then, as the Soviet Union began to collapse, she saw an important pattern emerge. In the United States and Western Europe, politicians, businessmen, intelligence operatives, and criminals tended to stay in their own orbits. But amid the scramble for power and economic wealth in Russia and the newly independent republics, such players were forging alliances and operating together. A businessman from Kiev might be a KGB operative, and a politician from Moscow might be allied with a major gang. To make policy, U.S. officials needed to know how these people connected together, and "Anne-ski," as some colleagues called her, became their guide. Anne's "customers" were typically officials at the White House, the State Department, or the Treasury Department who needed information about an Eastern European politician, company, or criminal in order to shape a decision. Along with her own wealth of knowledge, Anne could draw on several sources of information to put together a report. The agency maintained a massive database of books, newspaper articles, journal reports, broadcast transcripts, and Internet postings, and she could tap the expertise of CIA consultants. Analysts could also ask operatives overseas to gather information about a target. Such requests were funneled through a CIA center, which prioritized them based on national security needs. Analysts needed to be aggressive to push their assignments to the top of the pile. Anne made sure everyone knew her requests were urgent.

In 2000, she officially became a star when she was included in the first class of analysts inducted into the senior analytical service, a new rank created by the CIA to reward its most valued intelligence researchers. Then 9/11 happened and no one cared anymore about Russia. Scores of Russia analysts within the CIA were ordered to place their personal belongings into cardboard boxes so they could be moved into new jobs with the agency's Counterterrorism Center. Because of her rank, Anne escaped that fate and was assigned instead to a group of CIA employees who provided early-morning intelligence briefings to top U.S. officials about overnight developments affecting the country's security. The job sounded impressive. The reality could be different. One day, after briefing the then attorney general, John Ashcroft, Anne told a colleague, "I'd rather brief my cat."

After, she continued to write intelligence reports about Russian organized crime that few people read. It was as though she spoke a forgotten language that only the aging members of a dwindling sect were trying to keep alive. Her husband, Robert Otto, who worked at the State Department, was among them. So was Bob Levinson. She and her husband would have dinner with Bob during his visits to Washington, and they would swap gossip about Russian gangsters the way other people talked about movie stars or baseball players.

"There is something very calming about spending time with people who have the same perspective, the same commitment, the same values," Bob wrote them after one get-together. "You don't feel as crazy as usual."

During the course of her career, Anne had gotten to know a lot of FBI agents, but she always felt particularly close to Bob. He wasn't the typical button-down choirboy who followed the rules. She viewed him much as she saw herself: as a free spirit caught inside a bureaucracy. The FBI and the CIA were competitors, and agents and analysts weren't supposed to work together, but she and Bob didn't care and they both got a kick out of knowing their collaborations were driving their colleagues nuts. When Bob retired from the bureau, Anne flew to Miami to attend the party for him at the FBI's office and then spent hours debriefing him before returning home. Their relationship, both professional and personal, continued from there. Every holiday season, she and her husband sent a Christmas card to the Levinson family. When Bob's daughter Sarah came to Washington for a summer internship at a foundation, Anne met her at Union Station and they spent an afternoon together shopping for shoes. Sarah had dreaded the meeting, expecting to be stuck with a frumpy, middle-aged spinster. She told her father afterward that he was right: Anne was a lot of fun.

In 2004, Anne found a landing spot with the Illicit Finance Group. The unit had been created a year earlier during a reorganization of the Office of Transnational Affairs, one of the major divisions of the Directorate of Intelligence. Since 2001, Congress had quadrupled spending on intelligence gathering, and the CIA had expanded, hiring new operatives and analysts. Some of the new funding filtered down to units like the Illicit Finance Group, which had bigger budgets to hire consultants and buy information from private investigators and other sources of "gray market" intelligence. One of the part-time consultants used by the Illicit Finance Group was a former staffer for the Massachusetts senator John Kerry named Jonathan Winer, who then worked as a lawyer at a Washington lobbying firm, APCO International. While in government, Winer had served on a Senate panel investigating a notorious financial institution, the Bank of Credit and Commerce International, engaged in money laundering, a subject that he was expert in. Anne wanted to bring Bob on board as a consultant, but his case was a little trickier. She was certain that he could supply great material to her group, the type of information only a seasoned developer of informants could collect. But his skills and methods of operating could also pose a problem.

Under CIA rules, the agency's analytical branch is barred from engaging in clandestine operations overseas, which are the province of the "other side of the house," the agency's Directorate of Operations. The division exists for many reasons. Analysts aren't schooled in the tradecraft of spying, and ad hoc missions can jeopardize real ones and endanger operatives. CIA spies also have long viewed analysts as beneath them, and at one time they were barred from setting foot inside the cafeteria where operatives ate. Analysts had a different view of the agency's pecking order. In it, they were the brains without whom operatives would be useless. CIA management wasn't above stoking the competition. One day in 2004, a top official of the Directorate of Intelligence convened a meeting of analysts inside the CIA's main auditorium, known as "the Bubble," and declared that, under his watch, they were "going to destroy" their rivals on the agency's clandestine side.

Even before Bob got his consulting contract, he occasionally sold information to the CIA on a freelance basis, and Anne found herself dealing with the agency's bureaucracy. In mid-2005, a woman working at the agency named Bonnie balked at paying Bob for an intelligence memo he had sent to Anne because it didn't read like the kind of report she was used to seeing from analysts. He told Anne about the problem and she wrote him back: "Ugh . . . Pay NO attention to Bonnie—she's interjecting herself in this in ways that are driving me nuts. NO! We don't want/need analysis from you . . . what we want is what you know/hear! I'm going to get that message to her."

A few months later, while his contract still was undergoing CIA review, he alerted Anne about a potential break in a big case involving

American hostages. In 2003, a surveillance aircraft operated by contractors for the Defense Department crashed in Colombia while
monitoring drug trafficking. The three men aboard, all employees of
Northrop Grumman, were captured by a left-wing paramilitary group
known as the Revolutionary Armed Forces of Colombia, or FARC,
which held them prisoner in rebel camps deep inside impenetrable
jungles. In October 2005, one of Bob's old informants, the fashion
photographer Baruch Vega, contacted him with a tip. His sister, Olga
Vega, who was a television journalist in Colombia, had just interviewed a top FARC official who told her afterward that the group
might be willing to cut a deal to release the three Americans. Bob
relayed the information to the FBI and the CIA and asked Anne if the
agency could pay his travel expenses to New York to meet with Baruch Vega, who had the videotape of the interview his sister had conducted. He formalized the request in a memo:

TO: Appropriate Recipients

FROM: Robert A. Levinson

DATE: 12 October 2005

RE: Kidnapping of 3 US Contractors by Revolutionary Armed
  Forces of Colombia

Re my e-mail of 12 October 2005.

Request consideration be given to authorizing my travel to New
York, New York for a maximum of two (2) days for the purpose
of meeting and debriefing the confidential source referred to in the
referenced e-mail.

A complete report of the debriefing of the source, as well as full
descriptive/biographic data will be compiled and transmitted after
the contact is made.

As independent contractor, a request for compensation for time
expended and expenses incurred will be submitted through established channels.

Anne was excited and promised to jump right on it: "I'll pass it
along to the right folks tomorrow (heaven help us if they are not in—

there are only TWO people who 'get it' on this thing) and get back to you ASAP!"

After seeing Vega, Bob arranged for the photographer to meet with an FBI agent, and shortly afterward, both bureau agents and CIA operatives in Colombia were in contact with his sister. Anne wrote Bob that she expected to get a briefing from CIA officials working with the bureau, or the "B," as she called it, on the case, adding she had asked an associate to try to find a way to pay Bob for his efforts: "I'll try and get a debrief from the people coordinating with the 'B' to find out what is going on. Sorry I was out of touch for two days—there was a bit of a crisis at work and no one was there to handle it but yours truly. I'll also work with Brian to see if it's possible to have you write up some of this so we can pay you for it."

By May 2006, Anne was ready to tear her hair out because Bob's contract still hadn't been approved and she was getting a constant stream of emails from him about projects on which he was ready to get started. She wrote: "I am sure you're weary as hell of these delays and I don't know what to tell you other than that EVERYONE wants this to happen . . . But moving the paperwork along is painstakingly unfast. I know that opportunities are whizzing by in the meantime . . . Hanging my head in shame at my bureaucracy's molasses."

A month later, the logjam finally broke. Brian O'Toole, an analyst with whom Anne worked, oversaw Bob's contract. But she acted as his agency handler, distributing his reports, depending on their subject, to the right people within the CIA. The contract's language was vague. It called for Bob to provide the Illicit Finance Group over the next year with "ten (10) papers on topics of interest to analysts such as, but not limited to: the mechanism of international organized crime groups, money laundering, narcotics trafficking, counterfeiting, corruption in key countries and regions of US government interest, repercussions of these activities in areas of interest and abroad, and possible US strategies to counter illicit activities." The contract's value was $64,688, of which $10,000 was earmarked for travel and expenses. That worked out to an hourly rate of about $57, a fifth of what Bob charged his private clients. Still, the arrangement had advantages.

Bob could work for the CIA, Anne told him, while traveling for his private clients and whenever he wanted. "You could work a few hours in some months, more in others," she wrote him.

But as soon as Bob got going, Anne was inundated by dozens of investigative memos from him on subjects ranging from Russian crime to narcotics smuggling to arms trafficking. Another of his sources wanted to sell the CIA a stolen database compiled by the Venezuelan government that listed the cell phone numbers and email addresses of political dissidents whom officials there were monitoring. In the summer of 2006, he traveled on the CIA's behalf to a federal prison in North Carolina to meet with Peter F. Paul, a con man who had been Hillary Clinton's biggest fund-raiser during her successful 2000 New York Senate campaign. Paul, once a business partner of the comic book legend Stan Lee, the cocreator of Spider-Man and the Hulk, wanted to trade information to reduce his prison term for fraud. He told Bob that while in Brazil, where he was on the lam from U.S. authorities, he had shared a jail cell with an inmate who claimed to be the nephew of Hassan Nasrallah, the leader of Hezbollah, the Iranian-backed terror group based in Lebanon. Paul said the man, Josef Nasrallah, told him that he once ran a major cocaine trafficking ring that operated under his uncle's protection and that Hassan Nasrallah had arranged for him to escape Lebanon after he was arrested there on drug charges. According to Bob's report:

> Nasrallah indicated to the source that during the late 1990s, he was arrested, tried and convicted of drug trafficking offenses, and subsequently received a sentence of twenty years imprisonment. Nasrallah confided, however, that he never served the sentence because his uncle, Hassan Nasrallah, intervened and was able to "spring" him from the Lebanese prison where he was being held. Subsequently, Hassan Nasrallah placed his nephew on an airplane to Brazil.

As more memos from Bob poured in, Anne and others in the Illicit Finance Group decided they needed to meet with him. For one, they wanted to get him focused on topics that were priorities for the unit. There was another problem as well. His reports read like FBI investigative memos, and people at the CIA who read them might conclude he was involved in clandestine work. In August 2006, Anne suggested to Bob that it might be a good time for him to take a breather and regroup. In her email, she also referred to the Illicit Finance Group's head, Tim Sampson.

> And for heaven's sake, take some time off. Pace yourself, my man! Tim said the other day, "Crikey, I thought he might produce this much in, oh, say two YEARS" . . . We're all delighted with the material. Now we have a new problem on our hands—how to PROCESS it without pissing off the folks who are SUPPOSED to be collecting this kind of material for us but are too busy jumping through bureaucratic hoops and making excuses. Really . . . we're having meetings to figure this one out! You rock our world.

A few weeks later, Bob traveled to Langley to meet with the CIA unit. Anne told him beforehand that her colleagues were looking for ways to reframe his reports, rather than change what he was doing. "We teeter on the edge of some legal issues here—since we're NOT anything but an 'analytical shop.' So we have to kind of shape things a bit differently (same info, different prism) and maybe work with you to change the 'format' of the material you send."

The solution presented to Bob was simple. Going forward, he would use a standardized format to make his reports look more like those written by an analyst. Each submission would be labeled as an "A.R.," short for "analytical report," be numbered sequentially, and contain a brief summation of its contents as well as an assessment of the reliability of its source. Previously, he had been faxing his memos to Anne at CIA headquarters. He was told to burn future reports onto compact discs and ship them by FedEx to her home, procedures he quickly adopted.

He was also given a list of the Illicit Finance Group's main targets for intelligence gathering. It was short. One subject was Iran. The other subject was Iran's principal ally in South America, Hugo Chávez, the president of Venezuela. To anyone following the news in 2006, those choices would not have been a surprise. Iran had recently elected a new president, Mahmoud Ahmadinejad, a conservative firebrand who had quickly gained the world's attention by describing the Holocaust as a "hoax." He had restarted Iran's nuclear enrichment program, putting it on the path to developing an atomic bomb. Pushing back, President George W. Bush called for a tightening of trade and financial embargoes against Iran. Some administration hawks argued for war. In neighboring Iraq, a growing number of U.S. soldiers were dying in explosions of improvised bombs known as IEDs, and American officials had evidence that Iranian operatives were teaching Shiite paramilitary groups there how to build ever more powerful devices.

In 2006, the CIA's presence in Iran was all but nonexistent. The small cadre of spies it retained in Iran after the country's Islamic Revolution in 1979 had all been imprisoned or executed as the result of a careless mistake by a CIA clerk that revealed their identities. The main tools that the agency used to peer into Iran were spy satellites, cell phone intercepts, and computer programs that could track the flow of money into and out of the country. There was little human intelligence coming from inside.

The CIA wanted the Illicit Finance Group to gather information to help U.S. officials anticipate Iran's response to new sanctions and also dig up dirt that could be used as political ammunition against its leaders. The Iranian government was rife with corruption and competing political and clerical factions. Its religious leaders had long operated supposedly charitable organizations, known as "bonyads," that they used to consolidate the country's wealth for their own benefit. Top officials of the elite military force, the Revolutionary Guards, operated major companies, and political power brokers in Iran controlled key industries.

When it came to Venezuela and Chávez, Bob felt covered; he had sources with ties to South America who could provide information about the Venezuelan president's finances and associates. Bob had never gone near the Middle East, though he knew someone who had spent a week in Tehran—his old television buddy, Ira Silverman. Ira had gone to Iran in 2002 to interview a fugitive American long wanted in the United States for murder and was still in contact with the man, Dawud Salahuddin.

In June, after a meeting at the CIA, Bob phoned the retired newsman and suggested they grab lunch. They met at Clyde's, a Washington-area bar and restaurant that bills itself as the place where "patriots of all stripes come to dine." When Bob strolled in, Ira saw a big change in his friend. He looked buoyant again, like his old self. As they ate, Bob filled in Ira about his meeting at Langley. "Iran is the flavor of the day," he told him.

He didn't have to say more. It was time to call Dawud.

3

The Fugitive

At about the same time as Bob and Ira's lunch at Clyde's, Dawud Salahuddin was standing in front of a television camera in Iran, talking about himself. A Canadian filmmaker was making a documentary called *American Fugitive*, and Dawud was strolling around a room lined with movie posters. His once narrow features, which had glared out decades ago from WANTED posters in the United States, had thickened with age. He had a neatly trimmed beard and wore a black beret perched above his aviator eyeglasses. As he walked, a knee-length brown tunic grabbed at the midsection of his out-of-shape frame.

When asked by the documentary's director about the names he had used over the years, Dawud ticked off his aliases and noms de guerre before mentioning his given name: "In the past, I was Teddy when I was a kid . . . Teddy. Short for Theodore . . . David Theodore Belfield." Asked why he was speaking on camera, since he could put himself in danger, Dawud let a few beats pass before responding. He had been through this drill many times before with journalists and he had learned long ago how to deliver a money quote. "At this point in time, I can't give you a lucid answer, because there is really nothing in it for me, okay," he said. "There could be trouble from . . . from different sides. It's exposure . . . Some people say I'm reckless . . . Maybe it's recklessness . . . But ah . . . well, if I had to really, if I had to really dredge up an answer for you . . . I guess one of the reasons that I am doing it is to say that there is life after America."

Dawud's life as a fugitive had started three decades earlier. Ayatollah Ruhollah Khomeini, the fiery Islamic cleric, was poised in the late 1970s to overthrow the shah of Iran, who had long enjoyed the U.S. government's patronage. In Washington, D.C., Dawud had spent years adrift, committing petty crimes and looking for a cause. He found one in Khomeini's ideals of a pure Islamic state.

He fell in with a cadre of Khomeini supporters based at Washington's Islamic Center, a white marble mosque near the Embassy Row section of Massachusetts Avenue. His group frequently clashed with the mosque's elders who supported the shah, and Dawud attracted the attention of the intelligence division of the Washington police department, which identified him as a potentially dangerous radical. One police surveillance report described him as the head of a little-known group called the Islamic Guerrillas in America, which distributed leaflets "containing threats of domestic insurrection in the U.S. and indicated that one of the targets should be Zionist females."

In November 1979, months after the shah's overthrow, Dawud and other Khomeini supporters traveled to New York and chained themselves to the Statue of Liberty. In Tehran, on that same day, students seized the U.S. embassy, starting a hostage crisis that would last fifteen months. Soon afterward, Dawud was hired as a security guard at Iran's remaining diplomatic outpost in Washington, an office, or "interest section," housed inside the Algerian embassy. At the time, the fate of Iran's religious revolution remained unsettled as supporters of the ayatollah vied with other factions for power, including former associates of the shah. Fearing a counterrevolution, Khomeini's confederates began dispatching assassins to eliminate the shah's allies, and Dawud, then twenty-nine, was approached about undertaking such a mission. He was assigned to kill a former spokesman at the Iranian embassy in Washington, Ali Akbar Tabatabai, who was close to the leader of a failed coup attempt against Khomeini.

In July 1980, Dawud drove to Tabatabai's home in Bethesda, Maryland, in a U.S. Postal Service jeep that he paid a mailman to let him borrow. He emerged wearing a postman's uniform and holding what appeared to be two special-delivery packages. Concealed inside one of them was a 9 mm Browning semiautomatic pistol. When he rang the buzzer, a visitor at Tabatabai's home, an Iranian-born graduate student, opened the door and offered to take the packages. Dawud insisted he needed Tabatabai's signature and the former diplomat, who was in his late forties, came to the door. A few weeks earlier, he had spoken on a television news program about the threats he was receiving from Khomeini followers. "They had left messages, numerous messages of threats, of physical harm to me," he said. "In fact, they very clearly said we are going to kill you."

The postman waiting at his doorstep didn't appear threatening. "I need your signature," Dawud told him as he moved the packages closer. He then squeezed off three rounds, each bullet hitting Tabatabai in the abdomen. Dawud turned and walked back to the postal jeep. Forty-five minutes later, Tabatabai was declared dead at a local hospital.

Dawud quickly ditched the postal vehicle and climbed into a car driven by an accomplice. His original plan called for him to escape the United States by taking a flight to Europe from John F. Kennedy Airport in New York, but as he approached the city, the radio was buzzing with news of the killing, including descriptions of the shooter as a young black man. He decided to divert to Canada and, after driving north through the night, crossed the border. In Montreal he boarded a plane for Paris. It was on the next leg of his journey, a short flight from Paris to Geneva, that he picked up a newspaper and read that he was the subject of a manhunt. He hid out for a week in Switzerland and then, with the aid of an Iranian woman, slipped onto a flight to Tehran and safety.

In the United States, the public was shocked that a homegrown terrorist could carry out a brazen assassination near the nation's capital at the behest of one of America's enemies. For weeks, reporters from *The Washington Post*, *The New York Times*, and other newspapers dug into Dawud's past to try to understand the path that had taken him to Tabatabai's door. Friends and family who had known Teddy Belfield were stunned. In Bay Shore, New York, the Long Island suburb where he grew up, he had been regarded as smart, sociable, and athletic. His four siblings were all straight arrows; an older brother was a police officer.

People expected Teddy to follow in his siblings' footsteps. In 1968, he started as a freshman at Howard University in Washington, but before finishing the year he dropped out. Soon afterward, he converted to Islam, taking his new name, Dawud Salahuddin, in honor of a twelfth-century Muslim warrior. Plenty of students dropped out of college during the late 1960s; the Vietnam War was raging, race riots flared throughout the United States after the assassination of Martin Luther King, and black power groups such as the Black Muslims were in ascendancy. But becoming an assassin was totally different. "I don't understand this at all," Dawud's aunt told reporters after the murder. "When I saw his picture flashed up on the television screen and heard what the newscaster was saying about him, I nearly died. People here are so shocked. They know the family is much different."

Journalists seized on Dawud's use of a postman's disguise, suggesting he had gotten the idea from *Three Days of the Condor*, a thriller released in the mid-1970s that starred Robert Redford and Faye Dunaway. In the movie Redford plays a CIA analyst, code-named Condor, who is marked for execution by the spy agency. Hiding out in a New York brownstone, he answers a knock at the door and finds a postman holding a special delivery package. Redford's character lets the man in, unaware he is a CIA hit man, and is forced to dodge bullets. The writer of the novel on which the film was based, James Grady, was so shaken by how closely Tabatabai's murder resembled the scene he had created that he wrote a newspaper editorial lamenting the collision of art and life. "When I came up with the idea in 1972, I meant to inject paranoia into the plausible, not to write a script for assassins," he wrote.

For Dawud, the glamour of serving the Islamic Revolution quickly faded. He intended Iran only to be a stopover on his way to China, where he wanted to study herbal medicine and martial arts. Decades later, he was stuck there, afraid to leave because U.S. officials might grab him if he left the country. He married an Iranian woman and worked on English-language publications in Tehran, including a website called Press TV. Before long, the only people outside Iran who remembered him were his family, the relatives of his victim, some cops, and a few reporters who came to Iran to interview him.

The stories Dawud told the journalists were colorful, and invariably he was at the center of the action. He claimed he had fought courageously in Afghanistan alongside the mujahideen to drive out the Russians and had traveled clandestinely through the Middle East as a trusted courier for Islamic activists. His email address also rang a dramatic and cultural chord. He used the name David Jansen, after David Janssen, the actor in the popular 1960s television series *The Fugitive* who played the role of Dr. Richard Kimble, a physician wrongly accused of murder.

Journalists had no way of knowing which, if any, of Dawud's stories were true. For most of them that wasn't a big problem. The fugitive was well-read and charismatic, and he shared his stories so freely that journalists were flattered into thinking that he was opening up to them because of their skills as interviewers. He was also a canvas onto which they could paint a portrait of their choosing. In some journalistic renderings, he was depicted as an unrepentant idealist; in others, as a sympathetic pawn in a global intelligence game; in still others, as a man caught between two countries and ideologies, uncertain of where he belonged. Writers tended to downplay his cold-blooded murder of Tabatabai or to absolve him entirely. "Who am I, who grew up privileged and white in a small and stable country, England, to take to task a man who grew up black in 1960s America? That would be intolerably arrogant," one writer responded when asked about his sympathetic portrayal of Dawud. Ira Silverman had embraced another view of the fugitive; he thought Dawud might want to seek redemption by becoming an informant.

Ira inherited the idea from one of his best law enforcement sources, Carl Shoffler, a celebrated police detective in Washington, D.C. Shoffler first gained fame in 1972 when he and two fellow plainclothes officers arrested five burglars breaking into the Democratic National Committee headquarters at the Watergate complex. He then rose through the ranks of the intelligence division of the D.C. police, developing close ties to the FBI and the CIA. Shoffler didn't look like a master detective. He was short and overweight with a choppy haircut and a bad complexion. He smoked and drank constantly. Fellow cops nicknamed him "Mr. Chips" because he always had one hand in a bag of junk food or a box of donuts while sitting in a car on a surveillance operation. But Shoffler possessed a sixth sense about how to work people for information, whether they were criminals he was trying to flip or journalists with whom he traded tips. He developed an infatuation with Dawud and became obsessed with cutting a deal for him to surrender and return home.

A few years after Tabatabai's murder, James Grady, the author of the book made into *Three Days of the Condor*, got an unexpected call from Shoffler, who invited him to meet at a greasy spoon diner in downtown Washington. Grady had never met the detective and found him seated at a back table talking on a shoebox-size portable phone, a rarity in that era. As the author approached, he could see Shoffler speaking excitedly into the device, saying, "He's here . . . He's here." Then the detective, covering the phone's mouthpiece, said to Grady, "It's him . . . It's him." The writer was baffled, and when Shoffler handed him the phone he found Dawud on the line. To score points with the fugitive, the detective had promised to introduce him to Grady and get him an autographed copy of his book.

Shoffler's interest in Dawud waned for a time, but it was reignited in 1993 after Islamic terrorists used a truck bomb to try to topple the World Trade Center. By then Shoffler had retired from the D.C. police force and was working as the chief fire investigator in a suburban Maryland county, though he still retained close ties with U.S. intelligence agencies. The detective feared that another terrorist attack was imminent and believed that Dawud, if he could be persuaded to return home, might share his insights about Islamic terror groups. Over the next few years, the two men exchanged letters and talked regularly by phone. Shoffler suggested he and Dawud had areas of common interest they could work on together, such as reducing the supply of opium from Afghanistan that was fueling heroin addiction in Iran and the United States. They talked about American politics and religion, and Shoffler relayed messages between Dawud and his aging mother. To further their intimacy, the detective confided in the fugitive about the health of his daughter, who suffered from juvenile diabetes. "Don't think I'm going soft with age, but over the past few months I have developed a bit of a soft spot in my heart for you," Dawud wrote him. "Ten years ago, we probably would have had to try to kill each other if our paths crossed. Life is strange indeed."

In time, Shoffler swung the conversation around to his real purpose, trying to negotiate terms for Dawud's surrender. The fugitive had made it clear in their talks that his own infatuation with Iran was over. "This country, this regime, I think it has seen its best days," he told Shoffler. "I think it is going to be history, not before too long. And any idea about this country leading the Muslim world, excuse the language, is pure bullshit."

The detective told Dawud that he thought he could get him a relatively short prison term for Tabatabai's murder, maybe about eight years, in exchange for information about terrorist organizations. Dawud, then in his mid-forties, was interested, but he wanted less prison time. He drafted a letter to the Justice Department that outlined the kind of help he was prepared to give and what he wanted in return:

I believe that I am in a position to increase your government's depth of insight into Iran, a state mistakenly perceived as the heart of the international Islamic movement; that is provided anyone really wants to know. The price for this service is freedom from all prosecution related to charges I face in the Bethesda affair. From what I see coming at America down the road in the Middle East, I believe that what I am offering to you is of no small value.

Soon afterward, Shoffler called him to say that prosecutors in Maryland were insisting that he spend his time in a state penitentiary rather than a federal prison. Dawud was disappointed. "Maryland is a slave state," he responded. "I don't think they'd appreciate a guy like me in Maryland." When Shoffler suggested he might have better luck working with another law enforcement official, the fugitive asked him not to hand off his case. "I'm not looking to be a notch in somebody's gun belt," Dawud said. Shoffler reassured him, "I don't need a notch. I gave you my word on certain things and I'd like to see that happen. I just wanted to make sure that you knew that I was shooting straight with you and that I will continue to shoot straight with you."

But by that time, Shoffler had realized that the fugitive's demands were absurd and that the only way to bring him back was to capture him. To do that, he needed to lure the fugitive out of Iran, and he decided to exploit what he had come to see as Dawud's biggest vulnerability—his vanity and incessant need for attention. Nothing would thrill Dawud more, he knew, than boasting on American television about his killing of Tabatabai.

Shoffler knew dozens of reporters and television producers, and every one of them would have jumped at the chance to get Dawud's confession. However, Shoffler needed to find the right journalist. He didn't want to burn any of his regular contacts like Ira by making them the bait in his trap, so he contacted a freelance journalist named Joseph Trento, who specialized in intelligence issues and tended to see the CIA's hand behind many events. Shoffler told him that Dawud was prepared to publicly admit to the Iranian diplomat's murder and asked him if he was interested in the story. Trento pounced, and brought the project to *20/20*, the ABC television news magazine, which agreed to hire him as a consultant to help produce the segment. Since an American television crew couldn't get into Iran, Shoffler suggested to Trento that he interview Dawud in Moscow. He then notified FBI agents there so they could arrest the fugitive as soon as he landed. At the last moment, Trento learned about the setup from an intelligence source and, without telling Shoffler, shifted the interview's location to Istanbul.

In his *20/20* interview, Dawud came across as an eager job applicant, dressed in a double-breasted sports jacket, a white shirt, a tie, and a tie clip. He recounted his killing of Tabatabai with calm and apparent relish, offering a description of the look on his victim's face after he realized he had been shot. "Our eyes locked and he gave me the very strong impression of a man who expected to die," Dawud said. The *20/20* correspondent who conducted the on-air interview, Tom Jarriel, then ticked down the checklist of questions journalists feel obliged to ask when speaking with a murderer. Had he felt any remorse about the shooting? Had he ever lost any sleep over it? Dawud assured him that he hadn't. "All governments kill traitors. So on that level, I never had any doubt about the man's death," he responded.

A few months after the interview was broadcast in 1995, Shoffler developed acute pancreatitis and died. When a CIA agent called Dawud to tell him, the fugitive broke into tears. He was so moved by Shoffler's death he sent flowers to his funeral. Ira also was distraught. He had felt as close to Carl Shoffler as he did to Bob Levinson; ever since meeting Carl some eighteen years earlier, he had spoken with him nearly every day. Some journalists maintain distance from their sources and avoid socializing with them. Ira was never like that. He treated his sources like family members and cherished friends. He and Shoffler also belonged to a circle of Washington journalists, lawyers, congressional staffers, and cops who met regularly for drinks or got together on weekends at one another's homes.

To honor his late friend, Ira wrote a eulogy of him for *The New Yorker* that praised his skills as a cultivator of informants and recounted his attempt to convince Dawud to surrender.

> Other cops call their informants snitches or stoolie and often hold them in contempt. Carl Shoffler . . . called them "sources" and, sometimes, friends. He gave out his home telephone number to mobsters on the run, to suspected terrorists and to defectors from hate groups. For most people engaged in police work, especially

those devoted to their families, such a practice would be unthinkable. But for Shoffler, it was a way to build trust. He needed those unsavory informants; he didn't coddle them, but they knew that he would always be upfront and straight with them.

The article was among several that Ira wrote for *The New Yorker* after he retired from NBC News in the mid-1990s. He had started his television career in the 1960s with the network's local affiliate in New York and had gone on to a high-profile career as a producer of investigative pieces for its flagship program, *NBC Nightly News*. As a producer, he was a behind-the-scenes workhorse, developing sources, digging out stories, directing film crews, writing scripts, and editing pieces. In the mid-1970s, NBC paired him with a young on-air correspondent, Brian Ross, whom the network brought to New York from Cleveland after he had won a prestigious journalism award for pieces about Jackie Presser, a corrupt Teamsters union official. The two men were polar opposites. The baby-faced Ross had blond hair and the looks of a choirboy. Ira was pudgy, balding, and bespectacled. He had grown up in Brooklyn and liked to spout Yiddish phrases and act like a street tough. But they clicked as a team, and Ira helped pioneer techniques such as stakeouts, hidden cameras, and confrontational interviews that soon became standard fare for investigative programs. The two journalists, dubbed "Batman and Robin" by their colleagues, became network news stars, winning awards for breaking big stories and appearing as guests on *The Dick Cavett Show*, a popular late-night program.

Ira also earned a reputation for tenaciousness and for the self-confidence to roll over his bosses when they got in the way of a story. In 1980, he got a tip the FBI was running a sting operation in which undercover agents, disguised as Arab sheiks, were making payoffs to congressmen in exchange for political favors. The head of NBC News thought the scheme sounded too crazy to be real and told Ira to forget about it. He didn't and secretly brought in a camera crew from outside Washington, parked a mobile home outside the Hill house where the payoffs were taking place, and, using night-vision equipment, filmed politicians going in and out. He and Ross then broke the story of the investigation, which was code-named "ABSCAM." It became one of the biggest political scandals of its time, and the FBI sting later served as the basis for the popular film *American Hustle.*

Not all of Ira's pieces were triumphs; some competitors thought he hyped stories, and the newsman, like other investigative journalists, sometimes was prone to obsession and even a little paranoia. After collaborating on a book with a New York City detective who had blown the whistle on police corruption, he turned up at NBC wearing a pistol. He told colleagues he had gotten death threats. By the mid-1990s, his relationship with Brian Ross had unraveled after the on-air correspondent accepted an offer to move to ABC News. Ross offered to take Ira with him, but Ira felt loyal to NBC and thought Ross's departure a betrayal. The men would never talk again.

After his retirement from NBC, Ira tried to make a fresh start in television, this time in front of the camera. He developed a show called *Ira's People,* on which he planned to interview the interesting criminals and scalawags he had met during his career. One episode of it aired on a cable channel, Court TV, before it was dropped. He also wrote crime stories for *The New Yorker,* and soon after 9/11 he pitched the magazine on a story idea—to profile Dawud as the prototypical Islamic terrorist. While he was writing Carl Shoffler's eulogy, the detective's family had given Ira his correspondence with Dawud and tape recordings he had made of their phone conversations. Ira's proposal was timely: in 2001, the fugitive had attracted public attention again, not as an assassin but as an actor in a critically acclaimed Iranian film, *Kandahar.* The movie tells the story of an Afghan-born journalist living in Canada who returns to Afghanistan to search for her sister after the country has fallen under the Taliban's oppressive rule. In one of the film's most memorable scenes, a doctor examines the journalist. Because of religious strictures, she has to stand hidden behind a sheet drawn across a room. The sheet has a peephole, through which he peers at her. They recognize each other as English speakers. The doctor explains that he is an American who originally came to Afghanistan to fight as a jihadist. But after weary-ing of endless battles, he says, he decided to teach himself medicine so he could do some good. He picks up a small bottle of liquid and pours its contents along the edges of his long beard, peeling off his fake whiskers. "I too have to come out from behind the curtain," he remarks.

In the film's credits, the actor playing the doctor is listed as "Has-san Tantai." When *Kandahar* was shown in the United States, Dawud was recognized and a flurry of newspaper articles appeared about the escaped killer's new film career. After Ira called him and mentioned he was a close friend of Carl Shoffler, the fugitive said he would be happy to meet. With the *New Yorker* assignment in hand, Ira con-tacted two Canadian journalists who worked for *The Fifth Estate*, an investigative television program that is Canada's equivalent of *60 Minutes*. A few years earlier, Ira had worked with the men, Linden MacIntyre and Neil Docherty, on a piece about Russian organized crime, and he had arranged for them to interview Bob Levinson on camera about his days tracking Russian mobsters in Miami. The Ca-nadians agreed to accompany Ira and do a piece about Iran for *The Fifth Estate*.

When the journalists arrived in Tehran in early 2002, oversized dump trucks were still hauling away debris from the site where the Twin Towers had once stood. After the 9/11 attacks, thousands of Iranians had taken to the streets in a show of solidarity with the United States, holding candles and shouting, "Death to terrorists." Behind the scenes, a diplomatic window also briefly opened—a crack in the decades-long wall of hatred and distrust that had characterized the relationship between the United States and Iran. Since the shah's overthrow, the countries had been engaged in what one historian called a twilight war, a hidden conflict in which they had used prox-ies to strike at each other. The United States had armed Iran's enemy Iraq during eight years of war in which three hundred thousand Iranians had died. Hezbollah, the terrorist group funded by Iran, had carried out a 1983 suicide bombing of a marine barracks in Beirut that killed 241 U.S. troops.

In the Taliban and Al Qaeda, Iran and the United States found common enemies. Prior to the U.S. invasion of Afghanistan, American and Iranian officials held secret diplomatic talks, their first in decades. Iranian officials, along with providing the United States with data on Taliban troop locations, offered to rescue American combat pilots forced to bail out over Iran. Then President George W. Bush, in his first State of the Union address after 9/11, named Iran, along with Iraq and North Korea, as a member of an "axis of evil," countries that were exporting terrorism and developing weapons of mass destruction. The diplomatic window between Washington and Tehran slammed shut again and the secret talks ended.

Dawud was waiting at the airport to greet Ira and the *Fifth Estate* crew when they landed. Despite his long exile in Iran, he looked so unassimilated he appeared as if he could have walked off the same flight. He was also homesick. All he wanted to talk about was American politics, movies, music, and books. In interviews with Ira, he displayed the same braggadocio he had shown seven years earlier during his appearance on *20/20*. He claimed that he tried to convince his handlers to let him assassinate a political bigwig like the former secretary of state Henry Kissinger rather than a nobody like Ali Akbar Tabatabai. He also expressed mixed feelings about the 9/11 attacks. While he thought it had been wrong to hit the World Trade Center because regular people worked there, the situation at the Pentagon was different. "I felt sorry for the people who died there, especially the civilians. But in a situation like that they knew where they were working," he said.

Dawud also repeated an old complaint. Iran, he told Ira, had not turned into the egalitarian, color-blind paradise that he had hoped to help create. Instead, its religious leaders, or mullahs, exercised autocratic control over all aspects of life, and people who questioned their authority faced imprisonment, torture, and death. "The Iranians of my immediate association turned out to be far from paragons of virtue," he said. "The corruption here among the highest levels of the mullahs is incredible. It includes financial malfeasance, gross human-rights violations, extrajudicial murder and two systems of justice, one for the mullahs and one for the citizens."

His wrath was especially focused on one figure—Ali Akbar Hashemi Rafsanjani, a religious leader who had served as Iran's president from 1989 to 1997. Since leaving office, Rafsanjani had become one of Iran's wealthiest men, with business interests spanning auto making, construction, real estate, and pistachio nut farming. Dawud contemptuously referred to him as the "pistachio man." One day he took the *Fifth Estate* team, which was doing a broad piece about the suppression of political dissent in Iran, to a Tehran mosque to film a prayer service. During it, Rafsanjani stepped out from behind a prayer screen to lead the service. Salahuddin told the Canadian journalists that the ex-politician had siphoned off millions of dollars from government oil sales while in office and then used front companies to secretly invest the money in Canada, both in real estate and in business ventures. Linden MacIntyre felt Dawud wanted him and his *Fifth Estate* colleagues to do an exposé of Rafsanjani, whom the fugitive called "the biggest thief in the history of Iran."

On their last day in Iran, Ira and the Canadians went to Dawud's home in Karaj, an industrial city not far from Tehran, to share a final meal prepared by the fugitive's wife. Afterward, the *Fifth Estate* crew left for the airport. Ira, whose flight departed later, figured he would be more comfortable spending time at Dawud's house than inside the terminal. Once alone with the fugitive, he began to regret that decision. He had seen a side of Dawud that hadn't come through in Carl Shoffler's letters or tape recordings. The fugitive told Ira that he suffered frequent bouts of depression, including some that lasted for months. At times, Dawud stammered or broke off speaking mid-sentence, staring out blankly for a few seconds before completing his thought. With the Canadians around, there had been safety in numbers. Now that he was left alone with Dawud, Ira's fears mounted. The fugitive told Ira that he would not hesitate, if needed, to kill again.

Dawud didn't drive, and when it was time for Ira to leave for the airport, he found a neighbor who agreed to take them. It was dark when the man arrived. Ira and Dawud climbed into the backseat. On the way to Dawud's home, Ira's taxi had traveled along a well-lit motorway. The fugitive's neighbor zigzagged along pitch-black roads that could have been headed anywhere. It was only an hour later, when Ira saw signs for the airport, that he began to relax.

His profile of Dawud, "An American Terrorist," appeared in the August 5, 2002, issue of *The New Yorker*. In the piece's conclusion, Ira hammered home Carl Shoffler's view of the fugitive, which he had come to share—Dawud knew secrets of enormous value to U.S. intelligence. Ira wrote: "Although his capture would be a triumph for law enforcement, Salahuddin may be, from an intelligence perspective, more useful left in place. His efforts on behalf of the revolution have afforded him a high level of access to the inner circle of the government, especially among moderates and others interested in rapprochement with the United States."

The article would prove to be Ira's last assignment for the magazine or any other publication. In 2006, he was seventy-one, and the years since his trip to Tehran hadn't treated him kindly. His career as a journalist appeared over, and, to stave off retirement, he tried his hand at writing screenplays, though none of them went anywhere. He also continued to speak regularly with Dawud. They talked about politics, events in the news, or whatever was on the fugitive's mind. But Ira kept hoping for more—a tip from Dawud that might point him toward one more big story, like the warning of a coming terrorist attack. In late 2005, Dawud told Ira he sensed the "curtain" was coming down on him in Iran. With the election of Mahmoud Ahmadinejad as the country's new president, the political protection he had enjoyed was disappearing and he worried he might soon be jailed or expelled. Iran was also becoming increasingly chaotic. People were falling ill with radiation sickness, he said, because the Iranian government was using nuclear waste to "harden" conventional bombs.

It was also in late 2005 that Bob started asking Ira about Dawud. The two friends had spoken over the years about the fugitive, but Bob's questions became more pointed and he wanted to know if Ira could connect him with Dawud. Ira knew Bob wanted to get government work, and if he could help him, he was happy to do it. He saw himself passing along to Bob the torch left behind by the journalist's other confidant, Carl Shoffler.

After their lunch in June 2006 at Clyde's, Ira and Bob started kicking around ways in which the investigator could approach the fugitive. Dawud had made it clear to Ira that he didn't intend to return to the United States to "face the music," but they figured that Bob could offer other favors, such as arranging a reunion in a safe place outside Iran where Dawud could see his mother before she died. To start the ball rolling, Bob suggested a strategy that dovetailed with the Illicit Finance Group's interests—Ira would tell Dawud he was a private investigator hired to locate assets in Canada purchased by former Iranian president Rafsanjani with looted money. Earlier, Dawud had told Ira and the *Fifth Estate* team that one of those ventures was a privately operated expressway that ran through Toronto called Highway 407. Ira sent Bob an email with information about it, referring to Iranians such as Rafsanjani as the "I" guys or people.

The link below gives you some of the history on the building and financing of the 407 Express Toll Route (ETR) which runs east-west just north of Toronto. As you'll see the 407 was originally constructed in 1997 for the Ontario Provincial Government by Raytheon. In 1999, it was taken over by an international consortium—here's where I imagine the "I" guys come in as players laundering their black money skimmed from the oil profits of the Islamic Republic.

Our guy says he can come up with the names of the "I" people who moved the money and set up the deals.

The "I" people feel comfortable in Toronto and have lots of clout there, our guy says, because of years and years of dealings involving the acquisition of heavy equipment for the "I" petroleum business, refineries, drilling, that kind of thing.

In addition, our guy says there are huge investments in shopping centers and commercial and residential real estate projects in and around Toronto and Vancouver.

Ira then called Dawud and told him that a private investigator friend was interested in the "pistachio man." A few days later, Bob, while in Geneva for a corporate client, made contact with the fugitive. Afterward, he sent Ira an email.

It turns out that our friend was waiting by the phone for a couple of hours thinking that I would call late into the evening. I later told him after we spoke this afternoon at 2:30 PM Geneva time that my parents on Long Island taught me never but never to call anyone's house after 9 PM, that it was bad manners. Anyway, our friend and I spoke for about thirty-five or forty minutes. I was very careful on the phone and used your "pistachio nuts" code. Very useful I might add. And what I hoped is that I became more than just another voice on the phone. I tried to accomplish a couple of things. One, I need his patience and trust in that I want to be as complete as I can when we sit down and talk about pistachios, etc . . . Second, I would like to sit down with him in a place other than where he is, despite his assurances of my safety, etc. I think that I was able to get that over for starters. I wanted to be able to sit down with him one-on-one, even if it's for a short time. I also specifically requested and tried to emphasize that if he or anybody else there has other leads I can pursue regarding pistachios in Toronto, he should send them through an email to you. I hope you can reiterate that for me. I don't want to jump the gun, claim I've got everything when I still have to nail many things down on the nut business . . .

Best wishes.

Talk soon. Returning home Sunday evening.

On behalf of Uncle, thanks (I really mean that!).

4

Boris

Bob Levinson arrived in Toronto in the early fall of 2006 to meet someone who knew a lot about the "pistachio man." He was an Iranian-born oil industry consultant named Houshang Bouzari who had served as a close advisor to Ali Akbar Hashemi Rafsanjani until he ran afoul of the politician. Then he had been nearly tortured to death.

Bouzari was among Tehran's best and brightest. After studying abroad and receiving a doctorate in physics, he returned home following the Islamic Revolution and attracted Rafsanjani's attention. The politician, then chairman of Iran's parliament, hired Bouzari as a speechwriter and appointed him an advisor to Iran's national oil company. After several years, Bouzari decided to leave Iran and moved to Rome, where he established himself as an energy industry consultant, setting up deals between multinational producers and the Iranian government. In 1990, he helped put together a $1.8 billion plan for oil companies to exploit a massive natural gas reserve known as the South Pars field that lay beneath the Persian Gulf between Iran

and Qatar. Over time, Bouzari's commissions on the deal were scheduled to reach $35 million.

After the deal was struck, Rafsanjani, who had become Iran's
president in 1989, summoned Bouzari to Tehran and asked him to
mentor his son Medhi, who was then twenty-one, in the energy business. Over the next two years, Bouzari would later say, he subsidized
Mehdi Rafsanjani's travel through Europe, including stays at five-star
hotels and evenings with escorts. Then Mehdi, through an intermediary, demanded a $50 million payment from Bouzari, threatening to
scrap the South Pars project if he was not paid. The consultant's
friends warned Bouzari to flee Iran and the wrath of the Rafsanjani
family, advice he failed to heed. In 1993, three Iranian intelligence
agents arrived at his apartment, arrested him, and brought him blindfolded to Evin Prison, where his nightmare began. Guards forced his
head into a toilet filled with excrement. Electric prods were applied
to his kneecaps, throat, and genitals. He was strapped down on a
table and a metal cable was used to whip his feet. On several occasions, he was informed he would be executed. Guards came to his
cell and escorted him to a scaffold, where they blindfolded him. He
heard a trapdoor drop open. After the blindfold was removed, he realized he hadn't been standing on the door. Eventually, through
bribes and guile, Bouzari managed to escape Iran.

Bob learned about him because of a lawsuit Bouzari filed in Toronto against Mehdi Rafsanjani. A Canadian organization working
on that lawsuit was affiliated with the Center for Justice and Accountability, the human rights group for which Bob did investigations, and
he used the connection to contact Bouzari. He told him he was conducting an investigation for a client interested in Iran's oil industry
and government. When Bob met the consultant, twelve years had
passed since his ordeal in Evin Prison but he still bore scars. Bouzari
was then in his fifties, and his hair and beard were prematurely
white.

By 2006, Mehdi Rafsanjani and the South Pars deal had drawn the
interest of law enforcement officials in several countries. Documents

seized by Norwegian officials during a raid on that country's biggest energy company, Statoil, uncovered multimillion-dollar payments to a London-based firm with ties to Rafsanjani's son. Statoil executives admitted they had retained Mehdi as a "political advisor" and were paying him to make sure the company's work in Iran ran smoothly.

When Bob told Bouzari he was eager to locate Rafsanjani family assets in Canada, the consultant laid out what he had heard over the years. He said the family owned condominiums near the city of Vancouver, investments made in the names of Ali Akbar Hashemi Rafsanjani's daughters. Along with the Highway 407 toll road in Toronto, the elder Rafsanjani had supposedly invested in an area shopping mall called Times Square. Bob drove out to the mall, a modest three-story suburban development, and took photographs of it. He called Ira. "I think we've hit the mother lode," he told him. He typed up an analytical report for the Illicit Finance Group summarizing what Bouzari had said and sent it to Anne Jablonski.

In mid-2006, Bob was also presented with an opening to push forward his relationship with Dawud Salahuddin. The occasion was a planned trip to the United States by the former Iranian president Mohammed Khatami, who left office in 2005 following the election of Mahmoud Ahmadinejad. Khatami was viewed in the West as a moderate, and the former U.S. president Jimmy Carter had invited him to speak at his public policy institute in Atlanta. Then Dawud called Ira to tell him that Khatami was considering canceling the trip because American officials hadn't notified him he would be treated as a diplomat, a status that would allow him to avoid fingerprinting and other humiliating entry procedures. The fugitive asked Ira if he knew anyone who could pull strings on Khatami's behalf, and Ira contacted Bob.

The former agent liked to tell FBI recruits when giving lectures about developing sources that it was critical to show a potential informant you possessed the clout to fix his or her problem. He emailed Ira: "Just so you know, I'm trying to be of assistance on the fingerprints issue. If I can, in fact, deliver, I'll let you know immediately so you can advise our mutual friend. If it's, in fact, possible, I would like to be the one who made even this small part possible—and be viewed as a problem solver."

Bob sent a note to a friend with the State Department's Bureau of Diplomatic Security, in which he hyped his CIA relationship to get traction.

> Have an op going w/Iranians for the "dark side" and would like to know if you or a buddy might be able to assist quietly. A former president of Iran, Mohammed Khatami is traveling to Washington for a speech . . . He's also going to hold some very hush-hush talks with former President Carter at the Carter Center in Atlanta. Hang up is that he has heartburn with being fingerprinted upon entering the U.S., saying it is, to him anyway, insulting to have to submit to same.
>
> If DSS is possibly going to afford security for a visit, is there any way you might be able to get DHS/Immigration to forego the normal fingerprinting. This, believe it or not, would assist me greatly in the op. Please advise ASAP if you can do me any good.

A few days later, Bob's contact got back to him to say he didn't need to worry; U.S. officials had already granted Khatami diplomatic status. But Bob still wanted Dawud to think he was the one who had made it happen. He wrote Ira: "Please tell our friend that MK is going to be met planeside. As a result of a personal favor, he will not be subjected to any indignities."

Along with his CIA work, Bob needed to find new private clients, and in the summer of 2006, he got a juicy assignment from a London-based public interest group called Global Witness. The organization specialized in high-profile exposés that revealed political and business corruption, particularly in the area of natural resource exploitation. Global Witness got much of its funding from the billionaire investor George Soros, and it had made its name in the late 1990s by revealing the trade in so-called blood diamonds, jewels mined in strife-torn African countries that were laundered by middlemen before ending up in shops such as Tiffany and Cartier. The cash generated by sales of the diamonds was then used to buy weapons, which were shipped back to Africa.

More recently, Global Witness had turned its attention to the natural gas industry in Eastern Europe. Much of the gas used to heat homes and generate power in Western Europe was extracted thousands of miles away in Turkmenistan, a former Soviet republic. From there, the gas was carried by a system of pipelines through Russia and Ukraine and to the West. In 2006, Global Witness published a report about possible corruption and political kickbacks in the awarding of contracts to middlemen involved in Ukraine's pipeline system. One of those companies was a little-known firm called RosUkrEnergo. On paper, a businessman, Dmitry Firtash, owned the company. But some former Ukrainian government officials had claimed to Global Witness that the real power behind RosUkrEnergo was the man then referred to by journalists as "the most dangerous criminal in the world," a Russian mobster named Semion Mogilevich.

Mogilevich, a bald, morbidly obese man, presided over an international network of gangs involved in extortion, prostitution, art theft, and fraud. He reputedly enjoyed the protection of politicians and police officials throughout Eastern Europe, and he had engineered a Wall Street scam in the mid-1990s that defrauded investors out of tens of millions of dollars. Following his indictment, Mogilevich never returned to the United States to stand trial, and he held a spot on the FBI's Ten Most Wanted list.

RosUkrEnergo denied any links to the gangster, but speculation continued. For Global Witness, tying Mogilevich to the firm would be a major coup. The group was funneling whatever information it was learning to U.S. prosecutors looking into the Ukrainian gas trade. To make a link between the mobster and the company stick in court, it would need hard evidence and witness statements. Investigating the business and political connections of Russian criminals was extremely dangerous. In 2004, an American journalist, Paul Klebnikov, who specialized in reporting on Russian political corruption, was shot to death gangland style on a Moscow street. At the time, Bob was working for SafirRosetti and he was hired to investigate Klebnikov's murder. Upon his arrival in Moscow, he met a former FBI official for breakfast at an American-style coffee shop there called the Starlite Diner. When Bob explained his assignment, his old colleague was stunned. "You need to leave right now," the man told him. "This is a high-profile assassination and it is dangerous doing this stuff."

Still, Mogilevich was the kind of criminal every investigator wanted to catch, and Bob drew up a proposal that would cost Global Witness $100,000 and take him to Kiev, Tel Aviv, and several other cities. Once the group signed off, Bob's first call was to another former FBI agent, John Good, who had also become a private investigator. Years earlier, Good had contacted Bob about one of his clients, a Lithuanian-born businessman named Boris Birshtein who lived in Toronto. At the time, Good was compiling a report for stock market regulators attesting to Birshtein's character, and he had run across newspaper articles and other material that gave him pause.

Birshtein was depicted in those articles as a politically connected financial Music Man, who had spent his career cutting questionable deals, first in the Soviet Union and then in two former Soviet republics, Moldova and Kyrgyzstan, that were economic backwaters. The businessman would arrive at a remote outpost by private jet emblazoned in gold lettering with the name of his Swiss trading company, Seabeco, check into a fancy hotel, and sign contracts with local politicians for commodities such as fertilizer, natural gas, and metals. Soon after his departure, scandals might arise involving alleged bribes paid to officials by Seabeco. Some newspaper articles also suggested ties between Birshtein and Russian organized crime, a link he vigorously denied. If asked about reports questioning his business practices, Birshtein would look hurt, place his hand near his heart, and swear he had never done anything illegal.

In 2006, Bob called Good and told him he wanted to meet Birshtein. Bob knew something about the businessman that he wanted to share with him. He felt certain that once Birshtein heard the news, he would be eager to tell everything he knew about Semion Mogilevich.

A decade earlier, just before Bob retired from the bureau, Mogilevich had met with federal prosecutors and FBI agents in an attempt to cut a plea deal and avoid indictment for his Wall Street scam. For two days, the gangster ratted out other reputed Russian mobsters. He also claimed that Birshtein, to nail down business deals, had paid huge bribes to top officials in the KGB and its successor agency, the FSB. Eventually, other criminals had declared Birshtein "out," or persona non grata, because he spoke too publicly about the bribes, Mogilevich said.

Prosecutors hadn't considered Mogilevich's claims worthy of a deal, and they did not take any action against Birshtein based on what the gangster said. But years later, the impact of Mogilevich's comments still lingered. When Birshtein went to an airport to take a flight to the United States or attempted to cross the Canadian-U.S. border by car, his name would flash up on a watch list and American customs officials would question him for hours about the reason for his visit. Over the years, he had spent a small fortune on lawyers and lobbyists in a failed effort to get his name off the watch list.

In mid-2006, Bob, accompanied by John Good, arrived at a three-story building in Toronto's elegant Yorkville district. A glass insert above a large wooden door was etched with the initials HTM, which stood for the Royal HTM Group, one of Birshtein's companies. The elegantly furnished offices could have been mistaken for a small, discreet wealth management firm. A photograph displayed on a credenza showed a short, stocky man in his late fifties with snow-white hair and a moustache flashing a wide smile as he posed alongside a dozen towering Africans dressed in colorful tribal robes. The photograph was taken in Nigeria's oil-rich and corruption-plagued Niger Delta region, from which Birshtein had recently returned after signing an agreement for Royal HTM to build a fertilizer plant, seaport, and power generating station. Nearby, there were two large diplomas awarded by a group called the International Informatization Academy to "Dr. Boris Birshtein." Bob sensed that Boris was just the type of guy with whom he could do business.

After some small talk, Bob told Boris about his FBI file and what Mogilevich had said. Boris, who spoke in a thickly accented English, said he had met Mogilevich only a few times and regarded him as a thug who tried to muscle in on his businesses. Bob made it clear he had come to seek Boris's help in his investigation of the Russian gangster. Then he played his trump card. One of the biggest lures an FBI agent can use to attract an informant is to get him a visa or clear up an immigration problem. Bob told Boris he was certain he could convince U.S. officials to take his name off the watch list. "I'd take whatever bullshit they give you at the airport one last time and let ME try to get this straightened out once and for all," he emailed him after their meeting.

Before long, Bob and Boris were talking on a regular basis about Mogilevich, the Ukrainian gas industry, Eastern European politicians, and gangsters. Then, about two months after their first meeting, Bob called the businessman and asked him whether he knew any Iranians. Boris understood how the game was played and he knew better than to ask why. He told Bob that a retired KGB colonel, Aleksei Sisoev, had introduced him in 2005 to an Iranian, Ali Magamidi Riza, who lived in Moscow. Sisoev described Riza as a businessman and a liaison between Iran and Russia in the weapons business. Boris spoke by phone with Riza in mid-2005 but decided not to pursue further conversations, he told Bob, after the Iranian started feeling him out about doing arms deals. At Bob's suggestion, Boris called Riza in August 2006 to discuss the possibility of meeting in Europe in the coming weeks. Bob sent a report about the conversation to Anne, identifying Boris in it as "the Russian businessman." In an accompanying email, Bob noted that the head of the Illicit Finance Group, Tim Sampson, was "definitely" interested in the subject.

> The Russian businessman who operates internationally indicated that Riza talked openly of being active and having interests in neighboring Tadjikistan [sic]. This country shares the same language

and culture as Iran, and has what he characterized as "Persian origins."

It was apparent to the Russian businessman, from both this conversation as well as with another well-connected Iranian businessman, Farshid Ali Zadeh, that a similar theme was being sounded; Iranians are seeking to "take over" Tadjikistan in order to gain access to its lucrative industries. The Russian businessman mentioned that two areas of great interest to the Iranians included aluminum resources and hydro-electric power plants.

The Russian businessman indicated that from the way both Aleksei Sisoev and Ali Magamidi Riza spoke in late August 2006, both could possibly be instrumental in the Government of Iran's efforts to circumvent any upcoming trade sanctions imposed by the United Nations.

Anne's response was quick. "Wow!!!!!! . . . Mucho thanks!" she wrote.

Along with pushing for more U.N.-imposed sanctions, U.S. officials in 2006 also blacklisted one of Iran's biggest banks and intensified their financial surveillance of Iran. Bob soon heard again from Houshang Bouzari, the oil consultant in Toronto. Bouzari liked Bob, but he wanted him to understand that the people he was asking about, the Rafsanjani clan, were ruthless. He suggested he contact an Iranian journalist named Akbar Ganji, who several years earlier had written a series of articles about the killings of dissident writers, an episode known as the "Chain Murders of Iran." In his reports, Ganji had pointed to the role of Ali Akbar Hashemi Rafsanjani in the deaths. Long after his final conversation with Bob, the consultant would remember telling him during it that he suspected he worked for American intelligence. Bouzari recalled, "I told him, Bob, whatever you do, never, ever, think about going to Iran."

5

A Gold Mine

A "gold mine," that's what the CIA was calling him, a goddamn gold mine. It was right there in Anne Jablonski's email, the one in which she quoted her boss, Tim Sampson, as saying, "This guy is a damn GOLD MINE!" Bob knew that stroking people to get information was a part of the intelligence business. He did it all the time. But he was certain Anne was telling him they were on the right track and scoring points with the right people. "Toots, say no more. You made my day—forget that, my year. Some of the best stuff is yet to be written up and sent you, so strap your seat belt on."

In the late fall of 2006, Bob felt the wind at his back. Even his kids noticed he looked happier and asked him what was going on. "I'm doing important work again," he told them. His second-oldest daughter, Stephanie, was about to deliver his first grandchild, and lots of work from private clients was coming in the door. A big consulting firm in Washington, TD International, was using him regularly to do background reports about Russian businessmen for American companies. A firm in London, Bishop International, which did counterfeit product investigations, assigned him work from one of its clients, British American Tobacco. He had so much on his plate he was farming out cases with links to Central America to a friend living there, a retired CIA agent named Robert Seldon Lady. The former CIA station chief in Milan, Lady had helped mastermind the 2002 kidnapping in that city of a Muslim cleric known as Abu Omar, who was grabbed on a street and flown to Egypt, where he was imprisoned and questioned while tortured. The episode was one of the first extraordinary "renditions" after 9/11 of a terror suspect, and when Italian authorities learned of the CIA's role in it, they tried to arrest the agency operatives involved, including Lady, who fled Italy for Central America, one step ahead of the police.

That fall, Bob banged out forty analytical reports over a two-month period for the Illicit Finance Group, including five on a single day. Anne's home on South June Street in Arlington was now a regular FedEx stop, and his CIA bosses were so pleased with his work they added $20,000 in travel money to his contract because he had already spent down its original funding. His arrangement with the Illicit Finance Group was lucrative because his reports to the agency often didn't require additional work but were rewrites of information that private clients were paying him to gather. For instance, he was giving Anne Jablonski constant updates about the status of his investigation for Global Witness into Semion Mogilevich and the Ukrainian gas industry. Global Witness would have fired Bob if it found out what he was doing, because his contract with the group called for his work to be kept confidential. But Bob didn't need to worry; Anne and her CIA colleagues weren't about to give the game away.

The kind of material Bob gathered was known in the trade as "raw" intelligence, a catchall category covering leads, hearsay, and rumors that needed follow-up to verify the information's accuracy, because often it wasn't true. His informants were often inhabitants of the shadow world among crime, business, and espionage who peddled information for a living. The two men who were his main conduits for material about Hugo Chávez and Venezuela were emblematic of the breed. One of them was a disbarred lawyer in Miami named Kenneth Rijock, who, after doing time in a federal prison for laundering Colombian cartel money, reinvented himself as a financial crime consultant. The other man, Thor Halvorssen, was a former business executive from Venezuela who became so infatuated with spying that a journalist described him in a profile as suffering from a "James Bond complex."

One report from Venezuela that Bob forwarded to the Illicit Finance Group detailed life aboard Hugo Chávez's presidential jet. It depicted Chávez as a vain, unbalanced, and sexually charged madman, who reportedly destroyed the plane's bathroom after finding a container of Nivea skin cream in it because he took the product's presence as a message from his staff that "he was prematurely showing his age." Rijock and Halvorssen also told Bob that their sources in Venezuela were reporting that Iranian engineers had arrived in the South American country to help expand its production of uranium, the key material in nuclear weapons.

In early November, Bob was scheduled to meet at Langley with the Illicit Finance Group and he checked with Anne to make sure it was on. "Yup! The 9th is definitely a go—8:30 in Tim's office," she replied. At the meeting, he discussed a report from Venezuela that Hugo Chávez was sending planes loaded with cash to Hezbollah, Iran's ally in Lebanon. CIA analysts apparently considered the information so important they told Bob to forward it to the National Security Council, the panel that advises the White House on intelligence and security issues. Bob had also prepared a memo for the Langley meeting outlining possible assignments he could take on in the coming weeks for the Illicit Finance Group, a process known in intelligence parlance as "tasking." His proposals ranged from a trip to Panama to meet a source knowledgeable about the FARC, the Colombian paramilitary group holding the Defense Department hostages, to gathering information about how Hugo Chávez was laundering money.

The memo also included several possible assignments involving Iran. Though Bob did not mention Houshang Bouzari or Dawud

Salahuddin by name, he outlined the type of intelligence he anticipated finding. He wrote:

An individual who has previously provided information concerning the alleged use of Canada as a safe-haven for funds obtained in bribery and extortion schemes related to the production and distribution of petroleum products in the Islamic Republic of Iran, has advised that he continues to acquire data concerning the names, businesses and locations of "fronts" for the former president of the IRI, Ali Akbar Hashemi Rafsanjani, as well as his sons Mehdi and Mohsen.

This individual can be contacted again on multiple occasions during the next thirty to ninety days at which time the information he provides can be included in appropriate analytical reports to be submitted. (Location of anticipated interview to be provided upon request.)

A second individual has indicated that he has access to data which concerns the same activity by former President Rafsanjani and his "clan" and it is believed that this person's information can be utilized to corroborate or substantiate the reporting of the first individual. (Location of anticipated interview to be provided upon request.)

Anticipated costs involved in the production of analytical reports concerning these matters over the next thirty to ninety days is $15,000 (this includes compensation for time and estimated travel expenses).

Another Iran-related project was outlined in the same memo, one involving Boris Birshtein. Since their first meeting in Toronto, Bob had cultivated his relationship with Boris, stepping up his efforts to resolve the businessman's U.S. entry problems. He had also arranged for a private detective in Belgium to recover one of Boris's most prized possessions, a collection of antique pistols seized by the court there during a legal proceeding against him. Boris had reciprocated by setting up a potential meeting with Ali Magamidi Riza, the Iranian living in Moscow, that Bob could attend. In his memo Bob wrote:

An Iranian businessman identified as Ali Magamidi Riza, who is operating between Teheran and Moscow, has been the subject of one previous analytical report (25 August 2006). Riza has been described by a Russian businessman who shared information about him confidentially as involved in the clandestine acquisition of arms and other sensitive material for the Iranian government.

An opportunity exists to acquire detailed and specific information concerning this individual, as well as his reported objectives for the Iranian government, and this data could be the subject of a future analytical report.

Days after the Langley meeting, Boris arranged to see Riza in Istanbul in early December. The timing fit with Bob's other travel plans. At the beginning of December, he was scheduled to be in the Austrian city of Graz to testify at the drug trafficking trial of Leonid Venjik, his former informant who had double-crossed him. Bob worried that some of the criminals involved with Venjik's counterfeit cigarette and cocaine trafficking operations might try to harm him there, and he asked a friend who was an FBI agent based in Budapest to try to coordinate protection.

I'm attaching a document I received literally in the mail which asks that I travel on my own dime to appear as a witness in Leonid Venjik's trial in Graz, Austria. I don't know if I'm being subpoenaed by the judge, the prosecution or the defense, but it really doesn't matter as I had travelled there in December 2004, giving a statement to the investigating magistrate about my investigation of the criminal networks involved in the case.

I'm going to ask your advice and assistance as I'm planning to go and appear as asked but since the case involves literally a dangerous mix of Latin American, Serbian and Russian organized crime networks actively trafficking in both counterfeit cigarettes (my interest, for Philip Morris) and cocaine, I am concerned about the possible security implications of my travel. It has become public in all of the documents that I was investigating all of these groups, using Venjik as my source, and my walking to the courthouse, in my opinion is going to be quite risky.

What I was hoping is that you or someone there in the task force might have some contact with . . . the Austrian National Police's Organized Crime Division, known as EDOK, or its local equivalent there in the town of Graz, with whom I could coordinate my arrival in town, my stay in the local hotel and my departure out of the city. I would just like to be in contact with someone so that if I do, in fact, spot someone either following me or attempting to do something, I could call someone.

In early December, Bob walked into the lobby of a courthouse in Graz, a city in southern Austria about two hours from Vienna. A DEA agent, Philip Scott Forbes, spotted him and introduced himself. Forbes was the DEA agent who had gone undercover to set the trap that snared Venjik, and he had concluded Bob was clueless about his informant's crimes. Instead, he thought of him as an old, tired agent who was paying the price for having taken his eye off the ball. But Forbes was having a hard time convincing Austrian authorities to share that view. He knew the case's magistrate wanted to question Bob with an eye toward possibly indicting him, and he guessed the former FBI agent's chances of walking out of court a free man were no better than fifty-fifty. Bob appeared nervous, and when he took the witness stand he insisted that he had trusted Venjik and hadn't known anything about his dealing drugs. After he was done, the case's magistrate remained skeptical and asked Forbes to stand and affirm Bob's testimony. Forbes noticed Bob turn in his seat and look at him. "I believe that Mr. Levinson has been truthful," the DEA agent said. With that, the magistrate told Bob he was free to leave.

Bob sent Chris a note from Graz. It wasn't about his close call but about their youngest son, Douglas, who had turned thirteen while he was away. Bob and Chris did their best to treat their kids evenly, and somehow they managed to pull it off; all of their children felt special and sibling rivalries rarely existed. He told Chris he felt bad about missing Doug's first day as a teenager.

> This is a short message from the Diaper Husband. You remember him: He's tall, dark (er, make that grey) and handsome. Sorry I woke you up. Make sure that Dudless knows we are celebrating his birthday once again when I get back.
> Love.
> The Bum Hus

Bob and Forbes bumped into each other again at the Vienna airport. Bob was his usual gregarious self and he urged Forbes to give him a shout if he ever needed his help or was looking for work after his DEA career. He said he was headed to the Middle East on behalf of a corporate client. A few hours later, when Bob landed in Istanbul, the charade that he was a CIA consultant gathering information for the agency while traveling abroad for corporate clients had ended. He had come to Istanbul for one reason alone: to spy for the CIA.

Boris Birshtein and Ali Magamidi Riza, the Moscow-based arms trader, were already at the Istanbul Hilton when Bob arrived. Another Iranian businessman, Ahmad Rowshandel, was due to check in the next day. Boris, who was still waiting for Bob to make good on his promise to get his name off a U.S. watch list, filled him in about what Riza had said about Rowshandel. According to Riza, the U.S. Treasury Department after 9/11 had frozen several bank accounts that Rowshandel had in South Africa, which contained a total of $17 million. American officials were still blocking Rowshandel's access to the money, and Riza asked Boris if he knew anyone in the United States who could help get the funds released.

The following day, after Rowshandel's arrival, the four men gathered in the hotel's lobby. Boris introduced Bob as a business associate. Rowshandel handed out business cards with the names of several companies he owned in Iran and Germany. One of them, called Oberlausitzer Feinpaplerfrabik, produced high-quality paper and was located in the German spa town of Bad Muskau, not far from the Polish border.

In the reports he sent later to the Illicit Finance Group, Bob described the two Iranians as though he was booking them.

Ali Magamidi Riza was described as follows:

Race: White
Sex: Male
Age: Approximately 42 years
Nationality: Iranian
Height: Approximately 5'10"
Weight: Approximately 180 pounds
Hair: Black
      Affects moustache and goatee
      ("Van Dyke" beard)
Eyes: Brown
Remarks: Speaks fluent Russian

Ahmed Rowshandel was described as follows:

Race: White
Sex: Male
Age: Approximately 60–65 years
Nationality: Iranian
Height: Approximately 5'10"
Weight: Approximately 180 pounds
Hair: Gray, balding with fringe
      Affects moustache and goatee
      ("Van Dyke" beard)
Eyes: Brown
Remarks: Has distinctive wide-set eyes
      Speaks Farsi, English, Arabic and German languages

Riza and Rowshandel got down to business. With the U.N. poised to adopt new U.S.-supported trade sanctions against Iran, they said their government was looking for foreign businessmen willing to go around those embargoes and supply their country with needed commodities. As an incentive, Tehran was prepared to reward cooperative companies by selling them oil at a sharp discount, which the businesses could then resell at market prices, pocketing the profit. It was the same strategy Saddam Hussein had used to convince companies to go around the U.S.-led embargo against Iraq. In his report to the Illicit Finance Group, Bob wrote:

> Ahmad Rowshandel said privately that he has what he termed "direct access to Iranian President Mahmud [sic] Ahmadinejad" and, further, that he held an unidentified position in the Iranian government.
>
> Rowshandel stated that he had the ability to arrange travel into Iran for international businessmen interested in doing business with that country's government.
>
> Rowshandel talked about the need for the Iranian government to have the assistance of international businessmen, particularly those based in Europe, as opposed to the United States and Canada, and it was looking for opportunities to develop the metals and urea businesses.
>
> Rowshandel said that he also had the ability to "reward" cooperative international businessmen with lucrative contracts from the Iranian government for quantities of oil at discounts of approximately seven dollars ($7.00) (US) per barrel.

During the meeting, Riza said Iran was particularly looking to buy large quantities of bauxite, an ore used in the production of aluminum. He explained that his country bought bauxite at one time through Marc Rich, an American-born commodities trader who had fled the United States for Switzerland in the 1980s amid tax evasion charges. More recently, Iranian officials had tried to negotiate a deal with the Russian government to get bauxite. Those talks had fallen apart, Riza said, because Russia was concerned the arrangement could limit supplies of the ore needed by its biggest producer of aluminum, United Company RUSAL, or RUSAL, as it was often called.

Bob was still buzzing with excitement when he returned home to Florida and finalized his reports about the Istanbul meeting. He sent them to Anne, who was coming back from a trip to Los Angeles, telling her he was certain Tim Sampson and others would be pleased.

This has got to be the REAL "welcome back" message.

There's a Fedex which should arrive later this morning which contains a personal note to you and a memo for Mr. B and Mr. T . . .

Hope we can talk later in the week, once you're back to work and back up to speed (hope THAT doesn't take too long.)

Glad you enjoyed L.A.—was stationed there in the mid-70s and literally had a blast running around in Hollywood and Beverly Hills chasing mobsters.

Bob also wanted to do something for Boris. The Christmas holiday season was approaching and the businessman planned to take his wife to Florida. He was driving there and his route would take him into the United States over the Peace Bridge in Buffalo, New York. Bob didn't want Boris to get hassled and sent a note to an FBI agent in New York City, asking him to make sure Boris's border crossing went smoothly. The note contained the date and time of his anticipated arrival at the bridge and the license plate number of his Mercedes: "Our friend, together with his wife, plans to spend a few days down here in my neck of the woods for the holiday season. He did us, meaning the U.S., a real biggie when we were overseas together."

Bob's note did the trick. Boris and his wife were soon enjoying the sun in Fort Lauderdale, about to board a relaxing five-day luxury cruise.

6

Christmas

Christmas was the best time of the year for the Levinson family. Everyone stopped what they were doing and gathered together, usually in Coral Springs. In 2006, only Dan, Bob's oldest son, was missing because he was in Japan teaching English while he waited to hear from law schools. A new addition to the Levinson clan was attracting much of the attention: Stephanie's infant son, Ryan.

One family tradition was to pile into cars and head over to a nearby mall, Sawgrass Mills, for a shopping spree. On Christmas Eve, Chris and a few of the kids went to church. The holidays gave Bob a chance to catch up with Sarah, his third-oldest daughter. She was living in New York, working for Goldman Sachs writing business proposals about potential new investments the firm could make. Sarah saw her father less often than her siblings did and she was struck by the changes in him. He was only fifty-eight, but he was starting to look old and even a little frail. He kept promising his children, including Sarah, that he would take care of himself by eating better and getting more exercise. To prove he was serious, he would open his wallet and pull out a gym membership card. Sarah worried that her father might not stay healthy enough to celebrate many more holidays.

Since returning from Istanbul, Bob had tallied the amount spent in recent months on projects for the Illicit Finance Group and discovered that he had drawn down all the money available under his contract, including the extra $20,000 he had gotten. By his accounting, the CIA now owed him $12,000 in unpaid time and expenses. If more money wasn't added to his account, he would be dead in the water until May 2007, the time when his contract was scheduled to renew. He couldn't imagine Anne and Tim letting him sit on his hands for the next six months; the material he was providing them was too good. If anything, he sensed an opportunity. He wanted a bigger role at the CIA, and this seemed like the right moment to make his pitch.

He drafted a memo, recommending amendments to his contract. Currently, the agreement limited the amount of time he could charge to the Illicit Finance Group to 80 hours per month. He proposed raising that monthly cap to 135 hours, a 70 percent increase that would boost his contract's value to about $130,000, and suggested a proportional rise in his expense allowance. In a lengthy note to Anne, he cited the number of analytical reports he had provided since joining the agency in June, highlighting his contributions to CIA efforts in areas such as counternarcotics (CNC), counterterrorism (CTC), and counterintelligence (CI).

> Sorry to have inundated your front yard with FEDEX packages!
>
> Attached is a memorandum which requests that Brian and Tim consider augmenting the budget on the contract since, in effect, as of 31 December, my funding runs out.
>
> I know that when things were drawn up last spring, no one anticipated exactly how much would be needed or, in fact, how successful I might be at producing reports for the shop.
>
> It's six months later and, as I put it in my memo, I think I have written approximately 111 reports on a variety of subjects, all hopefully of interest to your shop, CNC, CTC, or the CI people.

Most recently, while you were away, I went over to Istanbul and, using Boris B., was able to meet with and fully identify two (2) people who appear to be covert Iranian government agents involved in recruiting European and Western businessmen for the cause—and identify the system the Iranians are utilizing to reward those who cooperate with them.

. . . I hope that at least some, if not most, of this stuff, has been both new and of interest to the guys and gals.

I have a number of opportunities to keep up the flow of reports but need to know that if I spend this amount of time on your work, I'll be 1) compensated (at the same rate, mind you—not looking for more money) and 2) have the ability to be reimbursed for those out-of-pocket expenditures I'm making on a regular basis, both for travel and for other things.

I do not want to be a pain in the butt and want to assure you that I am loving every minute of it—I just want to be able to continue . . .

If Brian or Tim need more information, either via documentation, by phone, or from me IN PERSON, for example, just whistle, and I'll be on a plane to DC to meet.

Please insure that the "powers that be" know that I continue to regard this work as a unique opportunity to serve my country and do not take anything for granted.

When Bob heard back from Anne, it wasn't the response he was expecting. She told him the legislation authorizing the CIA's new fiscal year budget was stuck in Congress and that agency expenditures were on hold until it passed.

Minor problem. We're OUT of cash on this contract for extras. Brian is searching high and low to scare up some cash to cover some recent expenses you billed. The well is sorta' dry thanks to some cuts here. So . . . feel free to take some TIME off, as right now we've got to start robbing Peter and paying Paul to cover things . . . Lovin' the stuff, though.

Bob could hardly believe it. During the past six months, all his feedback was positive and upbeat. He began to worry that maybe Tim Sampson or Brian O'Toole was unhappy he had used up his funding too quickly. He wrote Anne: "Wanted to make sure you knew that I was sorry for any aggravation caused, tried to stay within budget and get the job done. Also wanted to know if Mr. T. and Mr. B. were satisfied with what I've been doing."

She reassured him the agency's budget was the only issue: "Oh, Bobby, everybody's MORE than satisfied, they're thrilled. Right now the problem is the coffers are EMPTY and so there's just nothing to pay for the extra at this point. But trust me, everyone is THRILLED."

He managed to hide his disappointment from Chris and the kids. Some of his sources, including Ken Rijock, the ex-lawyer in Miami, were clamoring for money and he needed to hold them at bay. Rijock kept emailing Bob about the dynamite intelligence Thor Halversson was getting from his informants in Venezuela. Rijock said if the CIA wasn't going to pay, Bob should start shopping Thor's material to another part of the U.S. government, like the Defense Intelligence Agency: "T is losing faith that the sponsor will come up with the money. There is uranium activity by Iranians in VZ and T has 2 weeks of intel on many important subjects sitting on his desk waiting for funds. If the sponsor fails to deliver, what do we do? Go to DIA? I think that's our next move here. The stakes are too high."

Bob responded he was also frustrated with the agency. "I too am pissed off to a fare-thee-well . . . My feeling is that if this stuff is so important and so good, they should have begun re-funding the project on December 13th."

He sent Anne another memo listing projects he could pursue if funding was freed up. He wrote:

Enroute to your house for delivery on Friday 29 December is something I put together for you and the gang, dealing with your own favorite subjects. I know that I'm supposed to be a "good boy" and stand down but, as I explain in the accompanying note in the package, I felt an obligation to get what I got and get it in your hands. After more than 35 years of doing this stuff, I still love it and can do it in my sleep. Best wishes for a happy, healthy and successful New Year. Hoping that I can continue helping out!

His accompanying memo mentioned several projects, including a report about an upcoming meeting between Hugo Chávez and Mahmoud Ahmadinejad to discuss what Venezuela might do if Israel attacked Iran. Bob had also contacted Houshang Bouzari, the oil consultant in Toronto, and asked him to run down information about Ahmad Rowshandel, one of the Iranians he had met in Istanbul. Without mentioning Bouzari's name in his memo to Anne, Bob wrote that one of his sources had "conducted detailed inquiries concerning six (6) companies which were registered in the Islamic Republic of Iran by Ahmad Rowshandel of Teheran and Berlin—these inquiries show that Rowshandel is probably running these companies as 'fronts' for the Iranian Revolutionary Guards."

It was also around Christmas that a juicy case came through Bob's door, one he knew Anne would love. It had everything—Russian organized crime, Kremlin politics, espionage, and a mysterious murder—and the case was making front-page news around the world. The dead man was a former KGB agent named Alexander Litvinenko, who had been living and working in London as a private investigator. He was an outspoken critic of the Russian president, Vladimir Putin, and publicly blamed him for the murder of a Russian investigative journalist and other crimes. On a November day in 2006, Litvinenko developed severe stomach cramps and diarrhea. After he was hospitalized, doctors discovered that an assassin had slipped him a lethal dose of a radioactive material, polonium, and on his deathbed Litvinenko accused Putin of ordering his murder.

Bob's connection to the case was through another former KGB agent turned private investigator named Yuri Shvets. When Bob got assignments from clients seeking information about Russian businessmen, he often subcontracted the jobs out to the former Soviet spy, who had been living in the United States since the early 1990s. Shvets told Scotland Yard detectives that Litvinenko had asked him for similar help on a background investigation he was hired to conduct on a very highly placed member of Putin's inner circle. Their inquiry had turned up damaging material on the man, Viktor Ivanov, the chairman of Aeroflot airlines and a Moscow power broker known as the "Cardinal of the Kremlin." Then Litvinenko made a fatal mistake, Shvets told British detectives. He gave the report to another former KGB operative working on the assignment. Shvets said he was certain that the man, Andrei Lugovoi, was a double agent working for Russian intelligence and that when Putin and his allies learned about Litvinenko's findings, they ordered him killed.

Shvets shared much of his story with a British journalist, Tom Mangold, who had known Bob for many years. Mangold had the same type of relationship with Bob that Ira Silverman enjoyed; he tipped off the journalists to information and they reciprocated by treating him well. Mangold had suggested to Bob after his bureau retirement that they collaborate on a book about his law enforcement career that the British writer wanted to call "Manhunter." With England transfixed in late 2006 by the bizarre murder of Alexander Litvinenko, Mangold did a radio program about the case called The Litvinenko Mystery, on which both Bob and Yuri Shvets appeared as guests. Bob explained how the results of due diligence investigations could make or break multimillion-dollar business deals, suggesting the stakes were high enough to provide a motive for murder.

Around the time the program aired, a Canadian-born lawyer living in London, Robert Amsterdam, contacted Bob about the Litvinenko case. Bob had worked earlier for Amsterdam, who represented Mikhail Khodorkovsky, the former head of a major Russian energy company, Yukos Oil. In 2005, Khodorkovsky had been convicted of tax fraud charges and sent to a Soviet-era prison that once served as a forced labor camp. Many people suspected Vladimir Putin of engineering his downfall, and Amsterdam believed that any information tying Putin or his allies to Litvinenko's murder might help free his client. He hired Bob to find out what he could.

Right after New Year's Day, Bob sent Anne another note, alerting her to his involvement in the Litvinenko case. He also told her he was about to take another overseas trip for Global Witness as part of his continuing investigation into Semion Mogilevich and would be meeting in the coming weeks with sources in the United States and abroad who could provide valuable information for Illicit Finance Group. In the note, he abbreviated counterterrorism as "CT" and Russian organized crime as "ROC."

Can you give me any guidance on what to realistically expect regarding the possibilities of obtaining continued funding? I'm asking for the following reasons, which hopefully will show why this is on my mind.

I'm going to be meeting with a couple of people this week here in Miami, one of whom had been very helpful on the situation down south. The other has been helping on CT stuff down south.

Next week, I'll be in Tel Aviv in connection with the natural gas investigation.

I was contacted during the holidays by Khodorkovsky's Canadian lawyer, whom I helped out on a couple of international cases a few years ago, and he is interested in turning me loose to document connections between Yukos and the Litvinenko poisoning.

I'm going to Budapest on the 20th and while most of my time is to be spent on the natural gas thing, an intermediary is going to be setting up a meeting with a top level Russian "businessman" who should be able to assist us with the ROC program.

Please let me know if you can share anything, even at this early time.

When he didn't hear anything from her for two days, he emailed Anne again. "If Mr. Brian and Mr. Tim have any news, please share when you get a chance," he wrote. This time, she responded. Anne said that the CIA, like other government offices, had been closed an extra day over the New Year's break to mark the funeral of the former president Gerald Ford, who had died in late December.

Brian and Tim? Poor chumps got the flu! Our office is a dang sick ward. Everyone, myself included, is just coming back off a lonnnnnnng holiday weekend. We got Monday off for New Year's, Tuesday for Ford's day of mourning and I took Wednesday to burn up some use/lose leave. Lovely. And we were in NJ for the annual family holiday (dys)function. We're desperately hunting for money. The budget is AWFUL. We barely have travel money left for the analysts. But we're still hopeful. You're doing AWESOME stuff. Don't doubt that for a second.

He emailed her back:

Thanks for the update—trying to stay out of your way and keep what for me would be a very low profile (can't seem to do it, though!)—I truly and I mean TRULY appreciate the kind words—having been doing my best to keep all of my "friends" happy and hopeful—expect to be back from across the pond on the 13th. If there's anything new just email me.
    Best to Mr. Bob and the sick ward inhabitants.

Even while traveling, Bob couldn't let it go. A few days before his return home, he emailed Anne yet again, signing his note as "Buck," the nickname he often used for himself in his notes to her.

Hey Toots
    Heard anything good?
    Anyone recovered and back at work?
    Asking because lots of things are happening.
    Best wishes—home Saturday
    Buck

Anne responded that things were status quo and explained that even she was having trouble finding money to fly to Fort Lauderdale on CIA business. Bob wrote back:

> Hope they find YOU some travel money as I was planning to take you out to dinner with Christine Mary. We've got quite a few favorite restaurants we were hoping to find an excuse to try . . . Give my best to Mr. Brian and Mr. Tim and tell them I'm trying to keep everything and I mean EVERYTHING w-a-r-m.

When Bob returned in mid-January from his travels, he made plans to go to Washington. Robert Amsterdam wanted Yuri Shvets to give a formal affidavit about Alexander Litvinenko's murder, and he had arranged for him to do it at a Washington-area law firm. Bob let Anne know he was heading her way.

> Toots,
>   Look out!—I'm coming up around mid-week on another matter—would love to see you and Mr. Bob for dinner. Will be trying to stay in the same place as I always do, around the corner from your place. Anyway, wanted to share a few things, see how things are going in general and someone else is paying the freight.

Anne replied that she and her husband would be happy to meet him for a meal. Then a day later Bob followed with another email, wondering if, while in Washington, he could meet with managers at the "pickle factory," an old slang term for the CIA he liked to use.

> Planning now to fly into DC on Wednesday and, if you and Bob are free, we could do dinner on Wednesday evening. Now, separately, let me know about the possibility of (and I realize it is very, very short notice and probably impossible) getting to sit down with Mr. Brian and/or Mr. Tim there at the pickle factory on Wednesday afternoon

or Thursday morning. I would welcome the opportunity to show my face, let them know what's up and basically "check in." If you think they would consider it "pushing things" and something that wouldn't be appropriate, given the situation with funding just say the word—I'll leave everything be.

Both men were away, Anne replied, adding that the agency's money situation still hadn't improved. On January 17, she and her husband met Bob for dinner at Harry's Tap Room, a restaurant not far from their Arlington home. Bob was still weary from his recent trip overseas, and he told Anne he was about to leave on another one. He said he was feeling tired and his diabetes appeared to be getting worse. Then, when a waiter appeared, he ordered a rich meal. Anne looked at him. "You've got to stop this shit," she said. "You are not twenty years old."

Bob took off again and sent Anne several reports based on information he was picking up on his travels for other clients about Russian organized crime and other subjects. She shared them with her husband, Bob: "The first package came—holy SH**!!! . . . You really did hit the motherlode, my man. Bob and I were gasping reading what you sent. Damn we gotta find some money."

Two days later, while passing through Paris on his way home, he sent her another email, this one about the Iranians he had met in Istanbul with Boris Birshtein. He urged her to show the note to Tim Sampson, referring to him as "Mr. T."

Toots,

Greetings from Paris—coming home tomorrow night.

Can you get word to Mr. T that the parties with whom my friend and I met in Istanbul in early December are interested in meeting with my friend (and I) in Europe sometime in Feb. I just know they are going to discuss the kinds of matters of great interest, particularly now. I was wondering if you can just drop this stuff on him with all the other stuff that's coming to your house tomorrow—doing my best to keep things warm.

Anne assured him she would. He didn't get a response back. He had been pushing for two months, sending her email after email filled with bait without getting bites. His financial situation was getting worse. By January 2007, his work for Global Witness was winding down and he had failed so far to find a solid link between Semion Mogilevich and RosUkrEnergo, the gas pipeline company. His search had started on a high note in the fall when he went to Kiev to meet with Ukraine's former prime minister Yulia Tymoshenko, a politician best recognized in the West by the thick blond braid she wore wrapped around her head. Tymoshenko's supporters claimed that Ukraine's president had removed her from office after she questioned deals involving RosUkrEnergo, and they told Bob they had documents proving Mogilevich's role in the firm. But Tymoshenko, who was known as the "gas princess" for the millions she had made from natural gas companies she and her husband owned, never produced the records, leaving open the question of whether they existed. After that, Bob had spent months and nearly all of Global Witness's money chasing Mogilevich's shadow from country to country without results.

There was one possible stop left, Dubai. Early on, a source told him that police officials in Dubai had raided a May 2006 meeting at which Mogilevich and other crime figures were discussing a $500 million investment in Ukraine's pipeline system. Bob's source said the men were later released but insisted that authorities in Dubai retained photographs and surveillance tapes from the meeting. Bob suggested to Global Witness that he go to Dubai to try to get the evidence. It was a long shot and the group made it clear it was going to shut down the investigation if Bob came back empty-handed. Officials of the group wrote: "We don't have much money left. The Dubai trip seems to offer the best chance of getting what we need . . . I want to emphasize that we will need really detailed information confirming the who, where, when and exactly what was said. We would like you to ask if you can get a copy of the transcript or see a copy and make notes from it."

Bob replied he understood and assured the group he had numerous sources in Dubai who could open doors for him with law enforcement officials there. "I know the pressure is on to try and I repeat TRY (cause in these things, you really NEVER KNOW) to get something hard for you to write about." But Bob really didn't have any personal contacts in Dubai and he was soon scrambling to find some, reaching out to former FBI and DEA agents he knew to see if they had connections to investigators in the United Arab Emirates. One security consultant in Dubai warned him the local police were notoriously closemouthed, and he could end up in jail if he asked too many questions.

He wasn't put off. Dubai, with its ultramodern skyscrapers and man-made island in the shape of a palm tree, was a crossroads for deal makers, spies, and money launderers. It was also a major hub for smugglers and product counterfeiters. To Bob, a trip to Dubai was a chance to see a new part of the world and possibly make connections to generate future business. It was also his ticket to see Dawud Salahuddin.

For months, he and the fugitive, using Ira Silverman as their intermediary, had talked about places to rendezvous. They had for a time discussed Turkey as a possibility but then dropped the idea. Dawud kept coming back to one suggestion, Kish Island, a small spot of land in the Persian Gulf. The island was part of Iran but it had a unique visitors policy. Foreigners, including Americans, could visit Kish without applying to the Iranian government for a visa, a requirement for travelers anywhere else in the country. As a result, about one million people came annually to Kish, many of them Iranians who had fled their homeland for the United States or Europe during the Islamic Revolution and used the island as a spot to reunite with family members who remained behind. Businessmen and laborers working on short-term visas in the United Arab Emirates could take an hour-long flight from Dubai to Kish and then hop on a return flight to Dubai and get their U.A.E. visas renewed.

Ira told Bob it was clear from his conversations with Dawud that the fugitive wanted to talk. Bob wanted to meet him, too. At the FBI, he had seen how a single source could make an agent's career and how agents had coasted for years on the coattails of a key informant. Dawud could be that kind of informant for him with the CIA. All he needed was to see him for an hour or so, just long enough to be able to write up a report and send it to the Illicit Finance Group. Once Anne and Tim Sampson read it, they would have to stop and read it again—their guy had pulled off the unthinkable; he had landed a source inside Iran. It was hard to imagine that the CIA would have any more problems finding money for him. They would be begging him for work. Bob didn't know how much information Dawud had to offer, but with the right kind of stoking he might prove useful. Besides, a quick trip from Dubai to Kish wouldn't cost him much and the potential payoff was enormous.

Bob's travel plans for Global Witness put him in Dubai in the middle of February. Once he booked his flight there, he emailed Ira, telling him to let Dawud know he was available to meet him on Kish afterward: "I don't know if our friend has changed his mind or not about that meeting but I could do something toward the end of that week."

Ira checked with Dawud and wrote to Bob: "Whatever works for you. Very clear that our guy wants to meet with you when conditions permit."

7

The Black Dahlia

Chris would kill him, Bob knew, if she found out about Iran and Dawud, so he decided not to say a word about his plans. Still, he needed to tell her something. He always called her at least once a day while traveling, sometimes twice or three times. He liked to hear her voice and find out what was going on with the kids. Sometimes, while interviewing an informant, he would excuse himself, duck out into a hallway, and call home.

He planned to shut off his cell phone while on Kish so Iranian intelligence couldn't monitor it, and he needed an excuse to explain why Chris wouldn't be able to reach him for a day. He came up with a solution. About a week before his departure for Dubai, he told her that the Illicit Finance Group had contacted him with an urgent request—the CIA needed him to take a "side trip" while in Dubai as part of an important mission for "Uncle" and he would be out of contact for a day. The request was so last-minute he would have to pay his expenses out-of-pocket, and the agency would reimburse him when he got back.

Bob and Chris rarely fought, but when they did, it was usually about money. Chris knew as much about the state of Bob's business as he did. She also had more financial sense. She kept a close eye on his books, helping him out by depositing payments from clients and writing checks to pay sources. She knew their family was treading water. They had house payments, big college bills, and weddings ahead. They were also still in a hole from the lawsuit involving the Bank of Cyprus, the assignment Bob took on the "success fee" basis. A year later, the case's judge still hadn't rendered a decision and Bob's $100,000 bill remained unpaid. Before Bob could say another word about the side trip, Chris told him he wasn't going to do more for the CIA or advance Uncle Sam another dime until the agency paid him what he was owed.

Bob knew she wasn't going to back down. If he was going to meet Dawud Salahuddin, his only option was to make one final pitch to the Illicit Finance Group. He decided to send it to Tim Sampson. As head of the CIA unit, he was responsible for its budget, and if extra money was available, he was the person who could shake it loose. On February 5, Bob wrote a memo laying out what he could do for the Illicit Finance Group while in Dubai for Global Witness. In it, he abbreviated "organized crime" as "OC," and the former Soviet Union as "FSU." He didn't specifically mention Dawud or Kish in the memo and asked Anne to forward it to Tim.

TO: Tim
VIA: Anne
FROM: Bob L.
DATE: 5 February 2007
Best wishes from Florida.

I'm leaving on 13 February to go to Geneva on behalf of Global Witness, to meet with the folks in both the Surete de Geneva and the Swiss Federal Police, relative to information about possible Russian OC funds being invested in the FSU natural gas industry.

From Geneva, again, at Global Witness request, I'm flying to Dubai, U.A.E. to meet with officials there regarding the alleged meeting of Russian OC figures in May 2006 on this same subject.

In connection with ongoing research I am conducting for an analytical report on the foreign investment of kickback and bribe monies of top Iranian government officials, an individual with detailed knowledge of this subject, with whom I have been in contact by phone and e-mail over the past year, has agreed to meet with me. This meeting will take place either in Dubai or on an island nearby and should cost about two to three thousand dollars.

I would like to know if I do, in fact, expend my own funds to conduct this meeting, there will be reimbursement sometime in the near future, or, if I should discontinue this, as well as any and all similar projects until renewal time in May.

Please advise me as soon as possible as I leave in eight (8) days.

I hope that last week's papers on clandestine ties between Venezuelan officials and FARC, the three Venezuelan banks laundering FARC funds, and Hugo Chavez' brother's racketeering activities were of interest and contributed to your shop's production.

Levinson

Over the next few days, Chris kept seeing Bob at the kitchen table hunched over the telephone. She overheard Anne's name mentioned and assumed the discussions were about money. When Bob got off one call, he looked happy. He said the Illicit Finance Group had found another $10,000 to add to his contract, enough to just about wipe out his bill. Chris couldn't argue with that.

On February 9, four days after Bob sent the Dubai memo, he and Chris drove to a Best Buy in Plantation, Florida, not far from their home. He told her he needed to buy presents for an informant he planned to meet during his trip whom he couldn't pay in cash. Two days earlier, Ira Silverman had sent him a shopping list. Over their years of correspondence, Ira had gotten to know Dawud's tastes. He liked Miles Davis, John Coltrane, the Neville Brothers, Billie Holiday, and Ray Charles. The fugitive was also a fan of the comedians Richard Pryor and Chris Rock. Ira sent Bob photographs of Dawud and him taken during his 2002 trip to Tehran. "I wish I were hitting the stores with you, to say nothing of the trip itself," Ira wrote.

After buying a bunch of compact discs and videotapes at Best Buy, Bob and Chris went to a nearby BrandsMart, where Bob got a CD of Chris Rock performances. Bob also bought a book for Dawud that he had enjoyed reading—*The Black Dahlia*, a novel about a Hollywood starlet's unsolved murder, written by James Ellroy, an author whose own mother was killed by a man who was never caught. By the time the shopping spree was over, Bob had spent $170 on gifts and filed away the receipts so he could submit them to the CIA.

The next day, he called his travel agent and asked her to book him on a February 22 flight from Dubai to Kish Island on Kish Airlines, an Iranian airline, with a return flight to Dubai on the following day. He contacted a hotel on the island recommended by Dawud called the Maryam and reserved a room with two beds. There was one more preparation he needed to make. He needed a cover story to give Iranian authorities if they asked about his reason for coming to Kish.

In January, when Bob was in London, he had accompanied Jeff Katz, the head of the investigative firm Bishop International, to the offices of British American Tobacco to talk with company executives about counterfeit cigarette cases. One of the investigations Katz and Bob were pursuing involved a ring that was smuggling into Iran knockoff versions of a brand called "Montana," a product made by the Iranian Tobacco Company under an agreement with BAT. At their January meeting, executives of BAT had urged Katz and Bob to continue the inquiry, saying they would send their findings to Iranian officials. Using his home computer, Bob found a facsimile of British American Tobacco's letterhead and composed a letter supposedly written by a company executive, authorizing him to travel to Iran on the cigarette maker's behalf. The letter read:

> Dear Mr. Levinson
>
> In connection with our recent meeting together with representatives of Bishop International Ltd., you are hereby authorized to travel on our behalf to appropriate locations, including the Islamic Republic of Iran, in order to conduct research and interviews, as

necessary, relating to the trafficking in counterfeit British-American Tobacco brand products. Please forward the results of your efforts to our offices here in Globe House, London upon completion of this research and interviews.

Ira asked Bob if he wanted him to share his cigarette smuggling cover story with Dawud so the fugitive would be on the same page if police on Kish questioned them. "When I speak with him next, do you want me to mention BAT," Ira wrote in an email.

Everything was set. But on February 12, the day before Bob was scheduled to depart for Dubai, a problem arose. He had been expecting to get a formal notice from the CIA showing his account credited with the added $10,000. However, nothing had come. The last thing he wanted before leaving home was another fight with Chris about money, so he decided to take preemptive action. He contacted the agency's contracting office to find out the status of the funds so he could start submitting bills. The woman with whom he spoke appeared bewildered by his inquiry, and he sent an email to Anne.

Leaving tomorrow for Geneva and Dubai. Had a brief conversation with a nice lady in contracts . . . Asked her if I could submit anything in writing yet and she indicated that she had no paperwork or notice at all about the additional 10. I told her that I would reach out for the person in your shop who is handling this stuff and get them to give her a call . . . I am grateful for the confidence everyone has shown in my act.

As it turned out, Anne already knew about Bob's call because the woman in the contracting office had contacted her.

Hey there, hope you have a safe trip! The contracts people are NOT yet looped in on the additional money and by the time the news of the money officially finds its way to her, a month will have passed. She called, baffled and we had to explain that official notification would be forthcoming. Things have to first wend their way through our office bureaucracy before it reaches the contracts office. They'll need to amend the contract, get you to sign it, etc. Anyway, probably best if we keep talk about the additional money among "us girls" (you, me, Tim, Brian) and not get the contract folks involved until they are officially notified through channels!

Bob sent her a quick apology. "Hey, sorry about that—hope I did not cause any problems . . . In the future, I promise to keep it between us girls until told otherwise—my bad!!!" he wrote. "NO problem," Anne assured him. "I promise."

Switzerland was Bob's first stop on his way to Dubai and Kish. He took a train to Neuchâtel to meet a friend, D'Arcy Quinn, an executive in the division of Philip Morris International that investigated cigarette counterfeiting. Quinn's superiors had recently told him he was going to be fired because of his reliance on aging investigators like Bob whose sources were growing old and stale. Quinn wanted to dump dirt on the company before walking out the door and told Bob he had long suspected some Philip Morris executives were profiting from the illegal cigarette trade. He also warned him to be careful in Dubai because a major trafficker there had threatened to kill a company investigator.

In Geneva, Bob spoke with two Swiss detectives about Semion Mogilevich and RosUkrEnergo. He had known one of the men, Philippe Séchaud, since the mid-1990s, when Séchaud joined a newly formed Swiss police unit aimed at Russian organized crime. Bob served as a mentor to him, and after Bob's retirement from the FBI, Séchaud arranged for him to testify as an expert witness at the 1998 trial in Geneva of Sergei Mikhailov, a man who stood alongside Semion Mogilevich in the pantheon of Russian crime lords.

The case ended with Mikhailov's acquittal. Bob's former FBI supervisor in New York, James Moody, told a writer he thought the case collapsed because of Bob's poor courtroom performance, but Séchaud pointed out that key witnesses against Mikhailov were murdered prior to the trial's start. The Swiss detective had stayed close to

Bob and long admired his knowledge, enthusiasm, and tenacity. But when he saw Bob that February, he noticed a change in him. He seemed overwrought and anxious.

While in Switzerland, Bob found plenty of reasons not to go to Iran—all he had to do was watch television or read a newspaper. The twilight war was heating up. In early 2007, American troops raided an Iranian consular office in the Iraqi city of Irbil and arrested five "diplomats" who U.S. officials said were really officers in Iran's Revolutionary Guards. Militants infiltrated a U.S. military compound in Iraq and killed five American soldiers, an attack U.S. officials suspected was planned and financed by a special unit of the Revolutionary Guards called the Quds Force. It was also the Quds Force, White House officials believed, that was teaching Iraqi militia groups how to build more powerful improvised bombs. "I can say with certainty that the Quds Force, a part of the Iranian government, had provided these sophisticated IEDs that have harmed our troops," President George W. Bush said at a news conference in early 2007. "I'd like to repeat, I do not know whether or not the Quds Force was ordered from the top echelons of the government. But my point is, what's worse . . . them ordering it and it happening, or them not ordering it and its happening."

Bob had taken dangerous risks before. This time was different. He was going into enemy territory without a safety net or a fellow agent to bail him out. There wasn't anyone with whom he could talk about it besides Ira, because he had made certain his friend was the only person besides Dawud who knew about his plan. He decided to write him.

Uncle Ira:

Greetings from Geneva—getting ready to fly Sunday-Monday to Dubai to conduct some quiet inquiries there and hopefully not run afoul of the tribal leaders in charge of that part of the Emirates— was told this morning (and that's what prompted this e-mail) that one Western investigator made a routine question of one of his Emirates law enforcement contacts, something like, how many guys are in your unit, only to be told by his contact that he, the investigator, could literally be arrested for asking such a question. There is definitely a strong fear among even the most hardened of Middle East security guys that the climate is very, very hostile and one had to be very, very careful in this environment. I'm going to test the waters for a couple of days and if I don't like what I continue to be hearing, I'm gonna be out of there.

Which brings me to my visit to the island. I would like to share with you that prior to getting on the plane, I made an extensive number of shopping trips in Miami and picked up, using your list, a number of CD's and DVD's (Richard Pryor and the other kid)— stuff that should bring a smile to our friend's face. What I'm seeing on T.V., however, continuously on CNN International is the Middle East being worked up into a real paranoid state over possible invasion, airstrikes, etc. on that particular country. As a result, I am now really, really concerned that an American from Florida traveling over there in the midst of this environment is going to attract a great deal of attention (both from the natives as well as the services) and, as a result, put this man's ass in quite a bit of jeopardy. What I guess I would like from you is to ask our friend, prior to Wednesday, the 21st, to confirm that he believes the island is, in fact, a more relaxed environment, that the arrival of a tall, handsome, obviously American (overweight, as he is) is not going to place ME or HIM in jeopardy.

I guess as I approach my fifty-ninth birthday on the 10th of March, and after having done quite a few other crazy things in my life, I am questioning just why, at this point, with seven kids and a great wife, why I would put myself in such jeopardy. The answer, I keep telling myself, is that YOU went over there, to the capital, no less, and came back in one piece. My problem is that I'm not a journalist, will have no real live backup the BAT letter notwithstanding, and just wanted to be reassured that if I spend twenty-four hours there on the island, I'm not going to wind up someplace where I don't really want to be at this stage in my life . . .

If our friend says, hey it ain't gonna be like the mainland, it's a vacation spot, relax, etc. (and by the way, the local airline, the hotel people, all have been very, very pleasant and accommodating—all is confirmed for my arrival, with a room with two beds, etc. per our friend's recommendation) then I'm going to proceed and fuck it, do what needs to be done. If, as I'm reading, the stakes have been elevated over the last week or so, Bush's news conference, the military's efforts to document the supplying of better improvised things etc., well I'm going to reconsider and ask our friend to postpone things.

I truly believe that he has stuff worth going over and getting for this country. I'm just looking for a little reassurance that I'm not being too crazy at this age.

In his response, Ira pointed out that the circumstances of his visit with Dawud in 2002 after the release of the film *Kandahar* were different.

Not easy to assess this one. True, I did eight days in the capital but I was with the Canadians and that may have given me some cover. Also, we had press visas, and the Canadians had talked to the people in the embassy in Ottawa about going over to do a story about the movie he was in. My thought is to hear what he has to say, but if you are not at ease with this, we should wait for a better time.

Two hours later, after speaking with Dawud, Ira sent Bob another note.

Our guy just called. Very relaxed. He says you should just think about it as coming over for a long lunch. He sees no problems for himself or for you. Says he will be in the lobby early morning wearing a black beret.

Bob felt his fears ease. He told Ira he felt a little embarrassed about sounding the alarm.

Thanks so much for resolving this—

Couple of things to pass along if it's not too imposing:

1. Earliest flight I can get on Thursday morning leaves at 10:30 AM from Dubai and I have a reservation on it.

2. I have a reservation to return on the 8:30 PM flight on Friday from K back to Dubai—Is our friend planning to stay for only the day as I had made a reservation at the hotel for one night for one room with two beds. Should I stay for the day and take the 8:30 PM evening flight back? I know I'd feel a lot better spending as little time there as I have to. Also, will it cause him a problem if I don't stay overnight, because I will do so if needed—

3. Can you confirm, one more time, the amount of funds he's expecting to be reimbursed for time off from work—I also need to know if he is expecting that in USD or their currency, which I suppose I can exchange at the airport—just need to know how much and what kind.

Best wishes and thanks—again with the situation in the media, I needed to know from his perspective whether things were nice and calm.

Last thing, love that touch with the beret in the lobby. Sounds like something out of "Casablanca."

Not long afterward, Ira forwarded Bob a rambling note from Dawud containing the fugitive's thoughts about Iran's political situation. For months, Ira had told Dawud that Bob was collecting information about former president Rafsanjani's investments in Canada and that he planned to bring his dossier to their meeting on Kish. In his note, Dawud explained to Ira that he was rethinking how to best use the information, or the "North Country files," as he called the material. In early 2007, the former Iranian president was in the midst of a political comeback because of growing public dissatisfaction with the country's current leader, Mahmoud Ahmadinejad. Rafsanjani's past sins, Dawud said, seemed increasingly forgivable compared with Ahmadinejad's politics.

Have been concentrating on the matter at hand—and in particular the almost forgotten story of the North Country files. Perhaps it is too late to talk about this but after our conversation this morning I came up with a way in which the material could possibly be put to positive use.

The reason for the reluctance on this side, as I mentioned, is that the subject has been given a new political life thanks primarily to the Little Man with the big mouth. Our subject also seems primed for an upward change in fortunes and the simple truth is that despite the many deep blemishes, he remains the most dynamic and intelligent of his kind.

. . . If I had in hand the North Country stuff I believe I can put it to positive use PRIVATELY AND DIRECTLY and not for public consumption. Understand that things over here are done differently and that it would be to no one's benefit to do an expose but it could be an intangible and significant gesture to present the thing to him as a measure of both good will and a wake up call.

. . . Keep in mind that things here are complicated, few will try anything and I was lucky to be born black and in America, as it is a given that "niggers are crazy"—but that insanity sometimes unleashes bursts of creative energy that have an impact. I am feeling like that right now.

The following day, Bob went to the Geneva airport. He never made it onto his British Airways flight. When an airline purser checked his passport, he saw it contained an Israeli stamp. Bob was so inexperienced about traveling in the Middle East he hadn't known to ask to have his Israeli entry stamp put on a separate form rather than in his passport. The purser told him officials in Dubai might refuse him entry. He realized there was little choice but to return to Florida and get a fresh passport. Bob asked Ira to alert Dawud that their meeting needed to be rescheduled. When he touched down in Miami, he notified Anne he was back and they should talk soon. She responded:

Hey hey!! Glad you're back SAFELY. I always worry about you when
you travel. (I can only imagine what your wife goes through . . .)

Anyway . . . I'm traveling tomorrow (Wednesday and Thursday)
but can be reached on my cellphone around dinnertime tomorrow.
I plan to hunker down in my crappy hotel room in Columbus Ohio
and work on a yoga article I'm trying to write . . .

We missed you!

Tim sends his very best . . .

Back in Florida, Bob rescheduled his Dubai trip and told Ira to let
Dawud know they could meet on Kish on March 8. Ira sent him an article Dawud had just written for the news website run by Joe Trento,
the freelance writer whom the late Carl Shoffler tried to dupe in his
effort to capture Dawud. Since their initial meeting a decade earlier,
Trento had remained in regular contact with Dawud, and he asked
the fugitive in early 2007 to share his perspectives about relations
between the United States and Iran. Dawud focused his article on two
men, whom he described as inspirations to him. One of them was an
Iranian official who tried to curb drug use. The other man was Carl
Shoffler. In the article, he celebrated the deep personal bonds forged
between the late detective and himself, omitting any mention of
Shoffler's ploy to arrest him.

A lot of what we discussed dealt with how to overcome culture
divides and the reciprocal misperceptions and animosities bred by
misunderstanding that roiled then and even more so today the pul-
sating antagonism between Teheran and Washington. Of course
that agenda was impossible to accomplish but at least the two of us
gave it our best shot.

After Bob read the article, he wrote back to Ira.

He's obviously a brilliant guy and has a great way with words. I am
reminded of what you said about him having literally thrown his

life away with "Maryland." Talk soon. This was an enormous help in understanding him a little better.

On March 2, 2007, the day before Bob left home for the final time, he met with sources in Miami who provided him with information about money laundering techniques used by the FARC, the paramilitary group in Colombia. Couriers for the FARC were allegedly transporting huge quantities of dollars from the United States into Mexico and then on to Panama, where the funds were being deposited in banks. A $39 million shipment was about to be moved, and one of Bob's contacts was optimistic that he could recruit a courier and infiltrate the ring. Bob typed up the report and another one about FARC money laundering and sent them to Anne, who wrote him back: "OOH! Excellent . . . And very timely . . . thank you thank you thank you."

Bob told her he could get the CIA lots more: "My guys are very, very close to all the action and we are in a position to do more. I'd probably have to go there after my return from across the pond on the 12th. Pls let everyone know we can, in fact, do more on this."

Anne replied the Illicit Finance Group couldn't officially assign, or "task," him on more new projects, apparently until his contract supplement worked its way through the CIA's bureaucracy: "You hit a home run out of the park with the stuff!!! We can't, of course, task you on anything. But let's just say it's GREAT material."

Bob told her he understood: "Message received, no need to say more. I'm hoping that by the time I get back on the 12th, they will have had all those meetings and I get a call from the people re that add'l 10. I'll then do what needs to be done."

8

An Appointment on Kish

It was time to go. On the morning of Thursday, March 8, Bob left his room at the Marriott Towers in Dubai and rode the elevator to the lobby. He spoke to a desk clerk who took his large, hard-shelled suitcase and handed him a baggage check. It didn't make sense for him to lug it to Kish Island for one night. His big black binder filled with photographs of Russian gangsters was inside, and Bob didn't want to explain to a curious Iranian cop why he was carrying it. He filled a small roll-on bag with a change of clothing, his toiletry kit, and the presents for Dawud. He got into a cab and headed for the airport.

Dubai proved to be a bust for his Global Witness investigation of Semion Mogilevich. He tried to figure out how to approach the local police but none of the ways worked. Soon after arriving, he had met for lunch with four men who worked as investigators or security officers for the State Department, the DEA, and other U.S. agencies at a restaurant in the Emirates Towers, a Dubai landmark. Bob spent the meal telling stories about his FBI days chasing Russian gangsters. Afterward, he opened his binder and showed his companions photographs of Mogilevich and other Russian rogues. No one recognized the pictures, and the investigators told him they hadn't heard about any recent arrests by the Dubai police of Russian criminals. They exchanged business cards with Bob and wished him good luck.

The rest of his time in Dubai was spent on other business. The judge in the Bank of Cyprus lawsuit was finally ready to issue a ruling and Bob had started to worry that the law firm involved, Reed Smith, might balk at paying his bill. From Dubai, he emailed a lawyer in New York named John Moscow, whom Bob knew from Moscow's days as a top prosecutor in the office of Manhattan's famed district attorney Robert Morgenthau, and told him he might need his help getting the money.

> I've been a good, quiet boy for a year and a half now and am hoping that [they] are men of their words; i.e. if Reed Smith wins, I get paid in full ($108G). If you wouldn't mind following up on this, again, I plan to compensate you for time & expenses involved.

He exchanged emails with some of his children. Dan was still teaching in Japan and wrote his father that he had managed to fix his computer, which was making a strange whirring sound.

> Just a quick message to tell u Grandpa Harold would have been proud. I went out and bought a screwdriver set the other day. That night I couldn't sleep and realized I should check out my laptop. So I took it apart, found a giant thing of lint blocking my fan, and removed it. It is dead silent now and it doesn't get hot at the bottom. It was the best thing I've done all week. I might not need a new laptop after all. Anyways, I hope all is well in Dubai.

Bob wrote back.

> Hey, boy am I proud of YOU, pal. Ya know the joke I always use with your mother is "how many Jewish guys does it take to screw in a lightbulb? She always answers—one to make the call to someone to do the work. Oh well, congratulations on fixing your laptop.

I'm still gonna get you a new one for law school. That's a promise. Love ya, running off right now for an appointment and very proud of Daniel Levinson.

Bob also sent a note to his youngest daughter, Samantha, who was then sixteen. As a young girl, Samantha had been very shy, a little like her mother, and Bob had worked to coax her out of it. She would accompany him on Saturday mornings to the local bagel place. At first she hid behind her father. But he insisted she order, and eventually Samantha, whom Bob nicknamed "Turtle," started to get over her shyness. She was now a junior at Coral Springs High School and was giving a speech that day during a student government election. Bob offered his encouragement.

Gurlie
    Good luck with your speech today. I'll be thinking of you and know you'll do just fine.
    I truly enjoyed your "Fellow Turtlonian" e-mail. It was very creative and shows a mind with empathy for our fellow tortoises.
    As I said on the phone, please, please do-not-sweat-the-small-stuff—Just do your best and let everything else fall into place.
    And also know that your parents love you (despite the green shell and all!)
    Love
    Father of the silliest turtle in the United States

As he left his hotel, he sent a message to Ira: "Off today for that place. All is set. Best wishes and thanks for all your help in getting this arranged."
    Ira responded: "Bob, so good to have your words. Please get back to me when you can."
    Once at the airport, Bob called Chris. "I'm getting on a plane," he told her. The flight from Dubai to Kish took about thirty minutes. Upon landing, his plane taxied toward a small terminal building with a large red sign that said KISH INTERNATIONAL AIRPORT. It

stopped short of the terminal and Bob, after descending a stairway, boarded a bus for a brief ride. He walked up a short flight of black granite stairs into the building. A large round clock hung in the center of it. The waiting area consisted of about a dozen gray metal chairs. In twenty-four hours or less, he planned to be seated on one. He held his passport and the forged BAT letter ready for inspection by Iranian customs officers. Cleared, he walked out of the terminal and got into a taxi. It headed down a two-lane road divided by a wide median planted with palm trees and passed large, modern hotels resembling the types of places where he usually stayed.

Chris tried to reach him that day, but he had apparently shut off his phone, so she sent him an email with some updates from home. A client had paid a bill and St. John's law school in New York had made a provisional offer of financial aid to Dan if he kept his grades up.

Surprise!

You shut off your phone or it doesn't work.

So here is the fill in.

The check came in the regular mail.

The packet for St. John's also came for Dan. They are offering him $20,000 in tuition renewable each year if he is in the top half of his class. I tried to email him, I told him to call me for details.

Last, but not least, the bar in our shower broke in half and fell down. I hope it can be repaired.

Everything happens when you are gone!

Love, Chris.

The taxi pulled into the driveway of the Maryam hotel. It was a large white baroque-looking building with shuttered floor-to-ceiling windows that had seen better days. A doorman opened the door and Bob walked into an ornate, aging lobby decorated with plants and Persian rugs. A desk clerk greeted him and asked him to sign the reception book.

The following day, Friday, March 9, Ira waited at home, expecting a call or an email from Bob. He wanted to know about his meeting with Dawud and how it had gone. By evening, he'd heard nothing and he started to get anxious. It was early Saturday morning in Dubai, which was eight hours ahead of Washington. Bob should have been back there. Ira wanted to call Chris to see if she had heard anything, but his wife, Betsy, convinced him to wait until morning. Just after 11:00 p.m., Ira sent his friend an email: "Bob, how are you doing?"

Then he went to bed. When he awoke Saturday morning, he went downstairs to check his computer. There wasn't anything there. He sent another email: "Bob, how are you doing?"

It was March 10, 2007, Bob Levinson's fifty-ninth birthday.

9

The Missing Man

On Saturday, March 10, in Coral Springs, Chris awoke to the sound
of the telephone ringing on her bedside table. She was sure it was
Bob. It was his birthday and he always liked the kids to celebrate
with him. A big family party to mark the event was planned for
the following Saturday at Disney World in Orlando, but Samantha
and Douglas would still want to scream "Happy birthday!" into the
phone. When Chris picked up the receiver, she heard Ira Silverman's
voice. He wanted to know if Bob had called her. When she said no,
Ira told Chris that Bob had gone to Iran and that he hadn't heard from
him since. Chris sank back in shock. All of Bob's comments—about
the side trip, the presents, the back-and forth with the CIA over
money—suddenly made sense. He had also been more nervous than
she had ever seen him before a trip. Ira told Chris he would call Dave
McGee and ask him to alert the FBI.

When Ira reached Dave, the lawyer was speeding west along
Interstate 10, heading back to Gulf Breeze after spending Friday night
in Tallahassee. Ira laid out the story about Bob, the CIA, and Kish,
adding he thought their friend had been kidnapped. It was because of

Bob that Dave and Ira knew each other. They had met in the early 1980s, when Bob was with the FBI and Dave was trying to build a drug smuggling case against Robert Vesco, the famous financial swindler who had fled the United States for Cuba after his indictment on fraud charges. Dave had been trying to get information from his superiors at Justice Department headquarters about Vesco, but every request he made ran into some kind of roadblock. When Dave mentioned to Bob he thought that a Justice higher-up had put in a political fix to block his case, the FBI agent told Dave to expect a call from a friend of his named Ira who worked for NBC News. The prosecutor and the newsman struck a deal. When Dave wanted information from the Justice Department about Vesco, he gave his questions to Ira, who contacted his sources in the department, got the answers, and relayed them back to the prosecutor. Dave was never able to bring drug charges against Vesco, but he and Ira had remained friends ever since.

Dave's first call that Saturday morning was to a former Justice Department colleague, Greg Miller, the U.S. attorney in Tallahassee. Dave had stayed at Miller's home the previous evening, and Miller had mentioned in passing that a new prosecutor in his office used to work for the CIA. Dave got his number from Miller and asked the lawyer to alert the CIA that it had a man missing in Iran. He then contacted an FBI agent he knew in Tallahassee and asked him to call a twenty-four-hour crisis center in Washington, D.C., that notifies federal agencies about emergencies involving government employees.

Chris was also making calls. On his way home from Dubai, Bob had planned to stop over in London for several days to meet with clients, and she called the Marriott Heathrow, the hotel where he had a reservation. She was told he hadn't checked in as yet. Then she phoned a neighbor, Ron Jordison, a former DEA agent who sometimes worked with Bob. Jordison knew Bob was going to Dubai and had made a connection for him there, an agent for the Naval Criminal Investigative Service named Doug Einsel. But he hadn't been aware Bob had left on the trip until two days earlier, on Thursday, when Jordison had called Bob to suggest they go out and grab a bagel at a local place in Coral Springs. Bob laughed and told him he would have to take a rain check because he was in Dubai.

Chris decided for the moment not to say anything to the kids. It was still early and anything was possible. Her husband could be up in the air over the Atlantic or ill somewhere in a hospital. She was fiercely protective of her children and she did whatever she felt she needed to do to shield them. Chris was one of seven kids, and when her father fell ill, she dropped out of college and came home to help out.

Along with Samantha and Doug, who were sixteen and thirteen, two of the older Levinson children were at home that Saturday. Sue, who was thirty, had recently moved back in to save money while she worked at a nearby JetBlue facility training flight attendants. Dave, nineteen, was on spring break from Emory College in Atlanta. Chris did her best to pretend nothing was wrong. But as the day wore on, Sue sensed something was going on. Her mother kept darting in and out of her bedroom. Then, around noon, Chris emerged from her room and announced she was running out for a while to visit the Jordisons.

That's when Sue started to worry about her father. The Levinson children knew their mother usually left home only when she needed to buy groceries, run errands, or shuttle them back and forth from sports or events. Chris wasn't a hermit or a shut-in. But she was an intensely shy and private person, and spontaneously socializing with friends or running over to a neighbor to chat was the kind of thing she rarely did. Once in a while she hosted women from the neighborhood who got together to play bunco, a dice game. For the kids, it was a huge event. They almost never saw their parents entertaining, and suddenly card tables set with bowls of candy would appear in the house. Bob sometimes worried that Chris found being a mother to seven a convenient excuse to avoid social contact. He told friends that when their big nest was finally empty, he was going to take Chris traveling and find other ways to pull her into the world.

Chris didn't go to the Jordisons. Instead, she drove to a local Panera Bread restaurant, where she had arranged to meet Ron Jordison and an FBI agent who was driving up from Bob's old office in Miami. When the agent arrived, Chris told her that Bob had gone to Iran for the CIA. The agent replied that the bureau would start checking airline manifests and alert embassies in the region. She assured Chris the bureau would call her with updates.

While their mother was out, Sue told her brother Dave she was worried their father might be sick or in trouble. She thought Ira might know if something had happened to him, so she and Dave, without telling their younger siblings, snuck upstairs to call him. Sue spoke to Ira for a few moments and then put him on speakerphone so Dave could hear. Ira told them their father wasn't responding to phone calls and that people were looking for him. He didn't mention anything about Iran, but Dave assumed his father was somewhere in the Middle East. Sue then phoned her sister Stephanie, who was living in Tampa. Earlier in the day, Stephanie had called her mother to chitchat and give her the latest update on her infant son, Ryan. Her mother hadn't said anything specific then about her father, though she had mentioned in passing she was starting to worry about his health. At the time, Stephanie hadn't made much of the comment; maybe it was just her mother's attempt to get Stephanie to remind her father to take better care of himself when she saw him at his birthday party at Disney World. As Stephanie listened to Sue, her stomach dropped. She hung up the phone and burst out crying. Her husband, Randy, had left home about twenty minutes earlier for a rare evening out practicing with his garage band. She called him. "You need to come home, something has happened to my dad," she said.

When Chris arrived back from Panera Bread, she asked Dave to take Samantha and Douglas out for dinner at Chicken Kitchen, a nearby restaurant. Dave did his best to pretend nothing was wrong, and while he was at the restaurant, he got a text message from Sue that put him at ease. After speaking with their mother, she thought their father wasn't missing but had been detained briefly. Her impression proved mistaken. Around 7:00 p.m., after Dave returned home with Samantha and Doug, Chris asked her children to sit together at the dining table. "Your father is missing and I don't know where he is," she told them. Samantha burst out crying and ran upstairs to her room. Doug sat in his chair looking numb.

Meanwhile, Ron Jordison called Doug Einsel, the NCIS agent in Dubai. It was the middle of the night there and Einsel was startled out of a deep sleep. Einsel had been among Bob's luncheon companions at the Emirate Towers and he was alarmed to learn Bob had gone to Kish. Every American investigator who worked in the Middle East or knew about Iran knew that its intelligence agencies believed there was no such thing as a retired FBI agent and considered ex-agents like Bob to still be working for the United States. Einsel assured Jordison that a search would start at daybreak.

At 10:00 p.m. that Saturday night, two FBI agents from the bureau's Washington field office arrived at Ira's home, a pleasant, modern house at the end of a wooded cul-de-sac. An FBI supervisor had called Ira earlier in the evening to let him know the agents were coming. After they settled down in the Silvermans' living room, an agent named Paul Myers took charge of the questioning while his partner, Julian Sheppard, jotted down notes. Myers was assigned to a unit in Washington known as the Extraterritorial Squad, which investigated crimes against Americans overseas. The bureau operated similar squads in New York, Miami, and Los Angeles, and each was responsible for a different region of the world. The Washington-based squad covered the Middle East. There were about a dozen agents in it, and many of them, including Myers, were relatively new to the bureau. Working in the unit was grueling, required constant travel, and had a high burnout rate because of the strains it put on family life.

Myers walked Ira through a series of questions about his friendship with Bob, his understanding of Bob's relationship with the CIA, and Bob's meeting with Dawud on Kish. He wanted to know if Bob had ever gone off the radar before only to reemerge a few days later. At another point, he asked Ira and his wife, Betsy, whether either of them ever worked for the CIA. It was close to midnight when Myers and his partner left.

The following day, FBI agents came to the Levinson home in Coral Springs to examine Bob's files. Chris also gave them a memory stick onto which the contents of his computer's hard drive had been copied. There was a lot of activity in the house, with agents coming and going, and Doug became upset. To escape the chaos, he went into the den, the room where his father liked to sit and read. It was a shelter where Doug could be alone. Before Bob left Dubai for Kish, he had sent his youngest son an email telling him how much he missed him. Sitting in the den, Doug replied to his father's message. He was scared, he said. He was worried. All he wanted was for his father to be home.

U.S. officials in Dubai reported Bob's disappearance to the closest FBI official in the region, a legal attaché stationed at the American embassy in Abu Dhabi. The official did not appear to express much urgency about pursuing the case, but the American investigators such as Doug Einsel who had met with Bob in Dubai for lunch had their own reason to be concerned. If Bob was in the hands of Iranian intelligence officials, so probably were their business cards with their names and telephone numbers. Two of the investigators went to the Dubai Marriott and asked a manager to see any videotape taken by hotel cameras at the time of Bob's departure. There was a camera mounted above the building's entrance and they went into a security office to review the tape from Thursday morning. The men saw grainy images of Bob leaving the hotel, pulling a small wheeled overnight bag behind him. The manager explained that Bob asked the hotel to hold his large suitcase for a day and brought it out from storage. The U.S. investigators decided to break open the lock. Inside, they found Bob's big black binder and their business cards.

Ira called Dawud to ask what he knew. The fugitive said his first hours with Bob had gone well. They had met as planned in the Maryam's lobby and then gone for a walk before returning to the hotel for a meal. Afterward, they had gone to their room to talk more. Then, as Dawud put it, things went "south." There had been a knock on the door and two Iranian policemen entered. Dawud insisted the police were more interested in him than in Bob and that he was taken into custody and brought to a local police station, where he was questioned and held overnight. The following morning, Dawud said, he was released and went back to the Maryam, where a manager told him that Bob had just left for the airport in the hotel's taxi. Dawud assured Ira there was nothing to worry about; his friend was either in Dubai or on his way back to the United States.

A few days later, there was still no sign of Bob, and FBI agents returned to Ira's house with recording equipment to tape his calls with Dawud. They coached him on how to handle the conversations. "Don't be a reporter. Don't ask so many questions. Silence can be your friend," one agent said. With each call, Dawud's story changed. At times, two Iranian police officials were at the Maryam; in other versions, there were three. After a succession of calls, Dawud told Ira he had learned from his sources that Iranian authorities were holding Bob for questioning, though he expected he would be quickly released if his detention wasn't publicized. "Everyone just needs to stay quiet," Dawud insisted.

When Ira asked him if he could arrange for Bob to speak to Chris so she could hear his voice, Dawud went into a tirade about U.S. foreign policy. "What about all the oppressed people on the streets of Iraq?" he demanded to know. At the urging of the FBI, Chris also called Dawud and asked him what she should tell her children about their father. "That's not my problem," he replied. FBI officials concluded the fugitive was either an attention-seeking narcissist or a collaborator with Iranian intelligence who had lured Bob to Kish. Either way, taping his calls was a waste of time.

Chris was contacted by Jeff Katz, the private investigator who ran Bishop International in London. Katz had expected to see Bob during his layover there and had arranged for one of his associates to meet him at Heathrow when his flight from Dubai landed, so that Bob could hand over some packages of counterfeit cigarettes he had gotten from a source. After Chris told Katz about Bob, the investigator notified British American Tobacco about his disappearance. Katz also went to the U.S. embassy in London with a file folder containing copies of his correspondence with Bob about counterfeit cigarette cases and told officials there that he hadn't gone to Kish for British American Tobacco.

After the FBI sent a query to the CIA about Bob, word of his disappearance in Iran started circulating inside the agency. When Anne Jablonski heard the news, she walked into a Langley bathroom and threw up. An FBI supervisor contacted a friend in the CIA's clandestine division and was told the agency's spy side had never heard of Bob Levinson. The FBI got a similar response from officials at the National Counterterrorism Center, a large operation in McLean, Virginia, jointly run by the CIA, the FBI, and the Defense Department.

FBI agents also went to Langley to see agency analysts. Prior to the meeting, a CIA supervisor, Todd Egeland, who headed the branch of the Directorate of Intelligence that oversaw the Illicit Finance Group, asked Tim Sampson and others in the unit for information about Bob. He was told that Bob's CIA consulting contract had expired in late 2006 and that his work for the unit had never involved Iran. That same information was conveyed to FBI agents, and CIA analysts insisted to them that the CIA hadn't paid Bob to go to Kish and knew nothing about his trip.

On Saturday, March 17, a week after Bob went missing, Chris and her family went to Disney World in Orlando. She had paid weeks earlier for the vacation to celebrate Bob's birthday, and Chris thought the trip might offer a diversion, particularly for her younger children. It didn't. No one wanted to go on any rides and Doug, instead of having fun, became angry and upset. "This isn't supposed to be fun," Chris told him. "This is supposed to be a distraction." For the remainder of March, Chris, Ira, and Dave waited as the days ticked by, hoping for news of Bob's release. Then, at the beginning of April, a State Department official called Chris and told her several newspapers were about to publish articles about her husband's disappearance.

At the same time, Ira got a phone call from John Miller, the press spokesman for the FBI. Miller was a former television newsman and he had landed some coups during his career, including the first interview by a U.S. television reporter with Osama bin Laden. Some journalists disliked and distrusted Miller because he continually bounced between jobs as a reporter covering cops and jobs as a spokesman for cops. As a result, it was never clear whether Miller, during his turns as a journalist, was carrying water for his law enforcement sources because he had once worked for them or hoped to do so in the future. He asked Ira to provide him with an explanation he could give reporters asking questions about why Bob went to Kish. Ira suggested saying his friend was investigating cigarette smuggling and money laundering, but Miller said he didn't like Ira's idea and hopped off the phone to deal with another call.

The initial stories about Bob's disappearance appeared on April 4, 2007. An article in *The Washington Post* was headlined "Man Missing in Iran Named; He Worked for DEA and FBI." Spokesmen for the FBI and State Department insisted to reporters for the *Post* and other publications that Bob did not work for the U.S. government, adding they believed he had gone to the Iranian island on behalf of a corporate client or a documentary filmmaker.

Most of those first accounts described Bob as a highly experienced organized crime investigator. A piece in New York's *Daily News* struck a different tone. In it, Bob's old FBI supervisor in New York, James Moody, declined to say whether he thought Bob was a "competent investigator," and an unnamed former bureau supervisor was quoted as describing him as a "total nutcase" whose "grandiose schemes never panned out." Moody called Larry Sweeney, Bob's old friend from the FBI in New York, and insisted he wasn't the person who had made those remarks.

The burst of news about Bob caught Dawud's attention. On April 4, the same day stories about the missing man appeared in the United States, an article was posted on the website of Press TV, the government-run English-language news organization in Tehran where Dawud worked. It carried the headline "Ex-FBI Man in Iran Not 'Missing' at All." From all appearances, Dawud both wrote or dictated the article and served as the anonymous "informed sources" quoted in it.

Informed sources have told PRESS TV that the story of an American businessman and retired FBI agent gone missing from Iran's Kish Island is somewhat misleading.

The truth of the matter is that he has been in the hands of Iranian security forces since the early hours of March 9, and his inability to communicate with his family or company has raised the alarm about his health, safety and whereabouts. Speaking to PRESS TV on condition of anonymity, the sources made clear that aside from the usual inconvenience, the person is being well looked after.

The sources also said that the matter, though routine, has been complicated by the mounting tensions stemming from repeated American threats against Iran, actual ongoing covert activities within Iran run by the Americans and the particulars of the man's background with the FBI. Not a happy configuration under the circumstances. Nevertheless the authorities are well on the way to finishing the procedural arrangements that could see him freed in a matter of days.

It has been established that his retirement from law enforcement took place nearly a decade ago, his area of expertise was organized crime and not intelligence and that his trip to Kish was purely that of a private businessman looking to make contact with persons who could help him make representations to official Iranian bodies responsible for suppressing trade in pirated products which is a major concern of his company. The outstanding reason for making such a connection is the man has no prior experience in this part of the world.

The enterprise he works for deals in low technology high visibility brand name products sold worldwide and the Persian Gulf has been proving to be a major problem area for illegal production and marketing of these products. Iran is not the origin of this activity but is the largest market by far on the waterway and thus a primary target for the pirated goods.

His visit to Kish was supposed to be a one-day affair but drew the attention of the security forces because his Iranian national host registered in the same hotel room as he did and local police thought they had discovered some discrepancy in the Iranian's identification papers routinely handled in the hotel. Turns out, there was nothing irregular in the Iranian national's papers but this drew the attention of the local police onto the American and he was detained some 12–15 hours after arriving on the island.

It is a case of ordinary business running into extraordinarily bad circumstances. It is expected that the matter will be over in a few days time. The Swiss Embassy in Teheran is in the process of or had already delivered a note from the U.S. State Department concerning his welfare and whereabouts to the Iranian Foreign Ministry. One of the ironies of the retired FBI man's ordeal is that he had been instrumental in persuading his former colleagues not to put former president Mohammed Khatami and his retinue through the ordeal of fingerprinting when he traveled to that country in September 2006.

Chris found herself in a situation she had never faced, having to deal with the news media. Fortunately, one of her sisters, Suzanne Halpin, worked for a big New York public relations concern, Rubenstein Associates. Personality-wise, Suzi was the flip side of her older sister; she was hard charging and insistent. She handled one of Rubenstein Associates' biggest accounts, News Corp., the media conglomerate run by Rupert Murdoch. Suzi helped draft a press statement from Chris about Bob and distributed it on April 4 to reporters.

We miss him and love him very much. We are worried about him and want him home safe and sound as soon as possible. This has been a very difficult time. In the past 48 hours, as this has become public, we've heard from many of our friends. We are touched and so grateful for the support and prayers we've received.

Paul Myers, the FBI agent handling Bob's case, flew to Florida to meet with Chris. There was little doubt about his investigative tenacity. Along with other agents, Myers had spent years pursuing terrorists in Indonesia who had carried out a deadly 2002 attack on a school bus carrying ten American teachers, eventually capturing the group's ringleaders. He was also very tightly wound; his leg would jiggle up and down when he sat, and his bedside manner was not the best.

When Chris told Myers soon after his arrival about her husband's CIA connection, he almost snapped at her, saying the agency had insisted its relationship with her husband had ended long before Kish. Myers and a bureau colleague who had accompanied him to Florida then spent several hours going through Bob's files and copying documents. As they prepared to leave, he thanked Chris but didn't say anything particular about whether he had found anything of interest. Once outside the house, Myers called an FBI supervisor in Washington and told him he had copied documents showing that Bob had gotten recent assignments from the Illicit Finance Group. "I'm looking at tasking memos," Myers said.

The next morning at the FBI's Washington field office, Michael Heimbach, a senior manager, was holding his regular weekday meeting with the supervisors of the squads he oversaw, including the extraterritorial unit. At 9:00 a.m. each day, the supervisors would gather at a large conference table and, as Heimbach went around the room, give him updates about their cases. A CIA official also participated in the meeting. Since 9/11, the spy agency had stationed an operative at major FBI bureaus like the one in Washington as part of an effort to better coordinate intelligence gathering between the agencies. The move was largely symbolic. At heart, the CIA and FBI remained rivals, and most operatives and agents viewed each other with disdain and distrust. FBI agents at the Washington field office referred to the CIA official stationed there as "the Mole." Whenever Heimbach asked the Mole if he had any updates to share, his response was the same: "Nope. Nope."

At the meeting on the day after Myers's visit with Chris, Heimbach went around the table as usual. When it was his turn to report, the supervisor of the Extraterritorial Squad said there was news about the Levinson case. He recounted the discovery Myers made at Chris's house, adding that the agent was on a flight back from Florida with the agency records. He then looked across the table at the Mole. "Those sons of bitches have lied to us," he said.

10

One of Their Own

After word of Bob's disappearance became public, theories spread among his friends and acquaintances about what happened to him. Some of them believed Russian gangsters had caught wind of his Global Witness investigation, followed him to Kish, and made short work of him. Others of them suspected cigarette smugglers were holding him for ransom. Still other people speculated Iran would use Bob as a bargaining chip to be traded for the five Revolutionary Guards officials seized by American forces in Iraq.

Amid the heightening twilight war in early 2007, people were disappearing or being grabbed. A former Revolutionary Guards general, Ali Reza Asgari, who was involved in Iran's nuclear program, went missing while on a visit to Turkey, and Iranian officials said they suspected American agents had convinced him to defect to the United States. A few weeks later, Iranian naval forces seized fifteen British sailors and marines inspecting merchant ships for contraband off the coast of Iraq, claiming the British vessel had illegally entered Iranian waters.

In mid-April, the *Financial Times* broke the news that Bob had gone to Kish Island to meet Dawud Salahuddin. The article was based on an interview with the fugitive, who stuck with Bob's cover story, telling the newspaper that the former FBI agent had come to Kish to investigate cigarette smuggling for a tobacco company. He described Bob as an "innocent victim" of the political tensions between the United States and Iran and said Iranian officials knew his whereabouts. "I don't think he is missing, but don't want to point my finger at anyone," Dawud was quoted as saying. "Some people know exactly where he is."

With the disclosure of Dawud's role in the incident, reporters started connecting the dots among the fugitive, Carl Shoffler, and Ira Silverman. In a follow-up article, the *Financial Times* cited Ira's statement in *The New Yorker* about Dawud's potential value to American officials as an intelligence asset inside Iran. Ira, who had spent a career chasing stories, suddenly found himself at the center of one. He was getting emails and telephone calls from reporters eager to interview him, but he wasn't responding. He was in a state of shock. He had assumed that Bob's trip to Kish had the CIA's approval, and Bob never gave him any reason to think otherwise.

Throughout his career, Ira thought he understood the shadowy world he covered and saw himself as a player in it. Now he didn't know what to think. Despite everything, he still trusted Dawud. He didn't have a choice. The alternative—the possibility Dawud had used him to lure Bob into a trap—was too painful to consider.

The two Canadian journalists, Linden MacIntyre and Neil Docherty, who had accompanied Ira to Tehran had also returned home infatuated with the fugitive. Since then, they had gotten a reality check. The American public television program *Frontline* refused to air their documentary about Iran with Dawud in it because show producers felt he was being portrayed too sympathetically. They had also spent months searching for evidence to connect Ali Akbar Hashemi Rafsanjani to the Highway 407 toll road in Toronto but gave up after running into an impenetrable maze of corporate filings in Spain. Afterward, Linden MacIntyre asked his car mechanic, who was Iranian, if he had heard about any Rafsanjani assets in Canada. "Do you know about Highway 407?" the mechanic replied. When Macintyre asked how the man knew the rumor was true, he said, "Everyone knows it for a fact."

One of Dawud's other contacts in the United States, Tommy Cauffiel, soon got in touch with Ira. Cauffiel was a former Maryland homicide detective who had taken over Carl Shoffler's role as Dawud's main connection with law enforcement. In April, Cauffiel had emailed the fugitive after reading about Bob's meeting with him on Kish. In his message back, Dawud said he suspected Bob's trip had been part of a setup.

> To the best of my knowledge Ira and Levinson put their own collective ass in a crack in an attempt to somehow have me waylaid down the line. I had nothing to do with Levinson being disappeared or whatever has happened to him, that was all circumstances gone awry.
>
> They had been running a game up under me for I guess about a year and a half and it was all a game about getting me sensitive material, etc. I have not communicated with Ira for long days now and imagine he is too shamefaced to email me. I know he is your friend, but fuck Ira because with me he feigned friendship when his real intent was treachery. As for Levinson, I will leave him to the tender mercies of the Iranian authorities. Would you assist someone who was trying to cornhole you?

Ira was shaken. He didn't want to do anything to upset Dawud, for Bob's sake and his own. Since their ride together to the Tehran airport, he had feared the fugitive and believed he might be able to reach back into the United States and harm him or his family. He talked with Cauffiel, who passed on a message to Dawud.

> I talked with Ira and he asked me to convey this to you. He said "that he was not part of anything ever to harm you in any way and everything that we exchanged over the years is absolutely genuine. The relationship that we have should go on and should not be destroyed." I'm just the messenger but I think you two should exchange some

emails to work this out. You've known each other too long to end a
relationship this abruptly.

Joe Trento, the freelancer whom Shoffler had tried to use to snare
Dawud, was also in contact with the fugitive. He disliked Ira and
thought him arrogant. He remained angered by Ira's failure to give
him credit in his *New Yorker* profile of Dawud for the role he played in
setting up the *20/20* interview in which the fugitive first had admitted killing Ali Akbar Tabatabai. Trento considered Ira's omission intentional and had written a letter of complaint to *The New Yorker*
pointing it out, along with what he saw as other errors in the article.
He also believed the retired newsman was in the pocket of former
agency operatives still intent on capturing Dawud.

When Trento called Dawud after reading about his role in Bob's
disappearance, the fugitive revealed a fact to him that he hadn't disclosed to other reporters—that Bob was in Kish to give him damaging information about former Iranian president Rafsanjani. He also
told Trento a lot that wasn't true. He insisted it was Ira and Bob who
had proposed digging up dirt on Rafsanjani and claimed he had tried
to convince them to delay Bob's visit because of the increasing hos-
tilities in early 2007 between the United States and Iran. Trento accepted it all without question. He also agreed to abide by a condition
set by Dawud; he would not disclose Rafsanjani's name in his article
about Bob because the fugitive said doing so might jeopardize his
safety. A lengthy story appeared on Trento's website under the headline "Levinson Had Damaging Information on Iranian Leadership,"
in which the journalist referred to his operation as the National Security News Service.

Iran is dissembling. Despite official denials, the government there
has had former FBI agent Robert Levinson under their control since
March 8. The semantic game they are playing has to do with who in
Iran is holding Levinson. New information from the last man known
to meet with Levinson may demonstrate that the Iranians may have a

very good reason for not owning up to be holding Levinson. It seems the former FBI agent in their custody may have brought highly embarrassing allegations of wrongdoing about at least one top-tier Iranian leader. The National Security News Service has obtained the name of the Iranian leader in question but is not releasing it at this time.

Trento then went on to describe Dawud as a "very credible source" in whom he placed great stock. He quoted the fugitive as saying he was unimpressed by the material that the former FBI agent brought with him to Kish. Dawud said:

> I don't think there ever was any material, though Levinson knew some general information and he knows the language so it's easy for him to make something appear big when it's only him talking and his hands are empty. As I said earlier even the cigarette smuggling conversation was smoke, no meat and potatoes. And if they think I would get booted out of here, again they were off base and out of context.

For a month, Ira had refused to speak with other journalists about Bob. But in late April, an article in *Newsweek* magazine that portrayed Ira as a journalistic Captain Ahab obsessed with completing Carl Shoffler's quest to land Dawud forced him to respond.

> One acquaintance of both Levinson and Silverman told *Newsweek* he learned earlier this year that the former FBI agent was about to leave for the Middle East on a trip apparently designed to make renewed contact with Salahuddin.
>
> Silverman told this acquaintance that Levinson's plan was to meet the fugitive in Iran and try to persuade him to return to the United States. It is not clear why Levinson apparently believed he could convince Salahuddin to do this.
>
> Silverman did not return phone calls to *Newsweek*. He has made no public comments since Levinson's disappearance.

Reading the article on *Newsweek*'s website, Ira became agitated and called one of its writers, Michael Isikoff, to tell him the story's claims about Bob's intentions were wrong and needed to be corrected. Ira also pressed Isikoff for the name of the "acquaintance" who provided the information. The reporter replied he wasn't sure where the tip came from because a *Newsweek* colleague might have gotten it. Ira believed that the FBI's spokesman, John Miller, was the source of the story and that he had put Bob in more danger by planting it.

By the spring of 2007, many former FBI agents and private investigators were concerned about Bob's case for another reason—the FBI's seeming lack of interest in it. Larry Sweeney, Bob's old FBI friend, had expected bureau supervisors would treat the case as a "special," the FBI's equivalent of a five-alarm fire; after all, he had been one of their own. But months into the investigation, FBI agents still hadn't contacted many of the people with whom Bob had spoken in the weeks and days prior to visiting Kish. Also, when friends and colleagues of Bob called the bureau to offer information or leads, their efforts were ignored or rebuffed. Boris Birshtein, after seeing a news report about Bob, had contacted John Good, the former bureau agent who worked for him, and said he was eager to offer the FBI his help. Good called Paul Myers, the case agent, and left messages but he didn't hear back.

Meanwhile, Myers was struggling to get traction. While he had returned from Florida with some of Bob's "tasking memos" from the CIA, bureau agents involved with the case apparently did not systematically cull through the treasure trove of documents on Bob's hard drive. If they had, the FBI could have quickly reconstructed Bob's steps on his way to Kish and seen that the CIA's story didn't jibe with the facts. Myers complained that his FBI superiors weren't giving him much support. The agent had seen Bob's report about the Istanbul meeting and was eager to speak with Boris Birshtein about it. He suspected that the two Iranians at the meeting might have discovered that Bob was a former FBI agent and alerted their country's intelligence services. During Bob's days at the FBI, Myers could have jumped on a flight to Toronto, met with Boris, and explained the trip to a supervisor later. But the bureau was now top-heavy with managers eager to avoid risks, and laden with procedures that slowed investigations. Myers told Ira his supervisors had denied his request to call Boris or to fly to Toronto to see him, saying that under bureau rules, a request to interview the businessman first needed to be sent to Canadian law enforcement authorities. That never happened. He also wanted to fly to Dubai to speak with the U.S. investigators who met with Bob, but he said his supervisors denied that request, too. The FBI would not send agents to Dubai for five months, and bureau officials, despite suspicions about CIA duplicity, did not force a confrontation with the spy agency.

In late April, there was a brief moment when it seemed as though Bob had been freed. Dawud alerted the journalist Joe Trento that a high-ranking Iranian official was telling him that the former FBI agent was back in U.S. custody.

I was told this morning by someone far better connected than me that L is in the air. I have not been able to confirm this with the people I have been dealing with yet because they are not answering the phone but the one who told me could very well know what he is talking about—also told me to keep it under my hat so no mention of me to anyone PLEASE because the friend is a very valuable source of information.

Trento wrote back, saying he had checked with his CIA contacts and heard the same: "My CIA sources are confirming the release but say he has not left yet."

The government-run news website where Dawud worked, Press TV, posted a story about the supposed development, citing the U.S. National Security Agency as the source of its information.

A former FBI agent the US government claimed had gone missing in the Iranian island of Kish has returned to his country amid a news blackout.

The US National Security Agency had said that former FBI agent,

Robert Levinson, had been arrested following a meeting with a former US citizen on the Iranian island of Kish on March 8 and was
detained by Iranians until Sunday.

"The Iranian officials have concluded that he was merely a businessman with no ill intentions towards Iran," said a source in the
Agency.

The US National Security Agency reportedly received the news
of his release early on Monday US time.

U.S. officials, when contacted by American reporters about the
story, said it wasn't true, and Press TV ran another article retracting
its initial report. Trento wrote Dawud that his credibility was falling
fast and that plenty of people believed he had collaborated with Iranian intelligence to set up Bob. "People can think what they like and
I really don't give a rat's ass, but I really didn't do that," Dawud responded.

That spring, FBI agents worked with Bob's daughter Stephanie to
create a website called Help Bob Levinson, filled with photographs of
him and his family in happier times as well as news reports about his
case. The FBI used the Internet as a tool in missing person cases to
gather leads from the public. Much of what came in through such
sites was useless: Photoshopped pictures, rants by lunatics, messages
from con artists eager to scam a grieving family out of money. Still,
there was always a chance a lead would prove fruitful. A homemade
video was posted on the site, in which Chris made a plea. She seemed
uncertain and nervous.

*I'm Christine Levinson, wife of Robert Levinson. My children and I set up
this website to ask for your help in finding Robert so he can come home.*

*My husband went missing on March 8th while visiting Kish Island in
the Islamic Republic of Iran. Since then, there have been conflicting reports
about his condition and whereabouts. There were even reports that he had
been released but they were not true.*

This experience has been a nightmare for me and our children. We've

been living in darkness since this began. We just need to hear from him,
to see him, and to help him come home.
  We are seeking the truth. Someone knows where he is.

Chris was struggling to keep herself together. Since Bob's disappearance, she had not heard a word from Anne Jablonski or anyone
else at the CIA. She sensed that where the spy agency was concerned,
Bob had not only vanished but also ceased to exist. Some days, while
Samantha and Douglas were at school, she would go to a shopping
mall and wander around, hoping to distract herself. At night, she
would dream Bob was being tortured, or worse. Chris wanted her
family to feel nothing was different and that their crisis was temporary. Several months before Bob went missing, he and Chris had decided to help Stephanie and her husband financially so their daughter
could stay at home with Ryan rather than rush back to work. Stephanie was worried, though, that her mother was starting to run out of
money and told her she was ready to start working again. Chris insisted that everything was fine and kept sending her a check even
though she was nearly broke.

Chris couldn't understand why the FBI was treating her like an
outcast, a crazy civilian who was making up stories about spies and
secret worlds. She didn't know why agents like Paul Myers didn't believe her about Bob and the CIA. She had always thought of herself as
an FBI wife. She understood what that meant and she knew how to
keep a secret. She also knew that if this had been Bob's case, he would
have treated her differently. He would have sat with her and listened
to her for as long as she wanted to talk. Then he would have told her
that he wouldn't rest until the case was solved.

11

The Merchant of Death

Dave McGee was seething. He had been talking for months with Ira Silverman and Larry Sweeney and shared their view that the FBI's search for Bob was going nowhere. Dave expected more. Like Bob, he was a believer in the system and had spent his career in it. During his three decades as a prosecutor, first with the state of Florida and then with the Justice Department, Dave earned a reputation as a hard-nosed legal straight shooter—a "cop's prosecutor" was how some of his colleagues put it—and he still thought of himself that way. He originally wanted to work as an engineer for the National Aeronautics and Space Administration, but when he graduated from Florida State University in 1970 the aerospace industry was in a downturn and NASA, rather than hiring engineers, was laying off thousands of them. While at FSU, he had performed in the college's well-known student circus as a catcher in the trapeze act, but there wasn't much demand for that skill either, so he spent three years building houses and then decided to go to law school.

As a prosecutor, he frequently handled drug and money laundering cases. In the 1990s, he sent one of Bob's future informants, the lawyer Ken Rijock, to prison on money laundering charges. He prosecuted capital murder cases, including one involving an anti-abortion zealot, Paul Hill, who was executed following his conviction for killing a doctor at an abortion clinic. His most memorable case involved F. Lee Bailey, one of America's best-known criminal defense lawyers, who had worked for famous clients such as O. J. Simpson and Patty Hearst. Dave accused Bailey of keeping for himself as legal fees millions of dollars that a drug dealer client was supposed to forfeit to the Justice Department under a plea bargain. Bailey claimed he never made the forfeiture deal with prosecutors, but at a court hearing, Dave called other top defense attorneys, including Robert Shapiro, who worked with Bailey in the O. J. Simpson case, to testify the lawyer had reneged on agreements with them. Dave accused Bailey of betraying the government, the court, and his professional ethics. "He did it for the oldest, the most tiresome, and the least excusable reason—to put money in his own pocket," he argued. When the hearing was over, the judge ordered Bailey to pay back some of the money and the lawyer was imprisoned when he failed to do so. Years afterward, a framed copy of a New York *Daily News* front page with a headline screaming "IT'S F. LEE JAILEY" hung like a scalp on a wall of Dave's office at Beggs & Lane.

In the summer of 2007, Dave, a tall, trimly built man in his late fifties with dark hair and a thick moustache, was swamped with work. He mostly handled civil cases like lawsuits brought by one company against another over issues such as contract disputes or insurance claims. A big financial collapse on Wall Street was then unfolding and plenty of new clients wanted him to sue investment firms to recover money. But the more he spoke with Ira and Larry Sweeney, the angrier he was becoming. Over the course of his career, he had seen FBI agents relentlessly chase clues to solve an investigation. He had also watched while FBI bureaucrats made it clear through lack of action that they didn't care about a case. Dave didn't like what was happening where Bob was concerned. The final straw came when he got a call from Paul Myers, the FBI agent, who told him the CIA was still lying to him. Dave was overwhelmed by a sense of moral outrage. As far as he could tell, the U.S. government had abandoned Bob Levinson. It was that simple and appalling. Dave, Ira, and Larry suspected that someone high up in the CIA had asked an FBI buddy to soft-pedal the hunt for Bob and that if their friend was going to be found, they would have to launch their own search-and-rescue mission.

By then, the news media's interest in Bob's disappearance had waned and Chris's sister Suzi Halpin told her she needed to keep her husband's case in the public spotlight by doing television interviews. For a person as shy as Chris, the prospect of that kind of exposure wasn't pleasant. But if it could help bring Bob back, she would do it.

Her first interview was with one of television's biggest stars, Diane Sawyer, the host of ABC's *Good Morning America*. Suzi arranged the interview, and she was savvy enough to know that Sawyer would ask Chris if her husband was a spy. By then, FBI and State Department officials were consistently saying that Bob had gone to Kish to investigate cigarette smuggling, but plenty of news stories were hinting at the possibility of espionage, and Sawyer wouldn't miss the drama of asking the question. In 2007, authorities in Tehran were regularly detaining Iranian-American scholars, businessmen, and other visitors and subjecting them to public show trials on trumped-up spying charges. Some of those arrested were sentenced to lengthy terms in Evin Prison. With Bob, the opposite had happened. The Iranian government or some group there had grabbed someone who could qualify as a real spy, but instead of parading him as a prize catch before television cameras they were continuing to deny they knew anything about him. Chris didn't pretend to understand what was going on. But she was certain telling the truth about Bob and the CIA wasn't an option. Any suggestion of his connection to the spy agency, she believed, would make matters worse or get him killed.

During her interview, Chris described to Diane Sawyer how her children waited every day for news of their father's return and often cried themselves to sleep. Two of her daughters, Sue and Sarah, appeared on the program, and Sue said she sometimes called her father's cell phone just to listen to his voice on the recorded message. When

Sawyer started asking the types of questions Chris knew were coming, she answered them with a quiet, steely resolve.

SAWYER: Was he a spy?

CHRIS: No. Bob could not be a spy. As we said, he's such an open person. He went there under his own name. And so for him to, for anybody to think that he could be doing something like that, people who know him know it's not possible. Bob is just always Bob.

SAWYER: You would have known if he had a double life?

CHRIS: If he had any other life going on, I would know about it. And he doesn't. It's twenty-four hours at home. The business is his own home-based business. We'd go to breakfast, lunch, and dinner when he wasn't out of town. He took a lot of trips out of town. But at the same time, they were for major corporations and I knew the people who were in these corporations that he was talking to.

SAWYER: And no corporation has come forward, though, to say "We funded this. We were part of this. We wanted him to help with this"?

CHRIS: No, because he funded it himself. He's a subcontractor. He's not an employee of any of these major corporations.

By the late summer of 2007, Chris had decided to go to Iran, hoping that the trip's publicity might lead to Bob's release. Iranian officials rejected her requests for a visa and she wrote Dawud Salahuddin, asking whether he had heard any news about Bob.

Mr. Salahuddin,

Greetings.

I hope this message finds you well. I don't know if you are aware that I have been talking to the press lately. I have been asked about you and RL by everyone, but I have only talked about what has already been published. I am planning a trip to Iran myself to look for RL. I would like to be able to bring RL home with me. I am wondering if you have been able to find out where RL is. How is his health and who is he with? Any information would be helpful. Thank you.

Sincerely,

Christine

Dawud replied:

Perhaps the one good point is that in all these months your husband has been incarcerated here (of course I am not supposed to say that) no one has seen him. What that probably means is that he is not being held in a jail because people go in and out of jail and RL would stick out like a sore thumb and would be a source of conversation and certainly rumor which would have circulated around by now. My bet, and I have seen this before, he is being held in a safe house and most probably under the supervision of a high level security person. This would mean he is much better cared for than people in lockup. I can not guarantee what I am telling you and I am not saying this to make you feel good—all I am doing is passing along personal experience in how these things happen here. As always, please keep this between me and you as it could have repercussions for me. That does not frighten me because if it did I would not be writing you but obviously, if one can avoid trouble he does.

I pray you stay strong in what I know is a situation bordering or perhaps even going beyond the border of being intolerable. God bless you and the family.

The situation has impacted me in other ways. Was sent to CCU for 48 hours observation two weeks ago. First time I have been in a hospital in 26 years and then it was something related to a tear in my medial meniscus. My heart turned out fine but they say I am suffering from stress which in some way I relate to the events in March.

During that summer, the FBI finally put Bob's cigarette smuggling cover story to rest. Long after getting access to his hard drive, the bureau sent Scotland Yard a copy of the British American Tobacco letter he had created. A British detective took it to the cigarette company's offices, where executives declared it an amateurish forgery. They pointed out that Bob had misspelled the company's name by hyphenating it as "British-American Tobacco," and had dated the document two weeks before the actual date of his meeting in January at BAT headquarters.

Dave, Ira, and Larry had begun their hunt for Bob by hiring an investigative firm called SCG International Risk that did contract work for the FBI. SCG International was part of the new military-style security industry that had emerged after 9/11, and some of its employees, like those of similar firms, were former commandos. The best-known of the companies was Blackwater, which was accused of killing seventeen Iraqi civilians during a 2007 incident there. The head of SCG International, Jamie Smith, said he was a founder of Blackwater and a decorated military veteran who had once worked for the CIA. SCG International ran a training facility in the woods of northern Mississippi known as "G.I. Joe Fantasy Camp" where participants for a $1,200 fee could attend a course offering "real-world scenarios for real-world warriors." The retreat's programs included training on how to fire automatic weapons and interrogate captured enemy fighters.

One of SCG International's first actions for the Levinson family was to dispatch a female operative to Kish and the Maryam hotel. The woman, whom Jamie Smith called "Mila," told Maryam employees she was a headhunter for hotels in Dubai looking for experienced management personnel. She spoke with the hotel's manager and the supervisor of its restaurant and charmed both men, who allowed her to take their pictures and gave her their contact information.

Mohammed Para—Maryam Hotel Manager. He is a Muslim Indian. Determined that Mohammed Para could be very useful—especially since he's unhappy in his job—the carrot could be a new job. Need to elicit more from him—but he's scared.

He said it was very difficult to speak . . . and pointed out that the hotel staff (Iranian) were seemingly keeping a close eye on him as he spoke with us. In fact his contact details were obtained by way of a discreet handoff.

Ali Korakumjam—Maryam Hotel Restaurant Manager. He is a colleague of PARA and is also a Muslim Indian. He slipped SCG Asset his details while photo was being taken in the empty restaurant.

SCG Asset reports that both contacts approached at separate times and individually suggesting a further willingness to cooperate.

Mila walked around the Maryam, looking for surveillance cameras. She suspected people were monitoring her.

No spyholes in doors and feel CCTV maybe in corridors, difficult to confirm as yet. Have gone down in one lift and up in the other. Turned around and gone back to room. Suddenly both room doors left very, very slightly ajar. To the unaware would appear closed. Each time, I get back to my room—"they" do too. Building lends itself to many corners, objects to hide behind. Being careful.

Mila mentioned in passing to Mohammed Para, the hotel's manager, that she had seen news stories in Dubai about an American missing on Kish. "Oh, yes, he was my friend, he stayed here," Para said. He told Mila the driver of the Maryam's taxi took Bob to the Kish airport and watched him walk into the terminal.

She tried to speak to the driver, but there were always too many people around. After about a day, Mila decided to leave Kish after sensing Iranian intelligence agents were shadowing her. She suggested in her report SCG might want to lure Para and other Maryam employees to Dubai with sham job offers so they could be questioned outside Iran.

Dave turned to another avenue for help, an old Justice Department friend named Richard Gregorie who was a federal prosecutor in Miami. Gregorie had worked closely with Bob on a Russian organized crime task force and he was eager to do what he could to find him.

He put Dave in touch with an informant he had used for years on cases with Middle Eastern connections, a former international arms dealer named Sarkis Soghanalian, once known as "the Merchant of Death."

In his heyday, Soghanalian, a short, corpulent man with a moustache who bore a resemblance to the 1940s actor Sydney Greenstreet, supplied a wide range of customers—Lebanese Christian militiamen, Mauritanian rebel groups, Argentina's military junta, and others—with the tools of war. He was the principal seller of guns, tanks, aircraft parts, ammunition, and even uniforms to Saddam Hussein during Iraq's long war with Iran, and the CIA covertly blessed many of his deals. Soghanalian, who was of Armenian descent, lived lavishly for decades in Beirut and Paris, flying around the world in a private full-size jet named after his daughter. "You need that comfort, you have to show that you are not a cheap S.O.B. running in the street and you are running after somebody's buck," Soghanalian once explained to a reporter. He also loved publicity and told another journalist about a request he made to Lebanese fighters buying his weapons—he asked them for jars filled with the ears of their enemies as a testament to the quality of his weapons.

Gregorie met Soghanalian after his weapons-dealing career had fallen apart. In 1991, he was sentenced to six years in federal prison for conspiring to smuggle U.S.-made helicopters to Iraq in violation of export sanctions. Soghanalian asked the prosecutor to visit him because he wanted to share important information. When Gregorie got to the prison, Soghanalian said he knew about a counterfeit hundred-dollar bill so artfully made it was indistinguishable from a real one. Gregorie left thinking he had wasted his time, but a few weeks later one of Soghanalian's associates delivered a hundred-dollar bill to the prosecutor, who turned it over to the Secret Service. Experts examined the note and declared it one of the most skillful forgeries ever created. With Soghanalian's help, authorities traced the bill, dubbed the "Supernote," to a counterfeiting operation in Lebanon's Bekaa Valley. Within weeks, the printing facility used by the forgers was destroyed in an explosion, though Gregorie would never

learn who was behind the blast. As his reward, Soghanalian was released from prison early. A few years later, he was sent to prison
again, this time on a tax fraud charge, but won another early release
by assisting U.S. authorities investigating a clandestine arms deal involving Peru's intelligence chief.

Gregorie's faith in Soghanalian as a valuable informant remained
steadfast, but his credibility with the FBI and other federal agencies
sank with time. After 9/11, the aging arms merchant claimed to have
inside information on Osama bin Laden and FBI agents spent a year
on a global wild goose chase trying to track it down. Afterward, the
bureau viewed him as an intelligence welfare case and immigration
officials were dying to find an excuse to deport him to Lebanon, the
country where he held citizenship, but the old arms dealer still had
friends in the Justice Department who protected him.

When Dave contacted Soghanalian in 2007, he was seventy-eight,
broke, and living in a small, broken-down house behind Miami International Airport. His health was failing and he was confined to a
wheelchair. He spent most of his time in a small room containing a
bed, a bureau, and a folding card table upon which sat a telephone
and an old, battered address book. A large pulley was screwed into
the ceiling above Soghanalian's bed. By pulling on a thick rope he
was able to hoist himself up in the morning.

He insisted to Dave he could find out where Bob was and bring
him back. Within a few weeks, Soghanalian reported he had made
contact with two Iranians living in Paris who were willing to travel
to Tehran and ask questions. Soghanalian was too infirm to go himself, so he arranged for his son, Garo, a local maintenance worker, to
travel to Paris for a meeting with the Iranians. When Dave told FBI
officials about the plan they first tried to stop it, and when that failed,
the bureau insisted Paul Myers accompany Garo on the trip.

Garo met with the Iranians at a café. Myers observed the meeting
from a distance, and when it was over, Garo told him the Iranians
wanted $50,000 for their trip to Tehran. After checking with his FBI
superiors, Myers instructed Garo to arrange a second meeting at the

café and tell the men they would get paid but only if they returned from Iran with useful information. The haggling went on for several days but ended up going nowhere.

In the late summer of 2007, Ira checked his email and found a message with a subject line that simply said "Salam." It was sent from the Gmail account of someone named "Osman.Muhamad." The note read:

> My dear wife and friends
>
> I am safe and health. The group which has arrested me is complaining against American policies in the region. (Specially in Iraq and Afghanistan) they are also against the regions governments. Because these Governments have a much flexibility against U.S. policies.
>
> Please help me.
>
> I can not tolerate to be far from you anymore and I am worry about My future. I want to come back to my wife, house, 7 children and grandchild (Ryan) as soon as possible. Please Help Me.
>
> I love you forever.
>
> Bob

Ira sensed the email was from Bob's captors and that Bob may have played a role in sending it. It wasn't just the message's content that made him feel that way. It was the names of the people to whom it had been sent. Along with Chris and Ira, the message was copied to four people who seemed to share a connection. Each one of them was a friend of Bob's whose work put him in a position to publicize the email. Two of the people were journalists. One was Tom Mangold, the British correspondent, and the other was an investigative producer for ABC News named Chris Isham. The two other people copied on the email were lawyers, John Moscow, the former prosecutor in the Manhattan D.A.'s office whom Bob had written to about the Bank of Cyprus case, and Scott Horton, an American lawyer who had worked with Global Witness. Not all of the email's intended recipients received it. Chris Isham's copy, for instance, was sent to his email address at ABC News, which he had left a few weeks earlier for a post at CBS News.

To Ira, it seemed inconceivable the four names were selected randomly or without input from Bob. The investigator's cell phone contained hundreds of contacts, the numbers and email addresses of clients, friends, intelligence sources, and others. Ira expected the FBI would jump on the email as a big break. But bureau officials, after reviewing the note, dismissed it as a hoax.

One of the agents then working on Bob's case, Jonathan Beery, explained the bureau's thinking in an email to Chris's sister Suzi.

Some input my colleagues gave me in-house that their opinion leans strongly toward Osman being a fake. You're probably already thinking of these things, so this can just serve to shape the response that Christine sends back to Osman . . .

Two things that point toward Osman likely being an imposter without current access to Bob:

1. Lack of any singular facts or personal knowledge clues in content of email: It's highly likely that if Bob were attempting to (or being asked by captors to) get a message out to us, that he would include a personal fact or a memory that only the family would know. Instead everything described in the email is accessible on the internet.

2. The string of email addresses is somewhat of a mystery—but it is possible that it was obtained through hackers in months prior to March 2007 while Bob was traveling overseas using his laptop to link to the internet perhaps, or logging on at internet cafes overseas, or something similar.

Bureau officials wrote a note for Chris to send back.

Greetings,

I would like to thank you for sending me the e-mail from Bob. My children and myself are so happy and grateful to know that Bob is safe and in good health. I hope that you will be able to keep sending Bob's e-mails to me and giving my e-mails to him. Unfortunately, as I said in my other e-mail I did not see the August 6th e-mail until today and as you can imagine we have received a lot of e-mails from people pretending to have Bob or pretending to know who has him. This has made our very difficult situation nearly unbearable. So that we know you are talking with Bob or with people who are, please respond with the color of Bob's first car. I am giving you two of our children's e-mail addresses in the hope that if I do not receive your next e-mail they will receive it.

Bob can confirm that these are good e-mail addresses. Again, thank you, I know that if you have a family you know how important it is to finally be able to communicate with Bob.

Sincerely,

Christine Levinson

She didn't get a reply, and FBI officials considered the email of such little interest they didn't bother to send agents out to interview its intended recipients. Sarah Levinson, Bob's daughter in New York, was flabbergasted by the bureau's reaction. Her father raised her and her siblings to respect the FBI and complained to them whenever a news article or a movie cast it in a bad light. She couldn't understand how the bureau could ignore a possible signal from her father's captors. She began to wonder for the first time whether his faith in the FBI had been misplaced.

After Paul Myers returned from Paris, his frustrations with the Levinson case and the demands of his FBI job seemed to grow. He was juggling several investigations at once and frequently traveling on them. But nearly every day—and sometimes more than once a day—Chris would call him for updates about his progress or to ask what he planned to do next to bring her husband home. Within the bureau, officials had started referring to Chris and Suzi as "the Housewife and the Barracuda." Agents such as Myers who dealt regularly with Chris knew she could be just as aggressive as her sister when it came to Bob. Her calls became so constant, agents would recognize her number flashing on their cell phones and dread answering.

In the fall of 2007, Myers was still trying to figure out Bob's precise relationship with CIA analysts such as Anne Jablonski, and he asked Ira if there were any agency insiders who could help him. The only person Ira could think of was a former CIA operative named Ben Wickham, whom he knew through the occasional luncheons held by friends of Carl Shoffler, the late detective. Wickham agreed to speak with Myers and the three men started having get-togethers at the retired spy's home. Myers described the formal process through which the FBI obtained information from the CIA as bullshit. Inquiries to the agency were channeled through an FBI liaison who dealt with a CIA counterpart. The answers coming back from the agency were useless. The FBI agent was also unhappy with his supervisors because they were pressuring him to spend time on work that had nothing to do with solving cases. One manager wanted him to serve as the FBI's representative with a group of Arabic-speaking immigrants in the Washington area. "What the fuck, I'm not a diplomat," he said. "I don't want to be nice to these people."

At one of their meetings, Myers showed Ira and Wickham Bob's report from the meeting in Istanbul. He took care to make it clear that he wasn't breaking the law by pointing out that the word "Unclassified" was stamped on the document. Myers wanted to know if Colonel Sisoev, the former KGB officer who had originally introduced Boris to Ali Magamidi Riza, was a significant player. Wickham, who was once stationed with the CIA in Eastern Europe, replied he had heard of him. Myers also kept pressing the ex-spy to introduce him to lower-level CIA personnel who might help him understand how the Illicit Finance Group operated. Wickham, who had played a role in the Reagan-era scandal known as Iran-Contra, warned Myers he would put his FBI career in jeopardy if he went around bureau procedures.

Later that fall, when Myers arrived at Wickham's house for another meeting, he looked more relaxed than Ira and Wickham had ever seen him. He announced he was resigning from the FBI to take a job with a contractor for the CIA. He said it had long been his dream to work for the spy agency, and he appeared elated to be leaving behind his battles with FBI supervisors and Chris's calls. After leaving Wickham's home, Ira and Myers walked together to their cars. Ira told him about the dire state of Chris's finances and asked Myers if he could do anything to help Chris get the $12,000 she said the CIA still owed Bob. Myers turned to Ira. He told him that FBI officials, in going through Bob's records, had found instances where he had double-billed the CIA for expenses such as hotel rooms that he was also charging to his private clients. He warned Ira that making money an issue could backfire and end up embarrassing Chris. "I wouldn't push it," Myers said. Then he got into his car and drove off.

12

Passwords

Sonya Dobbs organized an annual charity event at Beggs & Lane, the law firm where she and Dave McGee worked. It was a skeet-shooting contest, with the winner getting a new shotgun. Sonya loved guns. She was certified by the National Rifle Association as a firearms instructor and drove around Pensacola with a pistol tucked beneath the seat of her car. Sonya, who grew up in rural Alabama and had a thick accent to prove it, was smart with a sharp sense of humor. As Dave's paralegal she kept him on track, solved his technological challenges with computers and other devices, and usually knew as much about his cases as he did.

In the fall of 2007, Dave told Sonya about a problem he was having with Chris. At the time, the lawyer had seen only a few documents pointing to Bob's relationship with the CIA, including his original consulting contract with the Illicit Finance Group. Chris had given the FBI a copy of Bob's computer hard drive, but Dave had been urging her for weeks to send him her husband's work files so he could examine them. The lawyer was growing increasingly concerned that Chris, without Bob's income, was plunging toward bankruptcy.

Banks were threatening to repossess the family's cars because the Levinsons were so far behind on their auto loans. Dave believed the CIA bore an obligation, both legally and morally, to financially provide for Chris and her children, and he needed Bob's records in case suing the agency was the only way to get it to do what was right.

Sonya, who was short with dark hair and eyes, offered a suggestion. Chris was probably too distraught, she said, to wade through Bob's office, so it might be easier to ask her for permission to review his email account. Sonya proposed the idea to Chris, who gave her the password to an AOL account she and Bob shared. Sonya logged into it and noticed something unusual. Bob had been using the AOL account as a kind of electronic way station to forward emails to accounts he had opened with Yahoo!, Hotmail, Gmail, and other providers. Sonya thought she wouldn't be able to go further. Like most people, she used separate passwords for each of her email accounts. But when she tried a slight variation of Bob's AOL password on his Yahoo! account, it worked, and soon she was able to get into all his accounts, using either the same password or a slight variation of it, such as capitalizing one letter.

Many of the emails had attachments. She started launching them and Bob's CIA life began to unfold. She saw his contract and some of his intelligence reports for the Illicit Finance Group. There were also messages between him and "Toots" as well as his note to Tim Sampson in February 2007 about his Dubai "side trip." She printed out some of the documents and walked into Dave's office. "You are not going to believe what I found," she said. As Dave went through them, he couldn't understand why FBI agents, if they had reviewed the same material, weren't pulling in CIA officials for questioning or arresting them. He picked up the phone and called Ira Silverman. "Whom do you know in Washington that you trust?" he asked.

Soon afterward, Ira was shown into the Capitol Hill office of Melvin Dubee, a staff member on the Senate Select Committee on Intelligence. Ira hadn't meet Dubee before, but an old source from his days as a journalist had suggested him because the Senate intelligence panel had oversight of the CIA. Dubee, who spoke with a slight

Texas drawl, listened to Ira's story and agreed to send an inquiry to the CIA's congressional liaison asking for information about Bob. Several weeks later, he called Ira to say he had gotten a response. It was the same one the CIA had given to the FBI six months earlier—Bob's contract had expired before his disappearance on Kish, and his agency work had never involved Iran.

By that time, Dave had figured out a way to get Bob's files. He told Chris that Sonya was going to fly to Coral Springs, come to her house, and pack them up. The prospect of Sonya poking around her home was the push Chris needed. Cardboard file boxes loaded with documents soon arrived at Dave's office. Inside were file folders labeled with the names of Bob's assignments, clients, or investigative targets. Several folders were marked GLOBAL WITNESS, while another was labeled DAOUD SALAHUDDIN. Bob's reports to the Illicit Finance Group were contained in five folders, labeled IFG and numbered sequentially in Roman numerals. Another folder, marked MAKE SEPARATE FILE AND ACTING FILE, contained a mix of material, including emails between Bob and Anne Jablonski, expense reports, proposed CIA projects, and billing records on which he logged the number of hours he had spent interviewing a source or writing up a report for the Illicit Finance Group, including ones about Iran.

Chris attached a handwritten note on one file, explaining to Dave how she and Bob had argued before his Dubai trip over the money the CIA owed him:

> In Feb. before his last trip, Bob & I had a heated discussion over the fact that the CIA had not paid him since his Nov. invoice and it was now Feb. I told him that he treated them differently from other clients and that he would never let anyone else get away with not paying him. This was after he took away a whole day to write reports for them knowing he was going on another trip. He told me that Anne told him that he would be paid because they had gotten funding but it would be another month before his invoices could be addressed.

Dave and Sonya made a rough pass through the boxes, pulling out records that grabbed their attention. Dave's fury was growing. It was one thing to hear Paul Myers say the CIA was lying. It was another for him to see mounds of evidence pointing to the fact. Bob's work for the CIA had clearly involved Iran, and the former FBI agent and Anne Jablonski had discussed money just before his disappearance on Kish. In October 2007, Dave flew to Washington and went with Ira to see Melvin Dubee.

Seeing the documents, Dubee became irate and contacted the CIA's congressional liaison to demand a meeting with agency officials in his Senate office. When they arrived, he showed them some of Bob's reports. The CIA officials acted as though they had never seen the records before, and an analyst with the Illicit Finance Group claimed that Bob's reports were considered to have such little intelligence value they were tossed into a storage box upon arrival without being read.

Dubee told Dave and Ira that to force answers out of the CIA they would need the involvement of lawmakers on the intelligence panel. He suggested they approach a Democratic senator from Florida, Clarence "Bill" Nelson, who was serving a temporary term on the committee. Nelson was already involved in Bob's case. By the fall of 2007, he was writing letters to Iran's ambassador to the United Nations urging his country to let Chris visit Iran.

Initially, Dave and Ira were not enthusiastic about seeing Nelson. A former state insurance commissioner, the Florida Democrat was better known for the space flight he took as a sitting congressman than for being a political heavyweight. But at a meeting in late 2007 at his Florida office, Nelson, a small, tautly built man with a wide smile, assured them he wouldn't hesitate to cross swords with the CIA. He assigned the matter to Carolyn Tess, his staffer on the Senate intelligence panel. Tess was young and idealistic about working in government. After speaking with Dubee, she was appalled by the CIA's handling of Bob's disappearance and decided that the agency needed to answer for its lack of action.

Soon afterward, a top CIA official, Stephen Kappes, arrived at the Hart Senate Office Building on Capitol Hill to give the intelligence panel one of its periodic briefings on national-security-related issues. The committee's hearing room is located on the building's second floor, and to reach it, lawmakers, staffers, and other officials must pass through a screening station manned by Capitol Hill police officers. The room itself has a thick, vault-like door and specially lined walls to prevent electronic eavesdropping.

Kappes, then the CIA's deputy director, had previously served as a spy in international hot spots and once headed the agency's "rendition" program, in which suspected terrorists were kidnapped overseas. Balding and with a graying beard, he was an old hand at doing briefings. After he made his presentation, lawmakers took turns asking him questions. When it was Senator Nelson's time, he looked at the CIA official and said, "What can you tell me about the status of an agency contractor missing in Iran?" Kappes sat silently for a few moments and then responded he didn't know what Nelson was asking about. The Florida lawmaker then started reading him excerpts culled by Carolyn Tess from Bob's emails and memos to the Illicit Finance Group. Kappes listened without showing any reaction. When Nelson was finished, he said that neither he nor the CIA's director, General Michael Hayden, were ever alerted about Bob's disappearance and they didn't know anything about the episode. He assured Nelson that he would investigate the matter and report back to the committee.

Around the same time as the panel's meeting, Chris stepped off a plane in Tehran accompanied by her oldest son, Dan, and her sister Suzi. Iranian officials had finally granted them visas. It was early December and the towering mountains to the north of Tehran, the Alborz, were covered with snow. At age fifty-seven, Chris was making her first trip outside the United States and she was spending it searching for her husband. Two officials from the Swiss embassy escorted Chris and her family to the Esteghial hotel, a five-star facility with luxurious rooms, a fitness center, and a twenty-four-hour coffee shop. After checking in, Chris and Suzi went up to the room they were sharing and Chris started looking around for a box of tissues. She asked Suzi if she had seen any and the sisters spent a few minutes looking for a tissue box before they gave up. The following morning, returning to their room after breakfast, they found five boxes of tissues strategically placed around it. They realized their room was probably bugged and Iranian intelligence was monitoring them.

Chris went to Iran's Foreign Ministry to meet with a top official there. Government officials remained publicly adamant that they knew nothing about Bob, adding that a police investigation on Kish had failed to yield any clues. Chris hoped they might be more forthcoming when speaking privately. Her meeting dispelled those illusions. After some initial pleasantries, the official turned hostile and told Chris that everything he had learned from media reports made him suspicious of her husband's real reason for coming to Kish. He also claimed a boat operator on the island told authorities Bob had offered to pay him $500 to take him to Iran's mainland and that the taxicab driver who drove her husband to the Kish airport reported overhearing him making cell phone calls to people elsewhere in Iran. Chris, who was keeping her hair covered in respect for Muslim culture, tried to maintain her composure. FBI officials had urged her not to challenge Iran's official line.

The following day, she, Dan, and Suzi flew to Kish and took a taxi to the Maryam hotel. When they walked into the lobby, Chris saw an English-language Iranian newspaper placed strategically on the registration desk, as if to catch her eye. A headline on its front page read "Wife of Missing American in Iran." A photograph showed Chris and Dan looking tired and jet-lagged after their arrival in Tehran. She was shown the room where her husband stayed and an entry in a registration book indicating he checked out at 11:00 a.m. on Friday, March 9. It was signed in Bob's handwriting. That afternoon, Chris, Dan, and Suzi took a taxi to the Kish airport and spent several hours handing out flyers with a photograph of a beaming Bob holding his grandson, Ryan, to ticket agents, baggage handlers, and airport workers. They asked everyone if they recognized him. No one did.

The family returned to Tehran to prepare for their flight home.

Suzi waited in her room while Chris and Dan went down to the hotel's lobby for one final meeting. It was with Dawud. Prior to coming to Iran, Chris was in touch with the fugitive and he had agreed to meet her. He appeared ill at ease. Seated in a chair, he repeatedly glanced around the room as if trying to spot Iranian operatives watching them. He stuttered at times. He told Chris and Dan how much he had liked Bob and how he felt he shared blame for what had happened. It was foolish, he said, to think two Americans—particularly, a white one and a black one—could meet safely on Kish without attracting police attention. Still, he was certain whoever was holding Bob was treating him well. "He might be sitting in a hotel room somewhere learning Farsi," he told Dan. Dawud then reached into a bag and gave Chris one of the gifts her husband had brought with him to Kish. It was the copy of *The Black Dahlia*, the murder mystery.

The flight back to the United States had a four-hour layover in Paris, and Chris, Dan, and Suzi took a taxi to Notre-Dame Cathedral, where Chris prayed for Bob. Snow was falling in New York when they landed at John F. Kennedy. Waiting FBI agents escorted them into a section of Air France's passenger lounge, which was cleared of other travelers. Agents questioned them about the trip, trying to get information while it was fresh. Chris handed over the copy of *The Black Dahlia*, which was sent to the FBI's forensics laboratory to be examined for fingerprints, DNA, and other clues.

A few weeks later, the Levinson family gathered for their first Christmas without Bob. His daughter Sarah kept hoping for a "Christmas miracle," imagining her mother's trip to Iran might have struck a humanitarian chord with her father's captors, who would release him in time for the holidays. There were presents under the tree just in case.

At Dave McGee's home in Gulf Breeze, the lawyer and his wife, Joyce, were also getting ready for Christmas. They had started a family tradition when their two children were young of making Cornish game hens rather than a turkey for their holiday meal, so each kid could have a bird. Their children were now young adults, but the McGees continued the tradition.

As Christmas Eve approached, the telephone rang at Dave's home. The call was from Jonathan Winer, the money laundering expert and consultant to the Illicit Finance Group. Dave hadn't ever spoken before to Winer, but Ira had known him since the late 1980s when he was on the staff of Senator John Kerry.

Not long after Bob's disappearance, Winer had called Ira and asked if he could be of help. Ira hadn't known at first that the lawyer worked for the Illicit Finance Group, and he told him about Bob's ties to the CIA unit. Ira also said he was trying to get ahold of Bob's agency handler, Anne Jablonski, and asked Winer if he knew of any way to do so. It was at that point that Winer told Ira he was a consultant to the Illicit Finance Group, adding that Anne was a close friend who had just helped him through a bad patch.

Over the previous year, a financial con man named R. Allen Stanford had tried to make Winer's life miserable. Prior to leaving government, the lawyer was investigating Stanford for running what appeared to be a massive Ponzi scheme. When *Businessweek* magazine published an article questioning Stanford's operation, the con man suspected Winer was its source. He hired Kroll, the big private investigations firm, and ordered it to dig up dirt on him. He "is a pure cockroach," Stanford told a Kroll investigator, a former DEA agent named Tom Cash. "Go after him hard on as many fronts as possible." Winer was going through a divorce and Cash started chasing rumors his wife had left him for another woman. Anne had stood by him through the ugly episode, Winer told Ira. He agreed to call her about Bob, and a few days later he phoned Ira back from his car while waiting to get cleared into Langley. He said Anne had told him her superiors had ordered her not to talk to anyone about Bob.

By the time of Winer's call to Dave in late December, Anne was under siege. After the CIA's deputy director, Stephen Kappes, returned red-faced from his Senate intelligence panel briefing, he had put together a team of investigators to look into Bob's work for the

CIA. The group included operatives from the CIA's Counterintelligence Center, the agency unit that hunts foreign spies and moles. They started examining files and interviewing Anne and other members of the Illicit Finance Group. Anne was in a panic and reached out to Winer and other friends for advice.

Winer told Dave he knew Anne and made it clear he was aware of the internal CIA investigation. He said it was his impression that it wouldn't go anywhere and suggested to Dave that the interests of the Levinson family might be better served if Dave reached a financial settlement with the CIA. Dave wasn't certain why Winer had called, but he sensed the lawyer was doing so unofficially to try to start a negotiation between him and the CIA to resolve the case. He told Winer he appreciated his interest in the Levinsons' welfare but added that Chris and her children had a goal besides money—they wanted to see justice done. "We aren't going away," Dave told him.

13

The Nuclear Option

Chris and her children held a rally on March 9, 2008, at a Coral Springs restaurant called Wings Plus, a favorite of Bob's, to mark the first anniversary of his disappearance and celebrate his sixtieth birthday. The event received some news media coverage, and after their meal, the family stood in the restaurant's parking lot and sang "Happy Birthday."

A day earlier, Chris had exchanged emails with Dawud Salahuddin, who had promised earlier to contact Iranian officials about her husband. In his reply, he told her he would have to wait a few more weeks to do so because Iranian government offices were closing for the Persian New Year, or Norooz.

> This is an odd and painful "anniversary" so to speak and I just want you to be assured that I have not forgotten it or one word of what I have said to you. On correspondence, bear in mind that there are some 11 days to the end of the Iranian calendar year and everybody is trying to get their desk cleared for the next year which following a two-week holiday will begin on April 1, give or take a day. That is

to say this is not a good time to put a sensitive letter on a person's desk so I will wait till the holidays and then make the submission I spoke of but that will be to a high-ranking judicial authority and as I have said many times in the past, this is not a judicial matter, it is not a police matter—it is a political question between two mule-headed governments, each suffering its own version of the disorder "center of the world complex" and as the Swahili proverb has it, "When elephants fight the grass suffers" 'grass' here of course meaning people and specifically in this context the family of Robert and Christine Levinson.

I know this past year has not been a good one for me and perhaps it is a blessing that you have kids to keep you busy. My situation allows for too much introspection and too much of anything is not good. Be aware too that our communications are read by interested parties besides us on both sides. Over here, I was told prior to meeting you to stay away and again last week was called in and given what I took as indirect but genuine threats. But not to worry it is simply not in me to be afraid of men. Don't want to get melodramatic but that is where I sit in all this and I am comfortable with that probably because discomfort had been a major theme of my adult life so bureaucratic nonsense does not move me very much and I have simply seen too much real mayhem to be fearful of the same—especially when I have done no moral or criminal action.

This started out as a just to let you know line but then I got carried away a bit. Forgive me for that. Hope your demonstration is a real success and be sure that I will keep up my part of the bargain but truth to tell, God hears the prayers of mothers in distress for their loved ones faster I think than those of anyone else.

That week, FBI officials invited Chris to Washington for an update about the status of the search for her husband. Dave McGee, Ira Silverman, Larry Sweeney, and Suzi Halpin also attended the meeting, which was held at the bureau's Washington field office. A senior FBI official named Sean Joyce presided, and officials from the CIA and the State Department were present. Joyce didn't delve into the details of the agency's investigation because there wasn't much new to say. In recent months, FBI agents had finally started to retrace Bob's activities prior to his trip to Kish, but even a year later they hadn't interviewed some key witnesses, such as Houshang Bouzari, the oil consultant in Toronto. Joyce assured Chris that the FBI, the CIA, and the State Department were now working together to bring Bob home. He also acknowledged the bureau had made "some mistakes" in its initial handling of the investigation. Joyce didn't go into details about what he meant, but upon hearing his comment Ira couldn't restrain himself. He first looked at Joyce and then at the CIA officials present. "Not mistakes, crimes," he said.

The CIA, eager to avoid another confrontation with the Florida senator Bill Nelson, had taken other steps. An agency lawyer, Joseph Sweeney, contacted Dave to discuss Chris's financial claims. It was a welcome call. For months, Dave had been hunting to find money to keep her afloat. Both he and John Moscow, the former prosecutor in New York, had contacted Reed Smith, the law firm in the Bank of Cyprus lawsuit, to collect Bob's bill. But the firm never paid the money, and Dave and Moscow concluded it had decided to stiff Bob because he wasn't around to collect.

At his meeting with Sweeney, Dave took an immediate liking to him. He noticed the CIA lawyer was wearing a graduation ring from the U.S. Military Academy at West Point, which Dave viewed as a sign he was trustworthy. He also appeared sympathetic. After listening to Dave's description of Chris's money problems, Sweeney said he could arrange for the CIA to immediately pay her $121,000, the amount Bob would have gotten in June when his consulting contract renewed. Dave added he wanted to discuss a global settlement to provide Bob's family with long-term security. One possibility was to set up a large annuity for Chris funded by the CIA that would provide her with enough annual income to make up for the loss of Bob's earnings. Dave ran some rough numbers. Looking at Bob's billings, he estimated his income in peak years ranged between $250,000 and $300,000. Taking Bob's FBI annual pension of $60,000 into account, a financial consultant advised Dave that Chris would need a $2.5 million annuity to make up the difference. When Dave mentioned the figure to Sweeney, he expected the CIA lawyer to start dickering. Instead, Sweeney said it sounded doable but he needed to run the proposal past his bosses.

Another CIA official met with Chris. He first explained he couldn't tell her his real name because he worked in the agency's clandestine division and suggested she call him "Mike." He then apologized to her on behalf of the CIA for the agency's behavior. Mike, who was a tall, athletically built man in his fifties with red hair, explained he was leading the CIA's internal inquiry into what had happened at the agency. He told Chris he believed what she was saying about Bob's work for the CIA but added that he needed to find out for himself. Mike assured her that when the review was completed, he would tell her the results. Chris thanked him. A year after her husband's disappearance, the CIA had finally broken its silence.

Within the agency, Anne Jablonski had experienced a roller-coaster ride. Not long after Bob went missing, life within the Illicit Finance Group had quickly resumed its normal rhythm. FBI agents, after asking a few questions, had gone away and did not come back. The book on Bob seemed closed. Anne's days took on their familiar pattern. A few months after Bob went missing, she agreed to be interviewed by *The Wall Street Journal* for an article about one of her favorite topics, the growing number of people preparing homemade food for their cats. "All of a sudden, the idea of making your own cat food didn't seem so insane," she told the newspaper.

At first the inquiries in the fall of 2007 from Mel Dubee, the Senate staffer, were viewed within the CIA as more of an annoyance than a threat. But when the agency's inquiry began in December, Anne's equilibrium quickly unraveled. During her twenty-three years at the CIA, she had watched witch hunts unfold as scared supervisors searched for scapegoats to protect their careers. Anne lost her appetite and lay in bed at night unable to sleep. In mid-January, she stepped on a bathroom scale, looked down, and saw she had lost a lot of weight.

Then, in February 2008, the questions about Bob suddenly stopped.

Anne took it as a sign that the agency's internal investigation was over and she had been cleared. She couldn't imagine any other possibility. She certainly hadn't done anything wrong. If she had any regrets, it might have been her decision to push for Bob to get a contract. He had made a terrible mistake and Anne felt awful for his wife and children. Her appetite returned and she started sleeping well again. Washington, D.C., was still in winter's grip, but Anne was close to completing her training as a yoga instructor and, inspired by her teacher, a man named Erich Schiffmann who had made a popular yoga video with the actress Ali MacGraw, she started writing essays.

Her period of tranquility didn't last. The internal CIA investigation hadn't stopped, and in March, around the first anniversary of Bob's disappearance, it resumed with a vengeance. Anne was summoned one day from her office and escorted into a windowless room by two former CIA operatives hired to work on the inquiry. She was told to sit in a chair and grilled for hours. Her interrogators said Bob's work for the CIA was worthless crap and she was probably glad to see him gone. "You were angry with your friend, you sent him to Iran to get killed," one of them said. Her heart was pounding and she protested, accusing the men of lying. She thought of Bob's efforts to help the Defense Department contractors held by the FARC. "What about those hostages in Colombia, was that crap, too?" she asked. Her inquisitors then changed tactics and told Anne it would all go away if she told them how her boss, Tim Sampson, concealed Bob's activities from his superiors. She replied he hadn't done anything wrong. When she finally was allowed to leave, Anne realized her days at the CIA might end in a way she had never imagined.

In the spring, Anne was notified she was being put on paid leave pending the outcome of the CIA's inquiry. When it was completed, an internal panel made up of senior CIA officials known as an "accountability board" would review the investigation's findings and decide what disciplinary actions, if any, to take. Those possibilities ranged from a mild reprimand to a brief suspension to a firing, an extremely rare, worst-case scenario.

Some agency officials saw what was happening. It was the same crap that had been going on within the CIA for years. Analysts in the Illicit Finance Group had been doing their job, gathering the kind of critical intelligence the agency's clandestine operatives either wouldn't or couldn't get. But now it was payback time, and the agency's spy side was seizing an opportunity to teach analysts a lesson about staying in their place. At home, Anne tried to put those thoughts aside and stay calm by concentrating on yoga, meditation, and her cats.

She wondered whether she should go back to the CIA, regardless of the verdict. She would feel like a battered wife going back to an abusive husband. Anne started looking for a new job. She knew that the types of private investigative firms for which Bob had worked doing due diligence inquiries would pay plenty for her knowledge about Russian crime. She didn't find the prospect of working in the private sector appealing. There was an opening for an analyst at another federal agency, the Office of the Director of National Intelligence. It didn't sound that exciting, but it would be a fresh start. Another possibility was working for a public interest group, such as Global Witness, which exposed political or economic corruption. Over the years, Anne got to know reporters who covered Russian crime, and one of them, David Kaplan, now worked at the Center for Public Integrity, a nonprofit group in Washington that specialized in investigative journalism. In the spring of 2008, he invited Anne to accompany him to an event at the Newseum, a local journalism museum, and introduced her to the heads of other public interest groups.

The CIA's board soon started issuing its recommendations. One by one, eight CIA employees were called into meetings. Five staffers, including personnel in the agency's contracting office, received mild rebukes ranging from an official reprimand to a two-week suspension. The panel's recommendations for the three other employees were more serious. Timothy Sampson was given the option of resigning voluntarily, with his security clearances intact, or being fired. Sampson, who would later publicly state he did not know that Bob's CIA work involved Iran, chose to resign. Todd Egeland, who headed the

CIA branch overseeing the Illicit Finance Group, was given the same option. Egeland would later say he had never met or communicated with Bob. But some analysts told CIA investigators during the agency's internal review that he had promoted a culture of risk-taking. Egeland was the official, they said, who had urged CIA analysts at the rally in "the Bubble" to take on the agency's spy side, and he supposedly rewarded subordinates who pushed the envelope. Egeland, who disputed those assertions, also chose to resign.

The board's harshest punishment was reserved for Anne. She was also given the option of resigning or being fired, but the panel recommended she lose her security clearances because it concluded she hadn't been forthright with agency investigators. It was essentially a death sentence as far as government intelligence work was concerned. Without a security clearance, she wouldn't be able to get a job with the Director of National Intelligence or any other sensitive post. She was being cast out from the circle of secrecy she had inhabited for two decades, never to return. Anne was devastated. She hadn't seen it coming. She told friends the CIA's clandestine side was throwing her under the bus, and to do so it needed to destroy her reputation and career. She insisted to friends she hadn't lied about anything. She had given the CIA panel a complete statement explaining all the facts of Bob's case and all the actions she had taken. But the board, she said, twisted her words and turned them against her. She was accused, she told friends, of not disclosing information she was never asked about.

The three forced departures were the strongest disciplinary actions taken by the agency in decades. For Anne, one step in the process remained. The CIA's director, General Michael Hayden, would review the board's recommendations against her and decide whether to adopt them. Her friends were furious. They believed that Anne was being cast aside to satisfy the demands of Senator Nelson and the Senate intelligence panel for a body. It was absurd to think she had kept her CIA colleagues in the dark about Bob, they said, because she was a "stickler" for agency rules. One of Anne's CIA mentors, a retired clandestine official named Paul Redmond, lobbied agency officials on her behalf. So did one of her closest friends, a former spy named Margaret Henoch. As far as Henoch was concerned, Bob had put his own neck into the noose by going off to Kish and there was no reason for Anne to take the fall for his misadventure.

Many of Anne's friends and acquaintances didn't know anything about Bob. Instead, they thought she had become the innocent victim of internal agency jockeying. After hearing about Anne's situation, Richard Clarke, a former top counterterrorism official, called her. Since leaving government, Clarke had become a bestselling author as well as an on-air personality for ABC News on national security issues. He told her he could arrange for media coverage about her mistreatment by the CIA. Anne begged off. If her case drew media attention, both reporters and Bob's captors would find out about Bob and the spy agency, and she wanted to avoid that happening in case he was alive.

At the urging of friends, Anne decided to hire a lawyer. She retained a former CIA operative named Janine Brookner who knew firsthand about agency infighting. In the 1990s, Brookner, a onetime station chief in Central America, sued the CIA, accusing it of widespread sexual discrimination. In her complaint, she detailed episodes where male subordinates refused to work for her because she was a woman and, as part of a campaign to sabotage her career, accused her of provocative sexual behavior. The CIA settled Brookner's claims for more than $400,000, money she used to pay for law school and start a practice specializing in suing the spy agency on behalf of former employees. Brookner helped Anne draft her appeal to CIA Director Hayden. They also discussed other steps Anne could take, including the "nuclear option," filing a public lawsuit in which the analyst accused the CIA of unjust dismissal.

Anne's friends were elated when they learned about her counterattack. Many of them were former CIA employees who had left the agency disillusioned with the imperious attitudes of its leaders. Anne felt like her decision to challenge the panel's decision was either the bravest or the most foolish thing she would ever do.

Anne was summoned to Langley and taken to the building's seventh floor, where the agency's senior officials are located. She was brought to see Stephen Kappes. When she was seated, he told her the CIA was adopting the accountability board's recommendations. He asked her if she had any questions. She looked at him. They had started their CIA careers at about the same time. She asked if he had anything to say to her, as one person to another. His response was a brief "No." With that, Anne left Langley.

A CIA official went to Capitol Hill to brief the staff of the Senate intelligence panel about the agency's findings and the actions taken against Anne and others. Committee staffers were told the Illicit Finance Group had violated agency policies by essentially running Bob as a "rogue" spy, who went on intelligence-gathering missions overseas without the knowledge of the clandestine division. Anne and others had known what they were doing was wrong, but technically speaking, they hadn't broken any rules because there weren't any rules in place for them to violate. During the agency's post-9/11 hiring boom, the CIA had failed to draft guidelines governing the activities of consultants such as Bob. To prevent similar episodes, the committee's staff was told, the agency was drafting rules for contractors, and Stephen Kappes was personally reviewing all existing contracts.

At a separate meeting, Anne's lawyer, Janine Brookner, made her case to panel staffers. Anne would later say she sent extensive memos immediately after Bob went missing to her boss, Tim Sampson, and to a senior official in the CIA's analytical division named Peter Clement that outlined all of Bob's activities for the Illicit Finance Group. She said she offered the FBI help and wanted to call Chris, but Sampson and Clement had told her they would "handle" everything inside the agency related to Bob's disappearance.

To committee staffers, Brookner's arguments were unpersuasive and Anne's story sounded convenient and self-serving. The Senate intelligence panel considered the inquiry over. Afterward, Anne still had one weapon; she could trigger the "nuclear option" and force a confrontation with the CIA by filing a lawsuit. But along the way, she lost the stomach to fight or thought better about it and decided not to sue.

The Senate intelligence panel's inquiry probably shouldn't have ended. If Anne's version of events came across as self-serving, so were the accounts the CIA gave to Congress, such as agency claims that Bob's reports were tossed in boxes and never read. CIA officials might have done so prior to his disappearance. But the idea that they would not have closely culled his reports immediately after he went missing to see if he might disclose agency secrets to Iran either was a lie or spoke to a level of agency incompetence that is almost unimaginable. In addition, if the Senate intelligence panel had probed further, it would have also discovered that the spy agency had long been aware of Bob's interest in recruiting Dawud Salahuddin.

Back in December 2005, when Bob was pitching Anne on projects he might take on when his CIA contract was approved, he sent her a lengthy memo about Dawud's potential as an informant, an idea based on his conversations then under way with Ira Silverman. It's not clear if Anne got it or responded. But Bob didn't stop there. That same month, he sent a similar memo to Robert Seldon Lady, the retired CIA spy who had fled Italy for Central America to avoid arrest. Bob asked Lady to pass along his memo to a top official on the CIA's clandestine side.

> Attached is something I would like you to review and consider forwarding on to your old buddy who is now way up in the stratosphere of your alma mater—it is, what I consider anyway, an extraordinary opportunity, operationally, if anyone has any balls or imagination left up there in the pickle factory. For your further information, I received this morning the subject's home telephone number in Iran, some additional background information on how he might possibly be, in fact, recruited, and what he's capable of providing, including political and potentially military-type data. What I was hoping for is an audience and a go-ahead to talk by phone with this guy. I could then set up a meeting in a third country with one of

our folks present. Anyway, take a look, have a great Christmas, best to your family and let's talk about this—I'd just like to run it up the flagpole as high as possible before being shot down.

In February 2006, Lady told Bob that he had been trying to stir interest at the CIA for the project, and while he hadn't succeeded, he was about to visit Langley and would try again.

I will personally push them when I go. I've been asking for an expression of interest, but so far all I get is silence. I'm afraid our bureaucracies have grown beyond their own usefulness. I won't let this just sit there and stew.

Two years after that memo was written, Joe Sweeney, the CIA lawyer, and "Mike," the counterintelligence officer, came to Pensacola to meet with Chris at Dave's office. They told her the inquiry hadn't found a "smoking gun," proving Anne knew beforehand about Bob's trip to Kish. But they remained suspicious. In examining emails and records of telephone calls between Bob and the analyst, they found evidence he had called his travel agent to book his Kish flight just after a long phone call with her, presumably the one in which she said the Illicit Finance Group had found more money for him. The events didn't prove Anne knew about the Kish trip, but the CIA decided to refer the case to the Justice Department for possible criminal investigation. The agency also finalized a financial settlement with Chris worth more than $2 million. In some ways, it was a small price. Dave was told by a congressional official that the CIA hadn't taken steps to try to locate Bob after hearing he had disappeared in Iran, such as alerting the National Security Agency to monitor cell phone conversations in the region for chatter about a captured American.

Both Chris and Dave were convinced Anne knew about Bob's trip. Dave viewed the analyst as a manipulative Mata Hari who had knowingly sent Bob into danger and then walked away when it went wrong. Chris's perspective was different. It was personal. She had never talked with Anne, but she had seen her at Bob's retirement party, sent her daughter to visit her, and gotten a Christmas card from her every year. The way Chris saw it, Anne had faced a choice. She could have called her when she learned Bob was missing and helped sound the alarm. If she had, maybe things would have turned out differently. But Chris also knew that Anne, by making that call, would have likely lost her job. So she had taken the route most people would; she had kept quiet. Chris could understand why she had. But that didn't mean she would forgive her.

Around the first anniversary of Bob's disappearance, a CIA official gave Chris an envelope containing a lengthy letter to her from Anne. In it, Anne described her long friendship with Bob, her admiration for him, and her concern about his safety. Chris was not a person given to displays of emotion. But as she read Anne's letter, she started to seethe. Every sentence rang hollow. Every profession of friendship seemed empty. Chris finished reading the letter. Then she put it back into its envelope, stuffed it inside a cabinet, and never read it again.

14

"Heloo Cheristi"

In mid-2008, an email arrived at the Help Bob Levinson website with the subject line "Heloo Cheristi," an apparent phonetic attempt at "Hello Christine." The accompanying message was written in Farsi and its writer, who said her name was Parisi, explained she had heard Chris talking about Bob on a recent Voice of America interview broadcast into Iran. Parisi described herself as a technician at a hospital in Gachsaran, an industrial city located five hundred miles south of Tehran. One night, she explained, she was called to the hospital to deal with a medical emergency. A male patient, described to her as a prisoner at a nearby detention facility run by the Iranian Ministry of Intelligence, was experiencing significant internal hemorrhaging caused by a bleeding ulcer. His hemoglobin count was at a dangerously low level. After doctors treated him, intelligence officers took the man away. Parisi said she had gone onto the Levinson family's website after hearing Chris's interview and looked at pictures of her missing husband. The man treated at the hospital appeared much thinner than Bob, but Parisi was certain it was him.

FBI officials took the message seriously. They drafted a response for Chris, and Parisi provided information in her reply about the patient's precise hemoglobin count, numbers FBI experts determined were consistent with diabetes. She also wrote: "You must rest assured that next time when they bring him in, I will talk to him; of course the Intelligence [Ministry] always has its own trusted physicians and that case was an emergency. But I will try to get some information about him and will try to send you a map of the location of where he is held."

Using the instant messaging feature on Chris's email account, FBI agents, pretending to be Chris, engaged in online conversations with Parisi and suggested she come to Turkey for a meeting. Parisi replied she was unable to travel because of work and family obligations, and as her correspondence continued, her comments increasingly took on a political tone. One note said:

> One day I will come to America because I like America very much.
>
> When you came to Iran, how did you find it? Our country is a good country with excellent people but this government is a government that supports terrorists and is not from the people. We young people have no freedom and do not share in the most basic human rights. We cannot even dress according to our own wishes, most of the people are looking for American help for their freedom. You must have full faith in the fact that your husband is in this very place and do not let yourself be duped by these leech-like people. May you succeed!

It was the last email Chris received from her and FBI agents were left to wonder if the earlier ones were genuine. If Parisi lived just about anywhere else, FBI officials could have sent an agent to see if she existed and possibly make contact with her. But in Iran, such moves were too dangerous.

Soon after Parisi's final email, Sarkis Soghanalian phoned Dave. For months, the old arms dealer had been putting him, Ira Silverman, and Larry Sweeney in contact with a succession of shadowy figures he claimed could help locate their friend. The men shared several qualities. They were all either French or Middle Eastern. They were all connected in some manner to intelligence agencies in France or the Middle East. They were also all involved in one way or another with criminal activities, such as weapons dealing, bribery, or money laundering. Dave realized early on that Soghanalian viewed Bob's case as an opportunity to find his way back into the arms trade. It was hard to see it any other way. His proposals to win the former FBI agent's release invariably involved the sale of embargoed products to Iran, such as helicopter parts or components for jet engines. Dave wasn't troubled. He knew governments cut deals all the time, and if a few helicopter parts could win Bob's freedom, it seemed like a small price to pay.

Soghanalian told Dave that Bob's Iranian captors had turned him over to Hezbollah for safekeeping and that the terrorist group was hiding him in Lebanon by moving him around the network of refugee camps it operated there. He said one of his contacts, a Syrian-born businessman named Fouad al-Zayat, was well connected to Hezbollah and was willing to negotiate the terms of Bob's release. "It's all in the oven," Soghanalian said. When Dave asked Senator Nelson's office to check out al-Zayat with the CIA, the feedback he received was encouraging. The businessman did have close ties to both Hezbollah and Syrian intelligence, the spy agency reported. Dave and Ira made arrangements to meet al-Zayat on Cyprus, where he had a home.

As their flight prepared to land in Nicosia, the largest city on Cyprus, Dave and Ira were buoyant. They sensed they were days away from seeing Bob and bringing him home. Ira felt a particular sense of relief. He had spent every day since his friend's disappearance hunkered down by the telephone, hoping for news and weaving the few threads he found into stories of hope. Chris and Bob's children didn't blame him for what happened on Kish. But for Ira, only Bob's return could relieve his sense of guilt.

Dave had contracted with SCG International to provide security for the trip, and they were met at the Nicosia airport by Jamie Smith, the firm's head, and two of his employees, Dino DeLaurentis and

Rocky Boudreau, both former commandos. Smith, a short, stocky man with blond hair, explained that his team had flown into Cyprus on a private plane loaded with weapons and telecommunications equipment. He said that SCG owned a large C-130 military transport plane that was stationed nearby, in position to pick up Bob when he was released.

The following morning, two black SUVs were waiting at Dave and Ira's hotel to take them to see al-Zayat at his office in downtown Nicosia. For security purposes, Smith told them, they needed to ride in separate cars. He handed each man a special pen containing a concealed video camera and a slip of paper on which he had written a name and telephone number. Smith explained it was the name of the police chief in Nicosia. "If the shit hits the fan, call this guy," he told them. The convoy departed. As the vehicles approached al-Zayat's address, Ira's driver, Rocky Boudreau, instructed the retired newsman on what to do if their car came under gunfire. He told Ira to throw himself down toward the left because he fired with his right hand and any returning rounds would be directed that way. He also urged Ira to stay calm even if bullets started whizzing in through the car's windshield. Ira sat frozen, wondering what the hell was going on.

Arriving at al-Zayat's office, Dave and Ira climbed a staircase and were ushered into a large, spacious room with white tile flooring and walls decorated with Christian icons. They were greeted affably by al-Zayat, a portly, balding man with an oversized face and heavy jowls who had been dubbed "the Fat Man" by British tabloids. The businessman had recently made headlines in England by refusing to pay off gambling losses at London's top casinos reportedly totaling $250 million. Instead, he sued the casinos, claiming his losses were the result of trickery by dealers who distracted him and managers who failed to provide him with services that were his due as a high-stakes casino "whale." "Casinos give a service, and if the service is not good, considering the price which you are paying, then you do not pay," al-Zayat told one newspaper. "If you go to a restaurant and you do not like the food, you do not pay. If you go to the whorehouse and do not get the pleasure you were seeking, you do not pay."

The Syrian's ability to attract controversy wasn't limited to Britain. He was barred from entering the United States and had been involved in a political scandal that resulted in the imprisonment of a congressman on bribery and corruption charges. In the mid-2000s, al-Zayat and a partner, Nigel Winfield, struck a deal to sell Iran replacement parts for Boeing jet engines. But since the parts fell on the list of embargoed materials, they needed to find a U.S. lawmaker willing to support a congressional exemption for the sale. Winfield approached a Republican representative from Ohio, Robert W. Ney, who agreed to fly to London to discuss the issue with al-Zayat. Once he arrived, the Syrian brought Ney to an exclusive casino, Les Ambassadeurs, and gave him fistfuls of gambling chips worth tens of thousands of dollars, money federal prosecutors later charged was a bribe to get Ney's support for the waiver.

At his office on Cyprus, al-Zayat introduced Dave and Ira to another associate, whom he described as a Jordanian colleague who would serve as his go-between with Hezbollah. Dave said the Levinson family didn't have money to pay a ransom, and al-Zayat said his advice was not to offer any. On the following day, another meeting was held, this one in the lobby of Dave and Ira's hotel. SCG was monitoring the proceedings and relaying reports about it to Dave's paralegal, Sonya Dobbs. Dave and Ira didn't know it at the time, but the CIA was also secretly listening in.

The talks soon shifted to al-Zayat's home, a walled compound occupying an entire block in a Nicosia suburb. Whenever Dave and Ira arrived, a lavish meal prepared by al-Zayat's cook always awaited them. During one meal, the businessman asked Dave why the United States made it so difficult for American companies to win business abroad by barring the payments of bribes to foreign officials, lamenting that this put U.S. firms at a disadvantage. During most of the meals at al-Zayat's home, seven or eight other men were present. They didn't take part in any discussions and Ira assumed they were Syrian intelligence agents. At one gathering, Ira thought he overheard al-Zayat's Jordanian associate mention the name of the former Iranian president Ali Akbar Hashemi Rafsanjani, the politician who had served as the link among Ira, Bob, and Dawud Salahuddin.

After about five days, al-Zayat finally announced that his Jordanian colleague was ready to leave for Beirut and would return with a Hezbollah representative. The Jordanian reappeared the following day accompanied by a man dressed in a white shirt opened at the collar and a thin gold necklace. The man, who spoke English, suggested Dave and Ira accompany him to Beirut to start talks about Bob, but they replied they preferred to conduct those discussions on Cyprus. At lunchtime, the man joined them at a poolside table. He explained their friend's release would cost $20 million. When Dave told al-Zayat about the demand, his host appeared angered. "We had made a deal that he was going to return Bob," al-Zayat said. "There are no terms other than he is going to give Bob."

The next morning, the supposed Hezbollah official was nowhere to be found and al-Zayat told Dave and Ira the terrorist group was now claiming to know nothing about Bob or his whereabouts. Dave and Ira were crushed. They had discussed every detail of Bob's return with Jamie Smith, including where he would be taken first for medical examination and the best place for his reunion with Chris. Now the only thing left to do was pack and leave Cyprus.

A few weeks earlier, Iran's president, Mahmoud Ahmadinejad, had agreed to a rare television interview in Tehran. International talks were restarting about the future of Iran's nuclear program and Ahmadinejad was on a charm offensive to project a more moderate image of Iran. He summoned the NBC News anchor Brian Williams to Tehran for the interview. Ahmadinejad remarked that he was hopeful that Iran and the United States were poised to enter a new phase of their relationship. "For more than fifty years, the policy of American statesmen has been to confront the Iranian people," he said. "Today, we see new behavior shown by the United States."

Toward the interview's end, Williams sprung a question on

Ahmadinejad—he asked him about Bob. The Iranian's response sounded more like a provocation than a reply. His country was willing to help the FBI find Bob, he said, but U.S. officials first needed to provide a better explanation of why he had come to Kish.

WILLIAMS: An American, a former FBI agent named Bob Levinson, . . . disappeared in Iran. How much do you know about his case and the status, the search for him?

AHMADINEJAD: There was a claim made some time ago, some people came over, the gentleman's family came over. They talked and met with our officials and were given our responses. I see no reason for a person who was given an Iranian visa and came into Iran, arrived in Iran through official channels, to have problems here. Our security officials and agents have expressed their willingness to assist the FBI if the FBI has any information about his travels around the world. We have said that we are ready to help, to assist with that matter. There is certain information that only the FBI . . . have.

After Dave and Ira's return from Cyprus, SCG International started sending bills to Larry Sweeney, who had agreed to oversee the company's payments. They were much bigger than he had expected and SCG hadn't provided receipts to support the expenditures. Some charges struck Sweeney as inflated or unrelated to the search for Bob. Jamie Smith had left Cyprus for a few days while Dave and Ira were there, apparently to go to London on other business. He had charged the Levinson family $15,000 in expenses and airfares for the trip to England. When Sweeney challenged the bill, he received a reply from an SCG official named Troy Titus, who insisted the charges were all appropriate.

Sweeney's old cop instincts went on alert. He started doing some research and discovered that Titus, who described himself as SCG's accountant, was a former lawyer who had been disbarred after his conviction in 2005 on fraud charges. In 2008, he was facing fraud charges again, this time in connection with a real estate investment scheme. "Well, this tops it all," Larry wrote Dave and Ira. "Our account is now being handled by an accused felon."

Dave and Larry made what they thought was a reasonable payment to SCG and broke ties with it. Years later, *Outside* magazine published an exposé of Smith, claiming he had embellished or manufactured key parts of his personal story, such as the extent of his involvement with the CIA. The article appeared just as Smith was set to publish his autobiography, *Gray Work: Confessions of an American Paramilitary Spy*. The book's publication was delayed for a time and Smith later filed a $30 million libel suit against the magazine, saying he had represented himself accurately.

Smith devoted a chapter in his book to SCG International's work on the Levinson case. In it, he wrote that he had warned Dave on Cyprus not to accompany the Hezbollah representative to Beirut, but Dave and Ira later said Smith wasn't involved in the discussion. Smith also said that the female SCG operative who had visited the Maryam hotel—the woman he called "Mila"—had quickly left Kish after discovering that someone had entered her room. Mila knew about the break-in, he wrote, because she had used an old spy's trick: she took a strand of her hair, wet it with saliva, and placed it across the gap between the door and its frame. Upon returning to her room, she discovered the strand on the floor, a sign the door had been opened. Mila might have told the story to Smith. But there was not a single word in her report from Kish about someone entering her room or a strand of hair.

15

The Hikers

Iran's mission to the United Nations is located on the eighth floor of a modern office building set back slightly from Third Avenue near the corner of East Fortieth Street in Manhattan. Inside is a small waiting area furnished with a few chairs, a love seat, and a coffee table. The walls are decorated with posters of tourist sites in Iran, such as Persepolis, the ancient capital of Persia. A woman wearing a bright blue headscarf and dark buttoned jacket appeared and smiled warmly at Chris. She introduced herself as Mrs. Kamali and said she recognized Chris from newspaper photographs, adding she looked much prettier in person. She said Iran's U.N. ambassador, Mohammad Khazaee, was ready to see Chris and her companions—her daughters Sue and Sarah, and her sister Suzi.

The diplomat, a short, trim man in his mid-fifties with graying hair, smiled and welcomed each of his visitors individually. He told Chris he had been hoping to meet all of her children, but she explained that several of them had other obligations or were traveling. Two of Khazaee's aides, a man and a woman, sat on either side of his desk with notepads on their laps. Chris was there to make another personal appeal to Iranian officials. Prior to coming to the meeting, she had discussed with FBI agents what she should and shouldn't say to the ambassador. Khazaee, an economist by training, had assumed his post in New York shortly after Bob's disappearance and served as his government's principal contact with U.S. officials and notables asking about him. Along with Senator Bill Nelson of Florida, those people included Bill Richardson, Bill Clinton's secretary of energy and a former U.S. ambassador to the U.N.

When Khazaee invited Chris to start their conversation, she mentioned she had watched Brian Williams's interview of Mahmoud Ahmadinejad and was impressed by the Iranian president's knowledge of Bob's case. But she became confused, she added, when he talked about Bob's failure to get an Iranian visa because her husband was visiting Kish, an area where he didn't need one.

The diplomat didn't respond directly. Instead, he explained to Chris that he had worked hard to set up her trip to Iran and was curious about how it went. She thanked him and said she greatly enjoyed the opportunity to meet Iranians. "Were they not hospitable?" he asked. When Chris responded that everyone had been very kind, the diplomat's demeanor abruptly changed and his voice got louder. If that was the case, he demanded to know, why was she continuing to make "false statements in the media."

He glanced down at four pages of notes spread out on his desk. They were written in Farsi and parts of each page were highlighted. For the next thirty minutes, he lectured Chris and her family members, coming back repeatedly to several points he wanted to emphasize. He said her husband's situation was as important for Iran as it was for the United States to resolve. He said he was tired of being asked about him because he didn't know about the case. He repeated that he and his colleagues remained suspicious of Bob's reasons for coming to Iran, echoing the Foreign Ministry official's claims that Bob might have offered $500 to a boat operator on Kish to take him to the Iranian mainland.

He asked Chris about the cigarette company for whom her husband was supposedly working and why he was traveling alone. Then he mentioned the FBI and the CIA and said it was entirely possible that a retired agent might still be doing work for the U.S. government. He said his government would not hesitate to put such a person on trial. "If we had him, we would announce it, we would accuse him of spying or whatever it might be."

Khazaee continued, adding that he found the congressional resolutions introduced about Bob by Senator Nelson and others to be insulting because they effectively accused Iran of lying. Dozens of Iranians were in U.S. prisons on trumped-up embargo violations, he said, and they were being held under degrading conditions without access to lawyers or their families. Khazaee then drew himself up, placed the notes into a folio, and leaned back, signaling it was the Levinson family's turn to talk.

Chris asked him if he thought smugglers on Kish might have seized her husband. Khazaee replied it was highly likely; smuggling was rampant in the Persian Gulf and Mafia-like gangs operating in places such as Kish routinely killed Iranian police officers. Her husband's captors, he added, may have taken him to Iraq, Afghanistan, or Pakistan. If U.S. officials learned of his whereabouts, Iran stood ready to assist in his rescue, the diplomat said. Several months earlier, Chris had hired a lawyer in Iran, and she asked Khazaee if he thought it would be helpful to retain private investigators in his country. He looked at her askance. "Have you not been listening to anything I just said? What makes you think this case is any more important to you than it is to us?"

Sarah Levinson reached into her bag and took out a photo album filled with pictures of Bob and Chris, their seven children, and Ryan, their grandson. Sarah, who was crying, defended her mother, saying she had always acted respectfully toward the Iranian government. She was a wife trying to find her husband and bring him home. "She is doing everything she can," said Sarah. "Our father is a wonderful man and in the end of the photo album are pictures of my sister's wedding. I know my boyfriend is waiting to propose to me until he can ask my father for my hand and it is so hard. We appreciate anything you can do to bring him home."

Khazaee took the album and leafed through the pages. His tone softened. He explained he had experienced the loss of a family member, the death of a son. He said he understood how the Levinsons felt. This wasn't their fault. It was a matter between governments. Sue Levinson was crying, too. Suddenly, she lashed out at Khazaee, telling him how they were all struggling to survive the trauma of her father's disappearance. "We just want you to send him home," she said.

The diplomat's reaction turned again. He became combative, though this time he wasn't reading from a script. "You say send him home, like you think that we have him. Well, to that I say to you, maybe you should ask why did the FBI send him over there in the first place!"

Khazaee stood up, indicating the meeting was over. Chris hastened to thank him, and Sue, still crying, tried to apologize. As the family left his office, the diplomat spoke to her. "Susan, be strong. Life has its ups and downs; we all go through these things. I told you I lost my son. You need to be strong."

About the time of that meeting, massive political demonstrations were taking place on the streets of Tehran. Iranians were about to vote in a presidential election, and it was not clear Mahmoud Ahmadinejad would win a second term. Political rivals blamed his strident stance toward the West for worsening economic conditions inside the country. The desire for political change was strong among middle-class Iranians and students. Pre-election polls put a reformist candidate, Mir-Hossein Mousavi, in the lead. The former president Ali Akbar Hashemi Rafsanjani was also running, having rebranded himself as a political moderate. When results were announced, the official tally gave Ahmadinejad a sizeable majority of the vote.

The news was met in Tehran and other cities with cries of derision and claims of election fraud. Large, spontaneous protests erupted and Iran hovered on the edge of a popular political uprising. Religious autocrats and ultraconservatives responded with a ruthless, bloody crackdown, one that was broadcast to the outside world through photographs and video captured on cell phones and posted on Twitter and other forms of social media. Leather-jacketed plain-clothes officers known as the Basij were seen riding motorcycles into crowds of protesters in Tehran, whipping bystanders with sticks. The dying moments of a young Iranian woman, Neda Agha-Soltan, were captured on video as she lay on the pavement after being shot. Hundreds of students and political dissidents were rounded up and taken to prisons. Reports emerged that dozens of them were tortured and killed.

Not long afterward, a twenty-seven-year-old computer engineering student walked into the American consulate in Ankara, Turkey. He showed officials burn and bruise marks and explained he had been tortured at a secret Revolutionary Guards prison following a roundup of students protesting President Ahmadinejad's reelection. After his head was shaved, he was brought to a cell, which reeked from the smell of blood. On the cell's door, a previous occupant had scratched three lines of text in English and a name. After his release from captivity, he said, he had gone onto the Internet and discovered the name's significance. It was "B LEVINSON."

President Obama and other Western politicians issued statements protesting the Iranian crackdown. A few months earlier, the American president had extended Iran an olive branch in an effort to coax its leaders into resuming nuclear control talks. In a videotaped message addressed to the Iranian people, he had referred to Iran as "the Islamic Republic," one of the rare times an American leader acknowledged its clerical government. But Iranian officials responded to the West's criticism of their repressive tactics with the same simple and brutal strategy they had used many times before—they seized foreigners and imprisoned them on trumped-up spying charges. In 2009, three young Americans became the newest political pawns in that game. The trio, Sarah Shourd, Joshua Fattal, and Shane Bauer, were on vacation, hiking in the Zagros Mountains in western Kurdistan, along the border between Iraq and Iran. They were trying to find their way to a scenic waterfall when they spotted a soldier on a nearby ridge. He waved at them and indicated he wanted the hikers to come over to where he was standing. They couldn't tell what uniform he was wearing, but when the Americans approached him they unwittingly crossed into Iran and were taken into custody. They were soon charged with espionage and sent to Evin Prison.

The seizure of the hikers came as FBI officials sensed they were about to make a breakthrough in the search for Bob. Ever since Chris's return from Iran, the bureau, under the watchful eye of Senator Bill Nelson, had been pouring more resources and more experienced agents into the case. In 2009, FBI agents, using the ruse suggested by Mila, the operative with SCG International, lured the Maryam hotel's manager and its restaurant supervisor, Mohammed Para and Ali Korakumjam, to Dubai with fake offers of jobs there. But the two men refused to talk when questioned by agents, and the driver of the Maryam's taxi, the person FBI agents wanted most to interview, had been sent back to Kish by airport officials in Dubai because he didn't have the right travel documents.

A few months later, FBI agents were again at Dubai International Airport, this time awaiting the arrival of a flight from Tehran. Aboard it was an Iranian judge who had passed word to the United States through intermediaries that he had seen Bob and could provide information about him. The Iranian judge was coming voluntarily and bringing his two daughters with him. Given the risks involved, U.S. officials were ready to offer him asylum if his story checked out. When his plane arrived, FBI agents escorted him and his children through the terminal to a connecting flight to Washington, D.C. Before they got to the gate, his older daughter, who was about eighteen, broke away and started running. An FBI agent took off after her, but she disappeared into a crowd of passengers. The man explained that his daughter didn't want to go to the United States because her boyfriend was in Iran. She also believed her father was betraying his country. FBI agents assured him they would find the girl and bring her with them on a later flight.

In Washington, the man and his younger daughter were taken to a safe house outside the nation's capital, where investigators questioned him. He said Bob was brought before him during a secret court proceeding and charged with espionage. But because he viewed the evidence against him as flimsy, prosecutors had transferred the case out of his court and given it to a more compliant judge, who found Bob guilty. For the bureau, assessing the judge's credibility wasn't easy. He apparently suffered from mental health problems. When FBI officials gave him an initial polygraph test, the result was inconclusive. A doctor was called to the safe house to examine him. He was polygraphed again, and this time the test suggested he might be telling the truth. However, the operation soon fell apart. When FBI agents in Dubai found his older daughter, she refused to come to the United States. Instead, she went back to Iran, where she denounced her father to authorities as a traitor. The man, fearing retribution against members of his family, decided to go home. FBI agents tried to talk him out of it and told him he could stay, but he and his younger daughter soon boarded a flight and left.

Meanwhile, another writer for *The New Yorker* returned from Iran, where he had interviewed Dawud Salahuddin. Seven years had passed since Ira Silverman spoke with the fugitive, but Dawud's act hadn't changed. He told the *New Yorker* writer, Jon Lee Anderson, that Iran's religious leaders were destroying the country. "The mullahs have industrialized the religion and turned it into a money-making venture, and they are the main beneficiaries," Dawud said. At some point, Dawud must have realized Anderson needed something fresh because, out of the blue, he said he was planning to leave Iran. When the writer asked him where he intended to go, Dawud simply replied, "The first law of a fugitive is not to tell anyone where you are headed."

16

The Young Man

The man seated across from Boris Birshtein in a Paris hotel room was in his forties, young enough to be Boris's son. But the divide between them was greater than age. The man, Oleg Deripaska, was among the best-known members of Russia's new business elite, the oligarchs, and stood atop one of his country's most strategic businesses, the aluminum industry. His company, United Company RUSAL, was an international industrial powerhouse. It was the same Russian company that one of the Iranians who met with Bob Levinson and Boris in Istanbul had mentioned while discussing Iran's need for bauxite.

Deripaska, whose Cossack heritage could be seen in his broad forehead and strong cheekbones, was worth an estimated $14 billion. He lived close to Vladimir Putin in a wealthy Moscow suburb, and Deripaska's wife, Polina, was the daughter of the top aide to Boris Yeltsin, the former Russian president. He owned homes in England, France, and Italy; a private jet; and an oceangoing yacht, the *Queen K*, which had a crew of twenty-one. But the State Department treated Deripaska much as it did Birshtein, as an undesirable. American officials never publicly said why they wouldn't issue him a visa, but it was apparently related to his meteoric rise in the aluminum industry. During the 1990s, southern Siberia, home to Russia's metal smelters, was the setting for the "aluminum wars," a period of Chicago-style gangland violence replete with murders and assassinations as rivals fought for control. Deripaska, who had earned degrees in economics and physics, was depicted in some accounts as a ruthless genius, and a lawsuit filed against him in an American court in the 1990s claimed he had made death threats against two competitors.

Deripaska denied doing so and insisted that the only payments he had made to gangs during the aluminum wars were to buy protection for his facilities. Over time, he had spent millions of dollars on lobbyists, including the former Senate leader Bob Dole, to get the State Department to change its stance. U.S. officials briefly lifted the ban, then reinstated it. Vladimir Putin was furious. "They give us nothing, explain to us nothing, and forbid him from entry," he told one newspaper. Deripaska also courted U.S. politicians, meeting in 2006 with the Arizona senator John McCain during the World Economic Forum, a conference in Davos, Switzerland. One of the lawmaker's advisors, Rick Davis, arranged the meeting for McCain, who was then gearing up to become the 2008 Republican presidential nominee. Deripaska later hosted McCain aboard the *Queen K*, while it was moored off the coast of Montenegro. Nothing the oligarch tried had worked, and Boris had come to Paris to offer him a chance to earn what his money and influence couldn't buy: a visa. To get it, he would have to finance a secret operation to find and rescue Bob.

It had taken FBI officials about six months to connect with Boris after John Good's initial call to the bureau to offer the businessman's help. Two FBI agents were assigned to deal with him. One of them, Martin Hellmer, was a member of the Extraterritorial Squad, and the other, Joe Krzemien, was a retired agent with experience on Russian cases who was working for the FBI as a contractor. Initially, Boris proposed an undercover operation in which Krzemien, posing as a business associate, would go with him to Istanbul and see the same Iranians whom Bob had met in December 2006. But the plan never materialized and Boris next spent months searching for someone who might have connections to Iran. The person he found was an ally of Turkey's most notorious terrorist, Abdullah Öcalan. For two decades, a group founded by Öcalan, the Kurdistan Workers' Party, had waged a guerrilla-style war against the Turkish government, ambushing troops and blowing up buildings and bridges in its campaign to create an autonomous Kurdish nation. Finally, in 1999, Öcalan was arrested during a joint operation between the CIA and Turkish forces and sentenced to life in prison.

Boris's contact, an ethnic Kurd named Madzhit Mamoyan, was still a backer of the Kurdistan Workers' Party, and he looked more at home in a leather jacket than in a business suit. A short, thickly built chain-smoker in his fifties with dark eyes, Mamoyan lived in Moscow and described himself as a businessman. He hated Turks with a passion; if he went into a restaurant where a Turk was working as a waiter, he would leave.

After meeting Mamoyan through a mutual acquaintance, Boris told him U.S. officials wanted to find an American private investigator missing in Iran and were willing to do favors for people who helped. As a Kurd, Madzhit had plenty of connections in the region. Along with Turkey, there are large Kurdish communities in Iraq, Syria, and Iran. He told Boris he had a friend imprisoned in Spain he wanted released. When the FBI discovered the link between Madzhit and the Kurdistan Workers' Party, they hesitated to move forward—the group, which is known as the PKK, was designated during the Bush administration as a terrorist organization.

But the FBI didn't have any better alternatives, so Martin Hellmer and Joe Krzemien told Boris he could bring Madzhit to Washington for an interview so long as he financed the trip himself. Boris did it in style. A black stretch limousine picked up Madzhit at the airport and ferried him to a luxurious hotel near the White House, where he popped out of the car wearing a worn tracksuit smelling of cigarettes. That evening, Boris hosted Madzhit, Hellmer, and Krzemien at a lavish dinner that included champagne, oysters, and several bottles of wine.

FBI supervisors, fearing Madzhit might conduct PKK-related business while in the United States, kept him under surveillance. They didn't see signs of problems, but bureau officials told Boris that the Kurd lacked the political clout they needed in an intermediary. That might have ended the FBI's interactions with Boris and Madzhit. However, the two men weren't the type of people used to taking no for an answer, and they soon devised a plan to which FBI officials couldn't say no—one involving the aluminum magnate Oleg Deripaska.

Madzhit had met Deripaska in the 1990s when the Soviet Union was collapsing. The Kurd ended up owning a chain of television stations in Russia but was squeezed out, he would later say, by a notoriously corrupt mayor of Moscow named Yury Luzhkov. Over the years, he had stayed in touch with Deripaska, and after his trip to Washington, he thought of the oligarch's campaign to get a visa and his many business and political connections to Iran. He told Deripaska that U.S. officials were willing to reward those who helped find a missing American and suggested he speak with Boris. Before long, the two men were flying to Paris aboard the oligarch's private jet. Prior to the meeting, FBI officials gave Boris his instructions. The message was simple—if Deripaska delivered definitive evidence showing that Bob was either alive or dead, he would get his visa. There were a few ground rules. The oligarch would have to sever his ties with Washington lobbyists and fund the search for information with his money. "I know that people are sucking your blood with all their stories about how they are going to help you," Boris told Deripaska. "I don't want anything from you, nothing."

Deripaska mulled the proposal. Boris sensed the younger man was seething with the same anger and humiliation he had felt for years. Leaders of other countries accorded them respect. But in the United States, which held itself out as the world's moral arbiter, they were ostracized and treated with contempt. Boris had agreed to help Bob for a reason: he wanted his name off the watch list. But Bob's disappearance had opened bigger doors. By rescuing a missing American, he and Deripaska would be publicly celebrated as heroes, their old reputations cleansed forever. There were other possibilities as well. Boris could envision business partnerships with Deripaska, or the "young man," as he called him, and the opportunity to assume his place among the oligarchs.

Boris was elated when Deripaska told him he was willing to meet with American officials. As their meeting ended, Boris couldn't resist letting him know that he had once been a major player in Russia. "Haven't you heard about me?" Boris asked. When Deripaska didn't reply, he explained that Boris Yeltsin, the godfather of the oligarch's wife, was his mortal enemy. In the early 1990s, the Russian president ran Boris out of the country after reports surfaced he had bribed Yeltsin's vice president to win baby food contracts for his trading company, Seabeco. Boris rejected the charge and chalked it up to political infighting. But Yeltsin didn't forget the incident, even mentioning Boris in his memoir. "I was to learn much more about him and Seabeco, his ill-reputed firm," Yeltsin wrote. Boris told Deripaska he was surprised, given the bad blood, that the oligarch had agreed to see him. "That is very interesting," Deripaska replied. "It was very nice meeting you."

A few weeks later, Martin Hellmer and Joe Krzemien walked into the lobby of the luxurious Le Grand Hotel, not far from Place Vendôme in Paris. Fashion Week was in full swing and celebrities were in town to see shows by designers such as Alexander McQueen and Stella McCartney. The hotel's lobby was swarming with willowy models, and the agents paused briefly to take in the view before finding the elevator and riding up to a suite. Before leaving Washington, Hellmer and Krzemien had read up about Deripaska, and they expected to find a typical oligarch dressed in a custom-made Savile Row suit with a gold Patek Philippe watch strapped to his wrist. Deripaska didn't fit the part. His suit looked like it was pulled off a department store rack, and a plastic strap secured his cheap digital watch. His closely cropped hair appeared unevenly cut, as though his wife trimmed it at home. Joe Krzemien's attention was drawn to Deripaska's eyes. They were pale and icy cold. Krzemien had spent much of his FBI career on dangerous assignments, chasing spies and terrorists. When he shook the oligarch's hand, he felt a chill. Deripaska was one of the few people he had ever met who scared him.

Krzemien did most of the talking. Being a contractor allowed him to take greater liberties with the truth than Martin Hellmer, and the partners had worked out a routine to cover occasions when Krzemien needed to ad-lib—he would give Hellmer a certain look and the young agent would say he needed to leave the room. Krzemien told Deripaska, who spoke fluent English, that he and Hellmer were representatives of the U.S. government but didn't specifically mention the FBI. The ruse wasn't necessary. Krzemien realized Deripaska would never have agreed to meet with him and Hellmer absent agreement from Putin's office and that Russian intelligence officials probably knew who they worked for.

The oligarch told Hellmer and Krzemien he needed two questions answered before deciding whether to go forward. The first question was whether Bob had been kidnapped or killed in retaliation for something he had done as an FBI agent. When Krzemien said he didn't believe so, Deripaska posed his second question. "Has he ever done anything to hurt Russia?" he asked. Assured that he hadn't, Deripaska announced he was willing to fund a search and pay any ransom needed to free Bob, expenses that could amount to tens of millions of dollars. That price was small compared with what the State Department's refusal to issue him a visa was costing. A worldwide economic recession then unfolding was devastating the oligarch's business. To build his aluminum empire, Deripaska had taken out billions in bank loans, but he faced the prospect of defaulting on them because the price of aluminum and other metals was plummeting due to reduced demand. He had hoped to raise capital from investors by selling shares of RUSAL on the London Stock Exchange. But British regulators did not allow the offering to go forward, and financial analysts speculated the State Department's refusal to give Deripaska a visa was a factor in the decision. Wall Street investment firms were interested in Deripaska's ventures, but to get their money he needed a clean bill of health from U.S. authorities.

The businessman insisted on one condition for his participation in Bob's case. His role was to remain secret so rivals in Russia wouldn't know he was cooperating with the United States, a disclosure that could put him in physical danger. It was agreed that the oligarch would remain in the background while Madzhit Mamoyan oversaw the search for Bob on the ground. Boris would act as the go-between, relaying information among Madzhit, Deripaska, and the FBI. Bureau officials were elated. Deripaska, who was also involved in the automobile industry and other ventures, had contacts in Iran who might know about Bob. One FBI official called Chris and, without mentioning the oligarch's name, told her the bureau was now dealing with someone who could "fly into Iran on his private jet" and bring her husband out.

By 2009, Chris was getting regular weekly briefings from the FBI and the State Department about her husband's case. Typically, there was nothing new to report, but speaking regularly with Chris limited the number of spontaneous calls she made to agents. U.S. officials wanted her to feel they were doing everything possible to bring her husband home. They feared she would grow frustrated and go public about Bob's CIA ties, an outcome they desperately wanted to avoid, both for his sake and for the fate of the three young American hikers who were still being held in Evin Prison.

Bob's friend in London, Jeff Katz, the private investigator who headed Bishop International, was losing patience with the FBI's lack of progress. A native New Yorker in his sixties, Katz had lived for decades in England and spent much of his career working for Kroll Associates, the big investigative outfit, before starting his own firm. His most high-profile case at Kroll involved the mysterious death of Roberto Calvi, an executive of Banco Ambrosiano, an Italian bank that served the Vatican. When Calvi was found hanged in 1982 underneath London's Blackfriars Bridge, police officials concluded that his death was a suicide. A decade later, Calvi's family, unable to collect his life insurance because of the suicide finding, hired Katz to reinvestigate. He assembled a team of forensic experts, engineers, and a stuntman to re-create events on the night of Calvi's death. The key to the case turned out to be the dead man's shoes. Calvi favored shoes made by John Lobb Ltd., a famous cobbler on St. James's Street in London. Katz had the stuntman put on an identical pair and walk along the same metal scaffolding Calvi would have needed to navigate to reach the point underneath the bridge where he would have hanged himself. Calvi's body was found partially submerged in the river Thames, so the stuntman's shoes were soaked overnight in a bucket of Thames water. Technicians then microscopically examined both pairs of shoes. Unlike the stuntman's shoes, whose soles showed flecks of paint and rust from the scaffolding, the banker's shoes were free of debris, suggesting murderers staged the hanging by hoisting him up onto the bridge from a boat underneath it. Katz's finding prompted insurers to pay millions to Calvi's survivors.

Through contacts, Katz was introduced to an oil industry consultant in Paris who had spent his career cutting deals in the Middle East, including Iran. The consultant, Xavier Houzel, also served as a courier of information between governments. After speaking with Katz, he agreed to call an Iranian official in Paris. The diplomat told him he knew nothing about Bob's case but offered to arrange a meeting in Tehran for Houzel with officials of the Ministry of Intelligence when the consultant next traveled there. Katz brought Houzel to London, where the two men went to the U.S. embassy and spoke over a secure video link with FBI agents in Washington. The agents appeared eager to use the consultant, but a few days later they called Katz back and said State Department officials wanted them to stand down because the United States was "getting results from other irons in the fire." Katz relayed the message to Houzel, thanking him and saying his services wouldn't be needed.

When Houzel next visited Tehran on oil-related business, intelligence operatives had been tipped off to his interest in Bob. Two agents from the Ministry of Intelligence came to his hotel room and told him to follow them. They escorted him to a small, unmarked building, where he was taken into a barren room without windows. He was questioned for two hours about the purpose of his trip and why he was so interested in the case of the missing American. Houzel tried to provide neutral answers. The two agents instructed him to remain in the room while they reported to their superiors. A young boy appeared with a sandwich and a bottle of water. When the men returned, they questioned Houzel for two more hours before saying the Intelligence Ministry knew nothing about Bob. The consultant was allowed to go back to his hotel. Not long afterward, another of Katz's sources made inquiries about Bob while visiting the Iranian city of Qom, the country's religious center. He was warned to mind his own business and told that Iranian leaders knew exactly why the former FBI agent was on Kish.

By then, Madzhit Mamoyan was hopscotching across the Middle East and Europe trying to pick up information. He met with leaders of the two most powerful Kurdish factions in northern Iraq, the Talabani and the Barzani. On his travels, he kept hearing about the Rafsanjani family and its involvement in smuggling, including the trafficking of counterfeit cigarettes and other contraband through Kish. Many of Madzhit's sources insisted that Ali Akbar Hashemi Rafsanjani and his sons had to know about Bob's arrest and might be playing a role in his detention. It wasn't an empty theory. During Iran's presidential campaign in 2009, the Fars News Agency, an outlet closely associated with the country's Supreme Leader, had attacked Rafsanjani by publishing an exposé of what it described as his family's Mafia-like grip on Iran's economy. The news service also called Rafsanjani the de facto ruler of Kish.

> Around 200,000 square meters of the most expensive lands in the free trade region of Kish have been exclusively given to the relatives of and aides to Mr Hashemi Rafsanjani, and they have made enormous investments in this region. This gang recognized itself as the owner and master of Kish and has grasped its economy in a manner that all the foreigners who come to Kish for trade have to pay a considerable amount of commission to the children of Mr Hashemi under different pretexts like donations to charities etc.
>
> In addition to all other activities, this mafia trend has established a landing ground for private planes in Kish through which they are able to directly import their commodities to Iran.

Madzhit also dispatched operatives into Iran who made it clear that the Kurd was willing to pay large sums of money for news about Bob. Before long, an Iranian who said that Bob was alive contacted him, adding he could secure the American's freedom for a price. FBI officials didn't take the man seriously at first; they had heard plenty of similar claims over the years from people such as Sarkis Soghanalian. But after they sent the Iranian's name to the CIA for any background information it might have on him, they sat back and took notice. The spy agency told them that the man, Seyed Mir Hejazi, appeared to be the son of Asghar Mir Hejazi, the top intelligence advisor to Ayatollah Ali Khamenei, Iran's Supreme Leader.

As bureau officials encouraged Madzhit to pursue Hejazi, Boris Birshtein was telling them that Oleg Deripaska needed to come to the United States. The oligarch's financial problems were growing and he wanted to meet with top Wall Street executives to discuss financing deals. The FBI was eager to keep Deripaska happy and asked the State Department to issue him a limited visa so he could make a brief visit. To the bureau's surprise, department officials refused to do so.

Up until that point, Dave McGee and Ira Silverman had been unaware of Deripaska's role in the hunt for their friend. The FBI didn't tell them about the operation because of its sensitivity. And they were happy to keep Dave and Ira in the dark for another reason. Over time, FBI managers had come to see them and Larry Sweeney as meddlers who regularly criticized and second-guessed bureau decisions. They figured the less they knew, the better.

But Boris, with his plan in jeopardy, needed new allies, and he reached out to Dave to tell him about Deripaska's involvement. He also warned him the oligarch might pull out of the operation if his visa request wasn't granted. Dave contacted Senator Nelson's office to see if the lawmaker could help, but the State Department remained adamant. Then, at a meeting about the visa, FBI officials encountered one of the State Department officials apparently opposed to letting Deripaska into the United States—it was Anne Jablonski's husband, Robert Otto, a department expert on Russian crime.

A year had passed since Anne's forced departure from the CIA. She hadn't gone to work for a public interest group, as she had once imagined. Instead, she followed a more predictable path and was employed by corporate investigative firms doing diligence reports about Russian businessmen and companies. The Justice Department, at the CIA's request, had looked into the question of whether to charge Anne or other agency officials with crimes, such as lying to FBI agents about Bob, but closed the investigation after finding insufficient evidence to do so.

During that inquiry, however, FBI agents had learned some things about Anne's husband and the information had left them with a bad taste. When Bob disappeared, a Russian analyst at the National Security Agency with whom he shared information had quickly alerted that agency about their relationship. But Robert Otto apparently had said nothing to his State Department superiors about his ties to Bob or disclosed to them that his wife was the missing man's CIA handler. When FBI agents encountered Otto participating in a meeting about Deripaska's visa, they were outraged. "What the hell are you doing here?" one agent shouted at him. "We know who you are."

In the end, FBI officials decided to make an end run around the State Department and secretly arranged to have the Department of Homeland Security issue the oligarch a special, short-term visa. In August 2009, Deripaska sat with Boris, Madzhit, Martin Hellmer, and Joe Krzemien in a hotel lobby in Washington. All of them felt Bob's release was imminent. Madzhit's Iranian contact, Seyed Mir Hejazi, had offered to arrange a phone call between Bob and Chris, but FBI officials, certain he was about to be freed, decided to forgo the offer, fearing the conversation might be intercepted.

Deripaska came again to the United States in the fall of 2009, meeting with top Wall Street executives, including Lloyd Blankfein, the head of Goldman Sachs. Earlier, he had traveled to Detroit to talk with General Motors executives. Deripaska already owned Russia's second-biggest automobile maker, and he was interested in purchasing GM's stake in Opel, a European car company. Initially, the oligarch's trips to the United States escaped the attention of the American news media. But he wasn't camera shy. In September, a Russian publication published a photograph showing him with GM executives, and in late October, reporters at *The Wall Street Journal* got a tip about his visits and the fight between the FBI and the State Department over his visa. The newspaper ran a front-page article under the headline "FBI Lets Barred Tycoon Visit U.S." Prior to its publication, reporters had called the FBI to ask an obvious question—why had the bureau allowed the barred oligarch into the United States? The reporters weren't told the reason. Instead, two unnamed "administration officials" were quoted in the article describing Deripaska's visits as part of "a continuing criminal probe." The newspaper reported that it had been unable to learn the investigation's focus.

FBI officials suspected the State Department was the source of the leak, and Boris was frantic that Deripaska might abandon the hunt because of the article. He asked Martin Hellmer and Joe Krzemien to fly to Vienna to meet the oligarch at a five-star hotel there, the Sacher, the birthplace of the famous Austrian pastry the Sacher torte. Boris and Madzhit also attended. Deripaska didn't appear upset. As he dined with his visitors inside a luxury suite on the hotel's top floor, he talked mainly about his businesses and the international economy, explaining how he felt a personal obligation to keep his companies afloat because they employed thousands of workers. Five waiters were present in the room, one for each diner. They moved cautiously as they served the meal, seemingly terrified of making a misstep that might upset Deripaska. When the soup course was brought to the table, the oligarch asked one waiter what it was. The man responded, describing it with a drawn-out, French-sounding name. Deripaska nodded and looked at the FBI agents. He smiled and said, "That's just a fancy name for gruel."

17

Proof of Life

Dan Levinson, Bob's oldest son, stepped out of a taxi in front of the Hotel Adlon Kempinski, a majestic building on Berlin's central square right across from the landmark Brandenburg Gate. More than three years had passed since his father's disappearance and Dan, like his siblings, remained haunted by it. All the Levinson children loved their father, though they tended to see him differently, perspectives shaped by their gender and age. Dan was one of his father's fiercest defenders and he had complete faith in his abilities. After 9/11, when it turned out that one of the terrorists, Mohamed Atta, lived for months in Coral Springs, Bob told Dan he might have stopped the attack if he was still with the FBI, explaining that Atta had gotten his hair cut at the same barbershop he used. Every agent who had ever carried a badge felt similar remorse. But Dan, then sixteen years old, sensed his father might have succeeded.

He had first heard about Iran and Dawud Salahuddin in 2002 when he was lying on the living room couch watching television. "Here, read this," his father said, walking in and tossing him a copy of *The New Yorker* with Ira Silverman's article about the fugitive. He had once passed his father's opened computer and saw a folder labeled DAOUD, and not long before Bob disappeared, he and his brother Doug were driving home with their father from a Steak 'n Shake, a fast-food restaurant, when a report about political unrest in Iran came on the car radio. "I'm working on something over there," Bob told his boys.

Dan was in his first year of law school when his father went missing. He found it difficult to focus on his studies and dropped out. He wrote articles for newspapers about his family's plight and accompanied his mother when she went to Iran. By 2010, he had gotten his academic career back on track but decided to switch out of law and pursue a master's degree in business. He was traveling in Ireland when he learned about an email that his mother had received through the Help Bob Levinson website from an Iranian living in Berlin. The email was about his father, and the Iranian, Amir Farshad Ebrahimi, had attached documents to it. He claimed they were the official records of Bob's arrest on Kish on charges of spying.

Ebrahimi described himself as a former officer in the Quds Force, the special unit of the Revolutionary Guards, who had fled Iran to start a new life in Germany as a freelance journalist and human rights activist. In his email, he told Chris that a friend in Iran, a police official, had found records related to Bob's arrest while going through a folder and photographed them with his cell phone camera. Ebrahimi asked Chris if she wanted him to release the documents to the news media. At the FBI's direction, she asked Ebrahimi to send her the records. In the photographs, they looked authentic. They were written in Farsi, appeared to be on official government stationery, and bore numerous signatures and countersignatures.

The earliest document was dated March 8, 2007, and authorized Bob's arrest on Kish. It referred to him as "Robert Anderson."

URGENT

Our Nation is Proud to Be the Student of the School of Prophet Mohammed

(Blessing of God be upon him and his descendants)

The Honorable Head of the Judiciary Office of the Armed Forces
H.E. Hojatollah-Aesalm Bahrami

Greetings, I hereby inform you that according to the report and the
security services of this Ministry in Kish, a member of the U.S. Federal [Bureau of] Investigation or may be [sic] CIA, Robert Anderson,
has recently entered the country with a regular passport and a tourist
visa. He is here as an undercover tourist while conducting various
meetings, taking pictures, and gathering information.

Since his spying activities and efforts to set up a network have been
established, please, make an arrangement to arrest him immediately by the end of the day, with the assistance of this ministry's
personnel at the headquarter[s] of the intelligence at Kish and transfer him to a detention center with a maximum security.
God Bless you with success.
3619172
274
03/08/2007
Signature of the Deputy of Counter Intelligence

CC:
1—Deputy of the operations
2—In the Name of God, the military prosecutor in Bandar Lange
   should be notified and the subject must be arrested.
Deputy for the operations: Expeditiously and with the help of the
   brothers should be arrested.

The second document was dated two months later and described
Bob's deteriorating health.

URGENT

AIR FORCE
Kish Air Base

No: 2619-42

Date: May 2, 2007

124

In the Name of God

From: Command Center of Sahafaja [PH], Kish Air Base

To: The Honorable head of the military prosecutor office of Bandar Langeh

Subject: Accused File No. 85/3598

Greetings, I hereby inform Your Excellency that according to your order, the above subject is under the arrest of this military unit at a detention center at this base.

The subject has expressed that he is sick and his blood pressure is low for the last three days. He fell into a coma. His doctor examined him and he was diagnosed to have diabetes and noted that he is not in a good condition and ordered to transfer him to a hospital.

In regard to the importance of this matter and the subject, please inform us about the necessary actions that should be taken in this regard.

Signed on behalf of

The Commander of Intelligence Protection, Kish Air Base

Mohammad Reza Jalali

(A messenger should hand deliver the result)

Receivers:

1—The Head of the Sahahagh [B-24] for information and taking necessary action

2—The Kish Intelligence Office for information purposes
3—Secret file

When FBI technicians analyzed the documents, they doubted they were genuine. Along with the misspelling of Bob's last name, the location of his hospitalization conflicted with the information they had received from Parisi, the laboratory technician. The CIA was also suspicious. Agency officials believed Ebrahimi may have previously circulated other fabricated documents and either was an agent provocateur working for Iranian intelligence or was being duped by operatives controlled by Tehran. Still, Dan wanted to see him and asked Jeff Katz, his father's friend in London, to go with him to Berlin.

At their meeting at the Hotel Adlon Kempinski, Ebrahimi, a man in his forties who shaved his balding scalp, told them that Bob was being held at a secret Revolutionary Guards facility near Tehran's airport. He explained that his sources were telling him that an Iranian intelligence officer named Shekari accompanied Bob wherever he was taken, and that while he was not in good health, the regime was taking care of him because of his value in a possible spy trade.

Dan and Katz didn't know what to make of Ebrahimi. He didn't speak English and they had to talk with him through an interpreter. They weren't ready to dismiss him, but they also weren't convinced the documents were real. Not long after they left Berlin, Chris received a phone call from a Fox News reporter named Richard Reilly. He said he was about to post an article on Fox's website reporting her husband was probably dead. The source of his information, Reilly told Chris, was Dawud Salahuddin. "I don't think he's still alive," the fugitive was quoted by Reilly as saying. "Levinson had some health issues, and somebody like him couldn't go from being free for fifty-nine years to all of a sudden thrown into jail and not being free." Reilly asked Chris if she wanted to comment. She tried to calm herself. "I just don't know," she replied. "The information is not confirmable. I still believe that Bob's alive. Dawud has been really ambiguous."

Afterward, Chris emailed Dawud: "I hope this message finds you in good health. I spoke to Mr. Riley [sic] and saw the articles he wrote after talking to you. I would like to know why you told him that you believe that RL is dead. Do you have any proof?"

Several days passed before Dawud responded: "Forgive this tardy reply but I rarely go online. To answer your question, no I have no proof or evidence whatsoever and was merely stating an opinion . . . I pray for you and your family and though your sense of loss is not comparable to mine you should know that RL remains a real sore spot in my heart."

When Larry Sweeney saw the Fox News report, he reacted angrily and sent out a blast email to former FBI agents following Bob's case: "This report is completely fictitious and his source is known to be completely unreliable . . . [Reilly] called Bob's wife to tell her he had received information that Bob was dead. Then he publicized this story on FOX."

Dawud was far from the only person to think Bob was dead. Many inside the FBI shared that view. By the fall of 2010, his case was stone cold. The bureau hadn't found a photograph of him, a shred of his clothing, a strand of his hair. They hadn't been able to corroborate any of the stories they had heard. Parisi had disappeared. The Iranian judge brought into the United States by the FBI had returned to Iran. Bureau officials were losing faith that Oleg Deripaska would swoop into Iran on his private jet and bring out Bob.

For months, Madzhit Mamoyan had been meeting with Seyed Mir Hejazi, the reputed son of Ayatollah Khamenei's intelligence advisor, in locations such as Vienna, Beirut, and Yerevan, the capital of Armenia. Hejazi, who didn't speak English, would arrive accompanied by a translator, another man who said he was an officer in the Quds Force, and a small coterie of attractive young Iranian women. Each time, he promised to deliver proof that Bob was alive and then never did. Then, in early 2010, it appeared the long waiting game was over. Madzhit told Boris that Hejazi had sworn to him that he would come to their next meeting armed with the proof. In return, he would receive $5 million. "We are expecting evidence and we will see heavy evidence," Boris said. The FBI agents working the operation,

Martin Hellmer and Joe Krzemien, also felt certain it would happen and alerted Chris, telling her to carry her cell phone at all times because Bob might call.

But when Hejazi arrived for the meeting, he told Madzhit that if he wanted to see the evidence, he would have to come to Tehran, surrender his passport, and turn over the $5 million. Only then could he examine the material, and he would not be permitted to take it with him when he left Iran.

Hellmer and Krzemien went ballistic. For more than a year, they had relied on Madzhit to act as their intermediary. They felt foolish and embarrassed before their superiors. FBI officials also couldn't figure out Hejazi's game. They suspected he was acting with his father's approval, because Iranian operatives were spotted keeping watch on the hotels where he met with Madzhit. But it was possible Hejazi was simply using the Kurd to underwrite his jaunts outside Iran while his father's underlings monitored the American government's interest in Bob's case.

Krzemien told Boris he needed to meet personally with Hejazi to try to assess his credibility. He and Boris flew to Rome for two days of discussions with him. Krzemien told Hejazi, who was thirty-nine years old and had dark hair and a Vandyke beard, that he was an investigator hired by the Levinson family, adding that cigarette companies were willing to pay a substantial sum of money to learn about Bob's status and secure his release. Later that day, Martin Hellmer called Larry Sweeney to say things were going well. Sweeney passed on the news in an email to Dave McGee and Ira Silverman, referring in the note to Oleg Deripaska as "O":

> Martin finally called tonight and was very encouraging based on his conversations with Joe. Joe met with un-identified representative(s) of the Russian (O was not physically present), unidentified Iranian(s), Boris and possibly others. The Iranians admit to having Bob although his physical condition is unknown to Martin. There were preliminary discussions about $ payments but Martin did not go into details. The Iranians were told that answers to proof of life

questions were necessary and they responded "no problem." They promised to have these answers very shortly. My old employer is somewhat concerned that the Iranians are trying to pull some kind of a scam on O but feel this is unlikely since they are aware of how powerful O is. Martin indicated he will continue playing a part in this matter at least until the O matter is resolved . . . I realize there are many more questions I could have asked Martin but I decided not to. I didn't want to turn him off by pressing too much. He did say that Joe thought Boris was an asset during these discussions. I'm anxious to learn if Joe's opinion is similar to Martin's. Hopefully, we can all sleep a little better tonight.

After the Rome meeting, however, Hejazi's pattern of behavior continued. He gave a videotape to Joe Krzemien that he claimed showed Bob. When FBI technicians examined it, there was nothing on the tape but garble.

In the fall of 2010, the Iranian president, Mahmoud Ahmadinejad, was scheduled to visit New York to make a speech at the United Nations. Several weeks before his arrival, Chris decided to use one of the few weapons she possessed, the documents she had received from the Iranian in Berlin, Amir Farshad Ebrahimi. She wasn't sure if the records were real, but that was of little consequence. After securing an appointment with Iran's U.N. ambassador, Mohammad Khazaee, she went to see him accompanied by her daughters Sue and Sarah, her sister Suzi, and her second-oldest son, Dave. This time, the Levinsons did not come as supplicants. Instead, they put Khazaee on notice. Chris told him her family was in possession of documents that indicated his government was lying about her husband. If it continued to do so, she would publicly release them. The world could then decide if Iran was telling the truth. A day later, Dave and Dan delivered a plain manila envelope to Khazaee's office, containing the material from Ebrahimi.

It was little more than a month later, on November 13, 2010, that Ira Silverman got the email with an attachment he could not open, the one that turned out to have the video showing Bob as a hostage.

Chris, after hearing Sonya play her the tape over the telephone, had tried to open the email's attachment herself so she could see her husband. When she couldn't figure out how, her youngest son, Doug, found a way to do it. She started calling her other children. "We've received a video from your father," Chris told Stephanie. "I'm sending it to you."

Stephanie's impulse was to race over to her computer to look at it. She stopped herself. Her youngest sister, Samantha, was standing a few feet away. Samantha, who was then twenty and a student at Florida State University, had come over to babysit Stephanie's children so she could go out to a local Tampa bar and watch her husband's garage band play. The older Levinson siblings felt a duty to protect Samantha. They saw her and her younger brother, Doug, as vulnerable kids who could be emotionally scarred by their father's disappearance. Stephanie didn't know what her father might look or sound like on the tape, so she decided to watch it privately before telling Samantha about it. Her concerns were soon swept away. Her father looked thin but he appeared healthy and there was nothing about the video that struck Stephanie as frightening or negative. Instead, she sensed its arrival was a signal his release was imminent. "This is the best day of my life," she thought.

After she told her sister about the tape, they sat down together to watch it. Stephanie expected to see her sister's face reflect the same joy and relief she had felt. Instead, Samantha appeared impassive. Inside, Samantha knew she should be hugging her sister and sharing her happiness. She couldn't allow herself those feelings. In the chaotic days immediately after her father's disappearance, her oldest sister, Sue, told her that an FBI agent or some other visitor to their house had said it was impossible to predict when he would be back. It could be "in six weeks or in six years," the person said. The words remained seared in Samantha's memory. Her father had lavished Samantha with attention and kindness. During her awkward teenage years, when high school boys had started buzzing around, he had reassured her he was watching her back. "I'm going to be sitting at the front door with a shotgun and a fingerprinting kit," he said. Then, in a flash, all his love and protection vanished. She might have fallen into despair, but she wanted her father to be proud of her when he returned. The only way to do that, she decided, was to ignore the future and push forward one day at a time. She allowed herself one small indulgence, her own secret yellow ribbon. Pinned up on the bedroom wall of her childhood room was the email her father had sent her just before he disappeared, the one in which he had wished his "Turtle" good luck on her high school speech. They were the last words he had said to her and she didn't plan to take the note down until she could tell him how much she loved him.

Sarah Levinson was in the kitchen of her New Jersey home that night when her phone lit up with her mother's number. A few months earlier, she and her fiancé, Ryan Moriarty, finally were married. Her brother Dan had walked her down the aisle. Among the couple's wedding presents was a ceramic oven stone for making homemade pizza, a gift from Chris. Sarah and Ryan were trying it out for the first time when her mother called. Sarah laughed as she picked up the phone. "We're using the pizza stone you gave us," she said. Then she heard the news about her father and dinner was forgotten.

In their joy, Sarah and other members of Bob's family didn't immediately examine the email to which it had been attached. There were striking resemblances between it and the email sent in mid-2007 to Ira Silverman and several other friends of Bob, the one that the FBI had dismissed as a fake. The 2007 email was sent through a Gmail account opened under the name "Osman.Muhamad." The 2010 email containing the video was sent through a Gmail account opened under the name "Osman.Muhamad90." A copy of the 2010 email was also sent to one of the journalists, Chris Isham, who was copied on the 2007 email.

The similarities weren't coincidences. FBI officials, through incompetence or sloth, had blown a huge clue by dismissing the 2007 email, one that could have dramatically altered the course of the bureau's investigation and Bob's fate. There was little question now that he had managed to get his captors to put his friends' names on that email. A hacker hadn't stolen them. They were his cries for help. His answer, day after day, was silence.

> *I need the help of the United States government to answer the requests of the group that has held me for three and a half years . . . And please help me . . . get home . . . Thirty-three years of service to the United States deserves something.*

18

Tradecraft

The video's arrival threw the FBI's search for Bob into high gear. Bureau officials kept its existence a closely guarded secret even inside the government. Investigators quickly focused on the email's message, the "last ultimatum" on which Bob's life supposedly hinged. Along with a payment of $3 million, the note demanded the release of three men—Salem Mohamad Ahmad Ghasem, Ahmad Ali Alarzagh, and Ebrahim Ali Ahmad. The names sounded Arabic, not Persian, and U.S. officials suspected they might be people that the United States was holding in American military detention facilities in Iraq. But a thorough search of records failed to find any trace of the men in U.S. custody there or anywhere else.

Using the email's IP address, FBI officials determined it had been sent from a computer in an Internet café in Pakistan. An agent was dispatched to stake out the shop. But that trail soon went cold. It became clear that the email, prior to being sent from the café, was routed through a network of cell phones to disguise its origins.

Inside the bureau's forensic laboratory in Quantico, Virginia, a glass-walled, industrial-looking building with a roof line studded with chimneys and vents, technicians pulled apart the video. Terror groups had turned to video as their preferred medium to spread propaganda and display hostages, and the FBI had developed expertise in analyzing it, compiling an informal cookbook to help technicians identify the organization involved based on a video's visual aesthetics and level of technical sophistication. While some groups preferred a bare-bones look and used a single camera and minimal lighting, others employed high production values involving multiple cameras and studio effects.

Audio specialists identified the music heard in the background of Bob's video as a song played at wedding ceremonies by Pashto-speaking tribes. Pashto is a common language, and groups speaking it are spread throughout Afghanistan, Iran, and Pakistan. The generic music was chosen by Bob's captors, analysts concluded, to both conceal his true location and mask any outside sounds, such as car traffic or the voice of a passerby, that might help investigators identify it. Psychological experts scrutinized Bob's words and gestures for signals. One comment that caught their attention was his reference to his "thirty-three years of service" to the United States. Bob worked a total of only twenty-eight years for the DEA and FBI, and it was possible he might be signaling that his captors knew about his CIA connection.

When Dave and Ira watched the video, they thought Bob might have chosen some of his words himself. To FBI analysts, everything about the email and video appeared carefully stage-managed and scripted to give the impression that Bob was in the hands of a group without any connection to the Iranian government. The demand for the release of the three men with Arabic-sounding names fit that scenario. So did Bob's comment that he was "running very quickly out of diabetes medicine." If anything, he would have run out of diabetes medicine, and every other prescription drug he was taking, within days of disappearing on Kish, not years later. That meant his captors were supplying him with drugs and taking care of his medical needs. When government doctors reviewed the video, they concluded that Bob appeared well given his circumstances and suggested all the weight he had lost as a prisoner might have improved his health.

Despite the intense review of the video, the FBI was unable to wring substantive leads from it. The only firm conclusion they made was that the video was shot shortly before it was sent. Officials from the FBI, the CIA, the National Security Council, and the State Department gathered to discuss what to do next. They felt fairly certain that either the Iranian government or a faction tied to the country's intelligence or religious hierarchy was holding Bob. Nothing else made sense. No one else would have a reason or the resources to hold him for so long. Cigarette smugglers or Russian thugs would have killed Bob long ago. Keeping him alive and hidden for years was costly and complicated. It required the involvement of a highly disciplined and organized group, one whose members obeyed orders because they feared death if they failed to do so.

When it came to deciding how to respond to the video, officials disagreed. The State Department was worried that using it to confront Iran over Bob might jeopardize nuclear control talks. The CIA suspected their Iranian counterparts were behind the video and warned that it might be part of an intelligence trap. The FBI had a different perspective. Iran's president, Mahmoud Ahmadinejad, while vehemently claiming his country knew nothing about Bob, had repeatedly boasted with smug satisfaction that his country would be happy to assist the FBI if new information about Bob emerged. It was time, FBI officials argued, to call him on it.

An FBI counterterrorism expert named James McJunkin was a vocal proponent of that view. A onetime Pennsylvania state trooper, McJunkin was short, bald, and built like a block from hours spent lifting weights. He imagined that the Iranians had first believed Bob was a big-time CIA spy. It probably hadn't taken them long to figure out he wasn't, but they had kept him, probably hoping that the United States would reach out to inaugurate a prisoner swap. That hadn't happened either, and McJunkin thought the Iranians might have sent the video to signal they were looking for a face-saving way to let Bob go while being able to deny any involvement in his captivity. It was fine with McJunkin if playing along with some Iranian fairy tale meant getting Bob back.

The FBI's argument prevailed, and in early 2011 Chris flew to Washington to meet with the bureau's director, Robert Mueller. A onetime federal prosecutor, Mueller had assumed his post just after the 9/11 attacks. He told Chris something she never expected to hear—that as a result of back-channel diplomacy, secret talks were starting between the United States and Iran aimed at winning her husband's release. Mueller was upbeat about the prospects. Just a few months earlier, Iran had released one of the imprisoned American hikers, Sarah Shourd, after the government of Oman intervened on her behalf. A senior FBI official told Chris that 2011 "was going to be a very good year for the Levinson family."

Chris felt Bob's return was near. After his disappearance, FBI agents specially trained to work with the families of kidnapping victims regularly visited her to check on her psychological well-being. More recently, they had started talking to her and the older children about the process Bob would need to go through after his release to help him overcome the trauma he had experienced. The government's plan called for him to be taken to the Landstuhl Regional Medical Center, a large U.S. military hospital in Germany, for a battery of physical and psychological assessments. During those first few days, Chris was told, she might not be able to speak with her husband. Once cleared for travel, he would go next to Brooke Army Medical Center, in San Antonio, Texas, a facility that specializes in treating soldiers and civilians held as prisoners or hostages, including those subjected to torture. Experts at the hospital were highly trained in treating emotional and mental trauma, and many of them had gone through the same course used to train members of elite military units, such as the Navy SEALs, on ways to withstand torture. Bob's stay in San Antonio could prove lengthy, and Chris was prepared to find accommodations near the hospital so she could be close to him.

Two FBI officials were selected to represent the United States in the talks with Iran. One of them was Sean Joyce, who had presided over the 2008 meeting at the bureau's Washington field office at which he acknowledged the bureau's mistakes in its initial search for Bob. The other was Carl Ghattas, who had overseen Bob's case during those early months. Both were veterans of terrorism-related operations. In the mid-1990s Joyce took part in a raid in Pakistan that captured a man named Mir Qazi, who had opened fire in 1993 on cars waiting to enter CIA headquarters at Langley, killing two people. Ghattas, a tall, thin man of Lebanese ancestry, spent two years heading FBI intelligence operations in Iraq and Afghanistan. He was a former prosecutor who came across as cold and aloof, and Ira Silverman took a particular dislike to him, believing that Ghattas was one of the bureaucratic stumbling blocks at the start of Bob's case.

Joyce and Ghattas were briefed prior to the talks by experts from the FBI and CIA in behavioral science, hostage negotiations, and Iranian culture and politics. Joyce was told it was critical for him, given the importance of hierarchy in Iran, to project authority and make it clear he was speaking for the United States. Agency specialists developed scripts of questions and replies, gaming out responses Joyce could make to statements by the Iranians. Hostage negotiators counseled the men not to show deference to their counterparts.

The first meeting between FBI officials and their Iranian counterparts took place in Europe, at a hotel closely monitored by intelligence agents from both sides. The CIA identified the Iranians attending the meeting as mid-level operatives in the Ministry of Intelligence with little authority. Whenever Joyce posed a question, the men would say they didn't know the answer and leave the room, apparently to confer with superiors. When they returned, it was typically with an empty response. They did throw out one piece of supposed information. They claimed intelligence gathered by Iran indicated a terrorist group opposed to their country's government was holding the former FBI agent in the rugged tribal regions along Iran's eastern border with Afghanistan and Pakistan.

The Iranians then made a demand. Their country was prepared to walk away from further discussions if the United States did not issue a statement absolving it from involvement in Bob's disappearance. They suggested President Obama should be the person to make the announcement. The ultimatum was absurd, but the FBI argued to the White House that the Iranians might want a public display of good faith by the United States as a prelude to Bob's release. Administration officials rejected the idea of President Obama making any statements and passed the job to Secretary of State Hillary Clinton. In March 2011, Clinton, without disclosing the existence of the secret talks or the video of Bob, released a statement saying the United States had recently received information showing he was alive. In deference to Iran, she added that American officials believed he was being held in "southwest Asia," a large geographical region that includes Iran and several surrounding countries:

> As we approach the fourth anniversary of Bob Levinson's disappearance, we have received recent indications that Bob is being held somewhere in southwest Asia. As the government of Iran has previously offered its assistance in this matter, we respectfully request the Iranian government to undertake humanitarian efforts to safely return and reunite Bob with his family. We would appreciate the Iranian government's efforts in this matter.

Afterward, the Iranians offered more details about Bob's supposed captors and claimed Iranian military units were conducting raids on suspected rebel camps, as part of a campaign to find and free him. Soon FBI officials realized the Iranians were playing them. Data from U.S. spy satellites didn't show signs of any military activity in the areas where the Iranians said it was occurring. James McJunkin began to worry. He still believed Iran wanted to create a narrative about Bob, but he wondered if it was a very different story from the one he had first imagined. Rather than manufacturing a story to explain away their involvement in Bob's captivity, the Iranians seemed to be devising a tale to set the stage for his execution. It would be simple enough to take Bob to a remote area, mount a raid on a supposed "rebel" camp, and announce afterward that he had been killed by cross fire during a valiant effort by Iranian forces to rescue him. There would even be a body to send home.

A few weeks after Secretary Clinton's statement, Chris received another email from Bob's captors, this one with five photographs of Bob attached. They were completely different in tone and appearance from the video. In the pictures, his hair and beard were wild and bushy and he was dressed in what looked like a bad Halloween costume of a Guantánamo prisoner. He wore a mock orange jumpsuit, and a cheap metal chain was draped around his neck and wrists. He stood in front of a dark blue curtain and in each picture held a piece of white paper on which a different message was written. A stencil might have been used to draw the characters, because the outlines of the letters were neat and clearly defined. The grammar was so irregular and sloppy that the mistakes appeared intentional. Some words were capitalized or written in boldface letters, others were not. All the messages had a political overtone. They said:

I Am HERE IN **GUANTANAMO**
DO YOU KNOW
WHERE IT IS?

THIS IS THE
RESULT OF
30 YEARS
SERVING
FOR **USA**

HELP ME

WHY YOU
CAN NOT
HELP ME

4 TH
YEAR . . .
You Cant
or you don't
want . . . ?

FBI technicians had trouble dating the photographs. But they suspected the pictures were shot before the video, because it was unlikely Bob's hair and beard would have grown that much during the five months since the video's arrival. When FBI agents traced the new email, they found it came from Afghanistan, not Pakistan. Using its IP address, agents identified the computer from which it had been sent and managed through sales records to track down its owner in Afghanistan. The man told investigators someone had stolen the computer several months earlier, and his story checked out.

FBI agents typically solve cases when criminals or terrorists make mistakes. Those missteps might involve a sloppy email, an impulsive Internet posting, repetitive travel patterns, or other fumbles. A mistake can provide the thread on which an investigator starts pulling. The more James McJunkin looked at the information in Bob's case—the emails, the video, the photographs—the more he was struck by a single impression. He couldn't find a mistake. Each possible lead had led investigators this way and that way before turning back on itself and evaporating. The supposed "clues" made sense only if seen in a different light: as part of a counterintelligence operation, a series of false leads and seductive crumbs scattered by an Iranian intelligence unit to lure the United States into making moves that would disclose how it spied on Iran. The Iranians even appeared to have used the talks about Bob for that purpose. At one point, they gave the FBI the names of several people who they claimed had information about Bob. But when the bureau ran down those names, they discovered they were aliases used by people held in Iranian prisons. At that juncture, U.S. officials decided further talks would be fruitless and broke them off.

The FBI's only remaining operation to find Bob involved Seyed Mir Hejazi, the man described by the CIA as the son of Ayatollah Khamenei's intelligence advisor. Hejazi kept insisting to Madzhit Mamoyan that all the previous hang-ups he had experienced in getting proof of life were the result of infighting among different factions within Iran over who would benefit financially and politically from Bob's release. In early 2011, he told the Kurd that the stars had finally aligned. He claimed that Ayatollah Khamenei had given his group authority to negotiate the terms under which Bob would be freed. Madzhit passed the message along to Boris Birshtein, emphasizing the potential dangers to Hejazi.

HE IS 99% SURE OF GETTING A RESULT. HE ALSO INSISTED THAT HE DOES NOT FIND ANY REASON TO BELIEVE THAT HIS PEOPLE NEED TO LIE TO HIM. THEY COULD SIMPLY TELL HIM TO STAY OUT OF IT INSTEAD OF GIVING HIM PROMISES.

HE ALSO SAID THAT WHAT HE HAS TOLD ME IS 2% OF THE WHOLE SITUATION AND WHAT HAS BEEN GOING ON. FOR EXAMPLE SOME PEOPLE TRYING TO ELIMINATE HIM. IF THEY COULD THEY WOULD HAVE DONE SO ALREADY.

Hejazi suggested an escape plan for Bob worthy of a thriller. He was to be brought by van from an undisclosed location to the Swiss embassy in Tehran. Once he was there, embassy officials would send a coded message to the State Department that would serve as the signal that the former FBI agent had been freed. Bob would then be spirited out of Iran by hiding him inside the trunk of a Swiss embassy car with diplomatic license plates. The vehicle would travel through northwestern Iran and across the Turkish border, delivering Bob into the waiting arms of U.S. officials.

FBI officials, having been burned by Hejazi, kept their expectations low. But Boris Birshtein started working on ways to get the Iranian the ransom payment he wanted for Bob's release while disguising that the source of those funds would be Oleg Deripaska, the Russian oligarch. Boris apparently had a knack for creating complicated chains of bank accounts, the kinds of networks money launderers use, and soon had devised a series of accounts in Cyprus, a country with loose financial regulations. When he showed his handiwork to Joe Krzemien, the FBI agent expressed appreciation for his skills. "I can show you how we can take over one of Deripaska's businesses if we want," Boris replied.

Hejazi's plan required the cooperation of Swiss diplomats in Tehran, and he told Madzhit that he would soon make contact with them. He also kept coming up with excuses to delay his visit to that country's embassy. Finally, Hejazi must have gone there, because U.S. officials received a message from Swiss diplomats warning them that the Iranian shouldn't be trusted, apparently because of his father's role in Iran's intelligence service. When Boris heard the news, he was irate. Throughout his career, he had rubbed shoulders with corrupt politicians and unscrupulous criminals. Those dealings invariably revolved around money, who needed to get it and who was going to get screwed. But the Iranians Boris had encountered seemed more interested in duplicity than in cutting a deal. "These fucking people are the worst," he said.

The FBI soon washed its hands of Boris, Madzhit, and Oleg Deripaska. The bureau considered them bullshit artists who had used Bob's case as a means to try to get the United States to do what they wanted without ever delivering anything. The three men hadn't succeeded, but the bureau's judgment was also a reflection of its inability to penetrate Iran. After years of investigations costing millions of dollars, FBI officials couldn't point to a single breakthrough they had made as a result of gumshoe work by agents.

Several months later, in the fall of 2011, the two remaining American hikers held in Iran, Joshua Fattal and Shane Bauer, were released from Evin Prison and put on a flight to Oman, where their families waited. The government of Oman had helped negotiate the pair's release and reportedly paid the $500,000 fines that an Iranian court had assessed against each man. There was plenty of speculation among political observers as to why Iranian officials chose to let the pair go, but it was largely seen as a public relations move by the Iranian president, Mahmoud Ahmadinejad, who took the action just days before he was to speak at the U.N.

Not long afterward, James McJunkin arrived in Coral Springs to meet with Chris. He did not bring good news. The bureau didn't see any purpose in pursuing further talks with Tehran, because the Iranians were continuing to claim that a terrorist or rebel group was holding Bob. Chris soon went to Washington to meet again with FBI Director Robert Mueller. He urged her to remain patient. She didn't have a choice. For Chris and her family, 2011 hadn't turned out to be a "good" year.

FBI officials decided there was no longer a reason to keep the video secret. In late 2011, the bureau distributed it to the news media on compact discs labeled LEVINSON FAMILY/PLEA/PROOF OF LIFE. The tape was preceded by an introduction in which a somber-looking Chris sat next to her son Dave. He had graduated two years earlier from Emory University with magna cum laude honors. Chris got to stand during the school's commencement ceremony with the other proud parents whose children had earned the achievement. Then parents who had themselves graduated magna cum laude were asked to stand. Dave's heart sank. Had his father been there, he would have stood with them. On the video distributed by the FBI, Dave spoke in a calm, steady voice.

My name is David Levinson. And I am speaking on behalf of my mother, Christine Levinson, and my entire family. I am making a plea to the people who are holding my father. My mother has received your messages. Please tell us your demands so we can work together to bring my father home safely. Thank you for taking care of my father and for continuing to provide him with the care and medical treatment he needs to stay alive. My father is a loving and caring man who has always worked hard to provide for his family. He is the father of seven children, a dear husband, a grandfather of two beautiful children, and the pillar of our family. We are not part of any government and we are not experts on the region. No one can help us but you. Please help us. We tried to contact you but you never responded. I am sending this message because we need to know what you want our family to do so that my father can come home safely. We will do everything within our power to bring him home. I don't know how else to communicate with you but my father knows how to contact us. We don't know what else to do.

19

Breaking News

A giant digital billboard in Times Square greeted President Mahmoud Ahmadinejad in the fall of 2012 when he arrived in New York to speak before the U.N. General Assembly for the last time. In nine months, Iranian voters were scheduled to elect his successor. The billboard, which was arranged by the FBI, consisted of a stark image of Bob as a captive and a message that diplomatically accused Iran of stonewalling. Video monitors located in subway stations near U.N. headquarters carried the same image:

United Nations Delegates
Please Encourage the
Islamic Republic of Iran to work
with the United States
Government to bring Bob home
On behalf of the Levinson Family

For Chris and her children, another year had passed in numbing silence. The FBI had hoped the video's public release would generate new leads. Bob's picture was plastered on billboards on roads leading into Iran offering $1 million for information, and in-flight airline magazines in the region contained similar announcements. Dave McGee, Ira Silverman, and Larry Sweeney continued their search, though there had been a turnover in the cast of characters claiming they could help. In late 2011, Sarkis Soghanalian, the old arms merchant, died of heart failure. Soghanalian had insisted up until his final days that he was cooking up a deal to bring Bob home. It was hard to know whether he believed that or whether he had been cruelly using the Levinson family to try to make one last arms deal. In either case, there were plenty of criminals, arms traffickers, and con men eager to fill his shoes, all swearing to Dave, Ira, and Larry that they were connected to Tehran.

About that time, Chris was contacted by a former movie star, Linda Fiorentino. The actress had portrayed a smoldering and double-crossing femme fatale in the 1994 noir-style crime film *The Last Seduction* and had starred in the 1997 science-fiction comedy hit *Men in Black* before her Hollywood career petered out. Fiorentino knew about Bob through an ex-boyfriend, Mark Rossini, a former FBI agent. Rossini had been forced to resign from the bureau in 2008 after it emerged that he had illegally downloaded FBI documents that ended up in the hands of lawyers representing one of Fiorentino's friends, Anthony Pellicano, a private investigator in Hollywood charged with blackmailing clients. Pellicano's lawyers tried to use the FBI records to convince a judge to throw out the case, arguing that prosecutors had withheld evidence from them because it could clear the investigator. The strategy backfired and a Justice Department inquiry uncovered Rossini's role in the theft of the records. Fiorentino insisted she did no wrong, and she was never charged in the incident, but law enforcement officials told reporters they believed she was the person who delivered the bureau documents to Pellicano's lawyers.

Before long, Ira and Fiorentino started speaking regularly. She told him that Rossini, before his downfall at the FBI, had recommended Bob as a private investigator to a close associate of Patrick M. Byrne, the head of an online retailer, Overstock.com, which sold clothing, jewelry, and other products. In 2006, Byrne was leading a public campaign to ban a Wall Street practice known as "naked" short selling, because he believed speculators were using it to manipulate the stock price of his company and others. Then, in early 2007, three of his associates received identical phone calls from a man calling himself "Paul Taylor" who said, "I am the messenger. Patrick Byrne will be killed by Russian entities," if he did not stop his campaign to ban naked short selling.

Bob had submitted a proposal to look into the incident not long before he disappeared. Fiorentino suspected the Iranians might somehow have learned about him through Byrne's associate, who had a brother living in Dubai. It was a far-fetched guess, and Ira and Dave could never figure out whether Fiorentino wanted to help, was bored, or had slipped back into the thrill-seeking character she had portrayed in *The Last Seduction*.

Throughout the frustrating years they had spent looking for their friend, the two men had stayed focused on another goal—trying to make sure those at the CIA who had concealed Bob's ties to the agency went to prison for doing so. They were certain that Anne Jablonski had misled investigators and that the CIA, absent the involvement of Senator Bill Nelson, would still be lying about Bob. But in late 2012, Dave realized they faced a problem. The last time FBI agents formally interviewed Anne and others about Bob had been in 2008, when the CIA referred the case to the Justice Department for possible criminal investigation. Dave viewed the department's decision to close that inquiry without bringing charges as more evidence of bungling by federal officials. He was certain that if he were still a prosecutor, he could have built a case against Anne. But the window to bring charges against her and other CIA officials was closing, because the five-year statute of limitations on any false statements made in those 2008 FBI interviews was about to expire. After that, they would be immune from prosecution even if evidence later emerged to show they had knowingly lied or withheld information. Dave's only option was to play for time. With Chris's support, he

started lobbying Justice Department officials to conduct new interviews of Anne and other witnesses. He knew they would likely
repeat their earlier statements, but the statute-of-limitations clock
would be reset for another five years, in case a "smoking gun"
emerged.

Justice Department officials eventually agreed. In early 2013, prosecutors invited Chris and Dave to come to department headquarters in Washington to hear the results of the new inquiry. Dave was
surprised to learn about a piece of evidence that he hadn't known
about and that wasn't anything he was expecting. Prosecutors said
they had found an internal CIA email that supported a key part
of Anne's testimony. She had sent the message on March 14, 2007,
four days after Bob's disappearance and right around the time she
would have learned of it. Justice Department officials did not show
the email to Dave but described it to him. In it, they said, Anne notified her CIA superiors about Bob's role as an agency consultant. In
her most recent FBI interview, Anne repeated that she didn't know
Bob was going to Kish and that if she had, she would have tried to
stop him. A top federal prosecutor, Michael Mullaney, told Dave and
Chris there was only one person who could challenge Anne's version
of events. "We're just going to have to wait until Bob comes back,"
he said.

Dave left dismayed. Soon after his return to Pensacola, he wrote
an email to Michael Mullaney. He pointed out that if Anne had told
the truth—and he still wasn't convinced she had—then others within
the CIA had covered up the information: "I have thought about your
disclosure that Jablonski reported to her superiors 'a relationship' with
Levinson on March 14, 2007 and find it hard to reconcile that with
what we were being told."

Dave never received a reply from Mullaney. The prime piece of
evidence on which Dave had relied to convince himself Anne had
known beforehand about Bob's Kish trip was a fairly thin reed. It was
his February 2007 memo to Tim Sampson seeking added funds for his
Dubai-related "side trip," though in the memo he mentioned neither

Dawud nor Kish. Still, given the weight that prosecutors such as Mullaney put on Anne's email to her superiors about Bob's CIA ties, Justice Department officials never made it clear to Chris or Dave whether they ever followed that thread to learn who at the spy agency had misled the FBI and Congress about his relationship.

Not long after Chris and Dave's trip to the Justice Department, Iranian voters went to the polls in the summer of 2013 and elected a moderate cleric, Hassan Rouhani, as their country's next president. It was a stunning repudiation of Iran's hard-liners, and Rouhani immediately made clear his desire to forge better relations with the West, calling for new talks to reach an agreement on Iran's nuclear capabilities that would also end economic sanctions against his nation. He also freed prominent political activists imprisoned during the regime of his predecessor, Mahmoud Ahmadinejad, and urged ultra-conservative clerics to loosen the cultural strictures constraining what Iranians could wear or read. "Everybody should accept the people's vote. The people have chosen a new path," he said.

For the Levinson family, the change in Iranian leadership meant renewed hope. Dave believed that Ahmadinejad and his cronies would have never freed Bob, and during his regime's last year, two Iranian-Americans—Saeed Abedini, a pastor, and Amir Hekmati, a former U.S. Marine—were arrested in Iran and sent to Evin Prison. In the fall of 2013, President Rouhani came to New York to speak for the first time. He gave lengthy interviews to several journalists, including the CNN correspondent Christiane Amanpour, intended to project a new image for his country. But when Amanpour asked him about Bob, Rouhani sounded as though he was reading from the same script his predecessor had used.

> You mentioned a person I've never heard of, Mr. Levinson. We don't know where he is, who he is. Sometimes, you are speaking of people who come before a court of trial and other times, there are people who disappear. It's not a clear question to put these two categories side by side. He is an American who has disappeared. We

have no news of him. We do not know where he is. We are willing
to help and all the intelligence services in the region can come together to gather information about him to find his whereabouts.
And we're willing to cooperate on that.

By then, more than six years had elapsed since Bob's disappearance. The last pieces of evidence showing him alive, the video and
the photographs, were three years old. Among journalists who had
been following Bob's case, there was a sense that the change in Iran's
government would bring an end to his story, with either his release
or the discovery that he was dead. A growing number of news organizations had learned over time about his CIA connection. In late
2007, Chris and Dave gave a reporter for *The New York Times* access to
Bob's files, but the newspaper decided not to disclose his agency ties
because of concerns it would jeopardize his safety. Brian Ross, Ira
Silverman's old partner and now the chief investigative correspondent for ABC News, also knew about Bob's role as a CIA consultant
but decided not to report about it.

Two other reporters who found out about Bob's secret worked
for the Associated Press. Matt Apuzzo and Adam Goldman covered
national security issues out of the news service's Washington office,
and both were relatively young and aggressive. In 2010, they learned
about Bob's connection to the spy agency and the internal CIA investigation that had led to the ouster of Anne and others. It is common
for news organizations to alert the CIA prior to publishing sensitive
information about national security. The practice gives government
officials an opportunity to comment on an article or to argue why a
story shouldn't be published. Upon learning about Apuzzo and Goldman's story, FBI officials called senior editors at the AP and urged
them not to publish it, citing its potential impact on Bob's safety. CIA
officials were so concerned that the story would appear they contacted other reporters who knew about the agency investigation and
briefed them about its findings. Such sanctioned leaks of classified
information are commonplace when officials hope to put their spin

on a potentially damaging story, and CIA managers were eager to get out the message that Bob's case involved a "rogue" operation run by a few analysts who had breached agency rules.

In deciding whether to publish Apuzzo and Goldman's story, AP editors faced a dilemma earlier confronted by other organizations, weighing the news value of disclosing Bob's role as a CIA contractor against the possibility that revealing it could get him killed or jeopardize efforts to free him. In 2010, they decided to hold the article rather than release it and adopted the same stance taken by other news outlets, such as *The New York Times* and ABC News. In an effort to protect Bob, the organizations, when reporting about developments in his case, didn't challenge the official U.S. line that he went to Kish as a "private citizen" to investigate cigarette smuggling.

But by 2013, the relationship between the government and the news media had become more confrontational. Over vehement protests by U.S. officials, two newspapers, *The Guardian* and *The Washington Post*, published a series of articles based on National Security Agency documents stolen by Edward Snowden, a contract employee. Federal officials said that publishing the stories would jeopardize national security. The newspapers countered that the NSA documents provided an unparalleled look at a U.S. intelligence-gathering apparatus run amok.

The previous year, Matt Apuzzo and Adam Goldman were part of an AP team that won a Pulitzer Prize for exposing another secret government surveillance program—an operation run by the New York City Police Department that clandestinely monitored Muslims in local mosques. The two reporters collaborated on a book based on that episode, and throughout 2013, they continued to push their reporting about Bob's case forward, visiting Dave and getting to know members of the Levinson family.

They kept urging their AP editors to publish their article, arguing that nothing had emerged since the video to show that Bob was still alive and that his captors already undoubtedly knew about his CIA connection. They also said their FBI sources had told them the bureau's investigation was at a dead end. Within the news service, executives still struggled to make a decision, and a factor in their deliberations was the question of whether they should disclose Bob's secret even if his family didn't want it revealed.

In the summer of 2013, editors at the AP contacted Chris's sister Suzi and told her they wanted to set up a meeting with Chris. Both Chris and Dave knew word of Bob's agency link would eventually come out and considered it a small miracle it hadn't already. But they both felt that they wanted to be the ones to disclose it, particularly since they believed Bob was alive. They saw the revelation of his CIA role as a kind of last-ditch Hail Mary tactic, the bombshell they would drop to embarrass the U.S. government into forcefully confronting Iran after every other option had been exhausted. Chris and Dave weren't ready to use that weapon, and with the change in Iran's government, they wanted to give diplomatic talks time to work. Suzi told a top AP executive that her sister wasn't ready to meet, and he assured her the news organization would contact her again to revisit the question.

Within the AP, editors were leaning toward publishing the article, and with the Snowden disclosures, everything related to U.S. government efforts to keep secrets appeared to be fair game. The AP didn't have a news "hook," a development or a change in Bob's situation, on which to hang his story because nothing new in it had occurred. Then something did happen that had nothing to do with Bob. In November 2013, Adam Goldman left the AP for a job with a competitor, *The Washington Post*. His job wasn't scheduled to start until December and Goldman *thought* the AP would publish the article before he joined the *Post*. In early December, when Goldman began his new job, the AP article still hadn't appeared, so he gave editors at the *Post* a version of Bob's story for the newspaper to run. Typically, when a reporter leaves one publication for another, he or she leaves behind any stories in progress, and AP editors had specifically told Goldman not to take his notes about Bob with him. The reporter would later say he didn't need those notes to write an article for the *Post*. All the information contained in his AP notes was in his head as well as in a book proposal about Bob's case that he and Matt Apuzzo had sent to their literary agent.

On December 12, 2013, a little more than a week after Goldman started at the *Post*, Suzi Halpin received an email from Apuzzo. It carried the subject line "Bob, a heads up for you and Christine."

> I wanted to give you a courtesy heads-up that, after many years of deliberations, A.P.'s top editors have decided to move ahead with the larger story about Bob's disappearance. I know this is probably not the decision you wanted us to make, but I hope you know that for the past three years, we have treated this matter as sensitively and personally as possible. I have nothing but warm thoughts for you and your family, and I know everyone here is ever hopeful that Bob comes home soon.

Suzi quickly notified Chris, Dave, and others about the email. An FBI spokesman as well as a top White House staffer contacted the senior editor at the AP, Kathleen Carroll, and urged her to hold the article. Senator Bill Nelson was irate and also called Carroll. "You are going to get him killed," Nelson said. The decision wasn't up for debate. Three hours after Apuzzo's email was sent, the AP released its story, breaking the news that Bob had been a CIA contractor. Along with the article, the AP released a statement by Kathleen Carroll explaining why the organization had gone ahead with the story. In her statement, the editor alluded to Edward Snowden and the NSA disclosures. It read in part:

> Publishing this article was a difficult decision. This story reveals serious mistakes and improper actions inside the U.S. government's most important intelligence agency. Those actions, the investigation and consequences have all been kept secret from the public.
>
> Publishing articles that help the public hold their government to account is part of what journalism is for, and especially so at The Associated Press, which pursues accountability journalism when-

ever it can. This seems particularly true on this subject at a time when the decisions of intelligence agencies are being extensively debated.

Other journalists saw a far less lofty motive behind the AP's move: simple journalistic competition. The news service was apparently so concerned Goldman might scoop it that editors there didn't notify him beforehand when the AP ran its article, even though it carried his byline. Goldman first saw it when it went online, and he alerted his editors at the *Post*, who posted the article he had written on the newspaper's website minutes later. The revelation of Bob's role as a CIA consultant was big news for days, and media organizations such as *The New York Times* that had withheld their accounts published them. Television and print reporters staked out Anne Jablonski's house in Arlington, Virginia, and stories about her role as Bob's secret handler appeared in numerous publications, including British tabloids. She was depicted in some as a yoga-crazed real-world counterpart of Carrie Mathison, the bipolar CIA operative played by Claire Danes on the popular television show *Homeland*.

When the news about Bob came out, Samantha Levinson, his youngest daughter, was twenty-three and working at Walt Disney World Resort in Orlando as a manager at the Magic Kingdom Park. Many of Samantha's fellow employees already knew from media accounts about her father's mysterious disappearance, and she had started a practice at the Magic Kingdom called "Pink Shirt Thursday" as a way to remember him. Back in the 1990s, Bob and a fellow agent in the FBI's Miami office wore pink polo shirts on Thursdays as a way of thumbing their noses at the bureau's straitlaced dress code. As word of Bob's CIA ties spread, the view of Samantha by coworkers changed from that of a girl whose father was missing to that of a girl whose dad was a spy. "My boss was like, 'Whoa,'" she recalled later. Another acquaintance took a cell phone picture of her and posted it on Twitter to the attention of Anderson Cooper, the CNN newsman.

The disclosure of Bob's CIA ties had a cathartic effect on Chris,

Dave, and Ira. They felt an immense burden lifted. They no longer had to lie. Chris and Dave made the rounds on television, speaking forcefully about what they said was the failure of U.S. officials to rescue Bob. "The CIA sent Bob Levinson on a mission, he got caught on that mission, and after he got caught, the CIA abandoned him," Dave said. The former Massachusetts senator John Kerry, who had replaced Hillary Clinton in 2013 as secretary of state, disputed that suggestion, telling reporters that he and other department officials had repeatedly asked the Iranians about Bob. "There hasn't been progress in the sense that we don't have him back," Kerry said. "But to suggest that we've abandoned him or anybody . . . is simply incorrect and not helpful."

Journalists also called Dawud Salahuddin, who was happy to provide them with his account of events on Kish. He told *The Christian Science Monitor* that six Iranian policemen had detained Bob and him in the lobby of the Maryam hotel, a rendering that included several more cops than earlier versions and moved the scene of the action from Bob's room to the lobby. He insisted to the *Monitor*'s reporter he had been unaware of Bob's CIA ties until reading about them and hadn't colluded with Iranian intelligence to set him up. "I can hurt people, but I won't hurt anybody like that, that's cheap stuff, man," he said.

Dawud pointed out, as he had in his emails to Chris, that he had also suffered as a result of his meeting with Bob. Since the incident on Kish, Iranian authorities had refused to give him a new passport or travel documents so he could move freely. As Dawud put it, he was "the last American hostage in Iran."

20

The Fellowship

On December 13, 2013, the day after the Associated Press article appeared, President Obama's press secretary, Jay Carney, strode into the White House briefing room to answer questions from reporters about Bob Levinson. The first came from a journalist who didn't mince words. "Why did the administration falsely say for years that Levinson was a private citizen in Iran on a business trip, and will you continue to say that now that it has been proven to be untrue?" she asked.

With their father's secret out, some of Bob's children wanted the U.S. government to stop its charade and honor him by telling the truth. If Iran was keeping him to force the United States to admit he was a spy, then the refusal of American officials to do so, they believed, was prolonging his confinement. The White House didn't intend to change its stance. Carney, standing behind a podium flanked by American flags, looked down at the prepared statement before him and read:

> Bob Levinson was not a U.S. government employee when he went
> missing in Iran. As there is an ongoing investigation into his

disappearance, I am not going to comment further on what he may or may not have been doing while in Iran. I am not going to fact-check every allegation . . . Since Bob disappeared, the U.S. government has pursued and continues to pursue all investigative leads, as we would with any missing American citizen missing or detained overseas. We continue to do everything we can to bring Bob home safely to his family. This remains a top priority.

By February 2014, a few months later, the media buzz about Bob and the CIA had faded when President Obama arrived at the Washington Hilton for the National Prayer Breakfast. Some three thousand people were gathered for the annual event, which is held by a Christian organization known as the Fellowship. The group, also called "the Family," is one of the most powerful and secretive religious organizations in the United States and counts leading politicians and businessmen among its ranks. Leaders of the Fellowship like to say that the group does not have members in the traditional sense, preferring to describe itself as a network of believers in Jesus and his ideals, who come together through prayer meetings and study groups to read the Bible and offer one another guidance.

Since the 1950s, every U.S. president has paid homage to the Fellowship by speaking at its Prayer Breakfast, and President Obama was no exception. In his talk that February, he spoke about the need to protect religious freedom around the world, singling out the cases of Kenneth Bae, a Korean-American Christian missionary then imprisoned in North Korea, and Saeed Abedini, the Iranian-American Christian pastor held in Tehran's Evin Prison. "Today, again, we call on the Iranian government to release Pastor Abedini so he can return to the loving arms of his wife and children," Obama said.

In the audience, a lawyer named Robert Destro bowed his head in prayer. Destro was aware of an episode involving Bob that had never been made public, one that might have resulted in his reunion with Chris and his family. In late 2011, around the time the FBI released the hostage video, a top official of the Iranian government admitted during a meeting arranged by the Fellowship that Iran controlled

Bob's fate and was ready to release him in exchange for American concessions at the nuclear bargaining table.

The Fellowship, using its religious affiliations, has long been involved in behind-the-scenes diplomacy, having established a network of contacts with countries worldwide, including Iran. In 2003, the group's leader, Douglas Coe, had headed a delegation of American religious figures to Iran. Three years later, in 2006, a member of that delegation, Cardinal Theodore McCarrick of Washington, D.C., hosted a reception in Washington for Mohammed Khatami during the former Iranian president's trip to the United States. The Fellowship's ties to Iran paid dividends in 2007 when it helped win the release of an Iranian-American scholar held in Evin Prison. The woman, Haleh Esfandiari, who was arrested while visiting her ailing mother in Tehran, later credited members of the group for drafting a letter sent to Ayatollah Khamenei by the former U.S. congressman Lee Hamilton, describing it as "instrumental" in securing her freedom.

The events leading to the Fellowship's involvement in Bob's case were set in motion by one of its more unlikely followers, Boris Birshtein. Though Jewish, Boris was a regular participant in the group's annual Prayer Breakfast, even putting up with the hassle he got from U.S. border officials to attend it. He also enjoyed a close friendship with Douglas Coe, whom he considered a spiritual mentor. Boris, despite his rebuff by the FBI, wasn't ready to step away from Bob's case, and in mid-2011 he arrived at Coe's residence, an expansive compound in Arlington, Virginia, known as "the Cedars." Boris was deferential and reserved toward Coe, and the two men began their meeting by praying together.

After they prayed, Boris told the Fellowship's leader about Bob and asked if he would send a letter to Ayatollah Khamenei, inquiring about the missing American. Coe agreed to do so and contacted Robert Destro, who taught law at the Catholic University of America in Washington and had helped draft the successful plea to Khamenei made on behalf of Haleh Esfandiari. Destro was a deeply religious person whose views shaped his work and his involvement with the Fellowship. For nearly a decade, he had played a central role in the high-profile legal fight over the fate of a Florida woman named Terri Schiavo. After suffering brain damage caused by a heart attack, Schiavo languished for years in a vegetative state, kept alive by a feeding tube. Her husband wanted to remove the tube, arguing that his wife wouldn't have wanted to live that way. Her parents, whom Destro represented, believed she might recover and wanted feeding to continue. The case became a cause célèbre for religious and pro-life groups over the issue of who had the right to determine Schiavo's fate. Destro asked, "What would Terri say to us about continued nutrition and hydration if she could speak to us today?" In 2005, after the lawyer's last appeal was exhausted, the feeding tube was removed and she died.

At Coe's request, Destro flew to Toronto to meet Boris. He had already read about the businessman's reputed crime connections and received Boris's standard lecture about why none of it was true and about how the U.S. government was mistreating him. Boris also told Destro that Madzhit Mamoyan was continuing to tap his sources inside Iran, hoping to glean new information about Bob.

Upon returning to Washington, Destro drafted a letter to Ayatollah Khamenei on behalf of Douglas Coe, containing an inquiry about Bob. The letter was sent to Madzhit in Paris, who was asked to deliver it to Iran's ambassador to France, Seyed Mehdi Miraboutalebi. The letter identified Madzhit, who was Christian, as an official envoy of the Fellowship, and Ambassador Miraboutalebi assured him that Coe's letter would be delivered to Iran's Supreme Leader. One paragraph read:

> As a believer and a follower of Jesus, to whom the Most High, "vouchsafed . . . all evidence of truth" (Holy Qu'ran 2:87), I pledge that I will continue to devote time and effort to the furtherance of dialogue, peace and understanding between our two great cultures. I would welcome your guidance and suggestions concerning more constructive ways in which we can bring about a peaceful dialogue, if not for ourselves, then for the sake of our children and grandchildren.

A month later, in September 2011, Madzhit was invited to Tehran to meet with the head of Iran's Ministry of Intelligence, Heydar Moslehi. At that time, two of the American hikers, Joshua Fattal and Shane Bauer, were still in Evin Prison, and Madzhit would later say Moslehi told him the Iranian government was planning to release them and Bob at the same time as a "goodwill" gesture to spur better relations with the United States. But when Mahmoud Ahmadinejad announced the hikers' release, he made no mention of Bob, and Madzhit later said Iranian intelligence officials told him the government of Oman secretly paid $50 million to Iran to free the hikers.

In October, a month after Madzhit's visit to Tehran, Ambassador Miraboutalebi contacted him and asked him to come to his Paris residence to talk. He told the Kurd his diplomatic posting in France was about to end and there was sensitive information about Bob he needed to discuss with an official of the Fellowship. Madzhit conveyed the message to Boris, who passed it along to Robert Destro. At that point, the lawyer decided it was time to alert the FBI about the group's involvement in Bob's case. He contacted an FBI agent, Dean Harp, then working on the investigation and also sent him a five-page memo summarizing the steps that the Fellowship had taken.

He also told Harp that Ambassador Miraboutalebi wanted to meet with representatives of the Fellowship on the following Sunday because Ayatollah Khamenei had called him back to Tehran on short notice. The date was just five days away, and Destro said that since he was unable to travel to Paris because of a prior commitment, he had asked Douglas Coe to recommend a replacement. In his memo to the FBI, Destro misspelled the name of the man, Ory Eshel, as Esher.

I called Doug Coe and asked him if he would suggest someone whom (1) he trusted implicitly; (2) who is discreet; and (3) who takes good notes. He thought about it for a day and then suggested that I call Ory Esher, a good friend of the Coe family, whom Doug has known since he was a young man. Mr. Esher is an American who has lived in Paris. I tried to call him yesterday but the result (so far) has been "phone tag." I will try again this morning and will send him an email as well.

Current plans are not completely clear at this point, but as I understand them now, Ory Esher will meet Madzhit and Boris for lunch in Paris on Sunday to go over some of the information that Madzhit can not share on the phone. Madzhit and Mr. Esher will then go to the embassy where they will meet with the Ambassador and get more information.

On that Sunday, Madzhit and Eshel rode to the ambassador's home in a chauffeur-driven Mercedes sedan that passed along the leafy streets of Paris's wealthy 16th arrondissement. The car turned through a cast-iron entrance gate and stopped in front of a nineteenth-century town house. The two men stepped out, and Ambassador Miraboutalebi welcomed his visitors and accompanied them up a flight of stairs to a large formal receiving room.

Eshel told the Iranian official he was attending the meeting as Douglas Coe's emissary and conveyed the religious leader's regrets he was unable to be present. Eshel explained his role was to provide Coe with a detailed and objective account of the conversation. Ambassador Miraboutalebi began by ticking through recent actions by American officials that he said were sowing distrust among his colleagues toward the United States. The episodes included speeches by Secretary of State Hillary Clinton attacking Iran; provocative propaganda broadcasts by the Voice of America into his country; and what he described as a "disappointing" response by U.S. officials to Iran's release of the hikers.

He then turned to his chief concern. It was a forthcoming report by the International Atomic Energy Agency, or IAEA, into whether Iran was using the country's nuclear energy program for peaceful purposes or to develop atomic bombs. In the weeks before the Paris meeting, newspapers had started reporting that the U.N. agency would disclose that Iran, contrary to its public claims, was secretly working on technologies used in nuclear weapons. Those stories also stated that President Obama planned to use the report's findings to call for additional sanctions against Tehran. The Iranian ambassador was apparently already aware of the report's findings, describing them to Madzhit and Eshel as "fake" conclusions adopted by the IAEA because of U.S. pressure. He added that the IAEA report would be devastating and set off a chain reaction that would make it difficult, if not impossible, to "reset" the relationship between the United States and Iran. Eshel wrote:

> The Ambassador added that Iran would not cooperate "under duress," and that the U.S. would not be able to push other nations against Iran. The challenge is to bridge this divide, through top-level discussions in both countries. The Ambassador acknowledged a common interest between "his" people and Doug Coe: both believe in God and can help overcome violence and war. Time is of the essence.

Ambassador Miraboutalebi went on to describe the political tensions within Iran and said it was important during his upcoming meeting with Ayatollah Khamenei to provide the Supreme Leader with a sign that the Fellowship could positively influence American foreign policy. But that signal needed to be sent quickly because the IAEA report was expected to be released in two weeks, on November 17. The Iranian diplomat made some suggestions, Eshel wrote:

> This week, the Ambassador will be meeting in Teheran with Khamenei. A tangible expression of good will would be especially useful, as an indication that our team can "deliver the goods":
>
> 1. An official letter from the Pope inviting a top delegation to meet in private in the Vatican, together with former US Presidents (specifically Bill Clinton and Bush I or II).
>
> 2. In view of the November 17 deadline, two actions to be taken urgently by the Secretary of State:
>
> delaying publication of the IAEA report

committing to a moratorium on public criticism of Iran and on "hostile actions" (for a few months)

Following these actions, the Ambassador estimated that it would be possible to release Robert Levinson prior to the Vatican meeting.

The Ambassador emphasized that unlike prior negotiations, this meeting would have to be conducted in a "truthful" and quiet way, leading to a positive outcome. In his opinion, success will depend on our common belief in God. "It was the guidance of our Lord and God that brought us here." He looks to God to protect both nations from nuclear bombs and military conflicts.

The Ambassador sends a "very special hello to Doug." We concluded the meeting with a prayer.

After the meeting, which lasted an hour and a half, the Iranian diplomat gave his guests a tour of his residence, which his wife, an interior designer, had decorated. One ground-floor room was lined with six decorative niches, each containing a garishly painted fresco depicting an ancient Persian city. Madzhit and Eshel were then driven to the U.S. embassy, where FBI agents debriefed them. Eshel also spoke by phone with Robert Destro and said it was his impression that Iranian government officials wanted to release Bob as a "gesture of good faith." Later that afternoon, the Iranian ambassador called Madzhit and asked him to return to his residence for a separate meeting. In a subsequent memo to the FBI, Destro summarized the official's comments to Madzhit in bold lettering:

1. That the Ambassador needs feedback this week.
2. The Iranians also want to discuss several Iranians held by the United States.
3. The Ambassador confirmed that:
   a. A deal could be reached if the November 17 publication of the IAEA report could be postponed; and that
   b. Robert Levinson would be released

In a memo to the FBI, Destro suggested several steps to help the Fellowship expand its efforts to free Bob. Among other things, Destro proposed a meeting between Secretary of State Clinton, Douglas Coe, Boris, Madzhit, and Ory Eshel so Clinton could hear firsthand what occurred in Paris. "This would provide the sufficient time ahead of the scheduled publication of the IAEA report for the Secretary to consider options," Destro wrote.

An FBI agent indicated that the bureau would pass the Fellowship's reports to the State Department. But Destro never heard another word about them. The IAEA report was released a week before its anticipated publication, and as expected it contained evidence Iran was working to develop components of a nuclear weapon. Iranian officials cast the IAEA report as a fabrication created by the United States, and Obama administration officials announced they would use the evidence of work on nuclear weapons technology as the basis for new sanctions.

Robert Destro would later wonder whether U.S. officials ever took seriously Ambassador Miraboutalebi's statements because of the FBI's disdain for Boris, or if senior State Department officials ever saw the Fellowship's reports. But whatever the case, it soon became clear to him that someone within the U.S. government wanted Boris out of the picture, once and for all.

In March 2012, five months after the Paris meeting, Boris's nephew, Jack Braverman, arrived at the Toronto airport with his wife and their children to take a flight for a vacation in Florida. Braverman was listed on corporate documents as an executive in several of Boris's companies, but the businessman treated him more like a personal assistant and general gofer. For instance, after Boris learned in early 2011 that Dave McGee and Ira Silverman were flying into Toronto to visit, he summoned Braverman back from a family vacation in Florida so he could chauffeur them around. When Dave and Ira saw him at the Toronto airport, he appeared so exhausted they thought he might have driven back nonstop from Fort Lauderdale.

As he waited with his family to board their flight, Braverman was pulled aside by U.S. border officials, who began to question him. They wanted to know if he knew a man named Madzhit Mamoyan and why the Kurd, who was on a U.S. watch list, was using a cell phone for which Braverman's company was paying the bill. They also asked him if he ever had met Madzhit or if the Kurd had come to Canada to meet Boris. The border agents also questioned him about his associations with Boris. Braverman's wife, who knew nothing about Madzhit or about Boris's problems getting into the United States, was horrified. Braverman was let go, but by then his family was forced to cancel their departure and return home. Robert Destro didn't view himself as a person given to conspiracy theories, but after the episode involving Braverman, it was hard not to think that some officials in the U.S. government were more interested in keeping tabs on Boris and his friends than in finding Bob. After the airport incident, Boris decided he was done with Bob's case.

In April 2015, American and Iranian government officials stood in a hotel ballroom in Lausanne, Switzerland, to announce a plan under which Iran would restrict its development of nuclear weapons in exchange for the lifting of economic and financial sanctions. The final details of a deal remained to be worked out. But the framework for that agreement, which followed months of talks between the United States, Iran, and several European countries, was hailed as a major breakthrough. President Obama, in a speech in the White House Rose Garden, called it "a historic understanding with Iran."

Obama administration officials had made it clear during the talks that Bob's fate and those of several Americans held in Iran were not a part of the negotiations. Along with Saeed Abedini, the pastor, and Amir Hekmati, the former marine, another Iranian-American, Jason Rezaian, a reporter for *The Washington Post*, had joined them in Evin Prison. U.S. officials insisted they didn't include the men in the talks because they didn't want the Iranians to use them as pawns they could play to their advantage. But if Ambassador Miraboutalebi's demands in 2011 were any indication, Bob had long ago become one.

After the announcement in Switzerland, Chris got a call from President Obama's top advisor on homeland security and terrorism,

Lisa Monaco. She told Chris she wanted to assure her the White House hadn't forgotten her husband and would continue to press Iran about him. "We plan to talk to them about Bob," Monaco said.

Chris hung up the phone. Since the start of her long ordeal, her faith in her family, her religion, and the FBI had sustained her. For seven years, she followed the instructions of the bureau and the State Department to the letter. She lied because it was necessary. She performed on cue when required. She swallowed her pride and exhibited respect to Iranian officials even as they treated her and her family with contempt. During that time, she watched happy reunions take place for families other than her own. She had endured it all for one reason—she believed if she did what U.S. officials told her to do, Bob would return home. Those close to her, including some of Chris's children, wondered at times if she wasn't blinded by her allegiance to the FBI. They didn't blame her because they knew she could not have acted differently. As Chris saw it, she and Bob had entered into a covenant of trust with the U.S. government when he had joined the bureau, a bond to which both sides were still obligated. She never imagined her government might have withheld information from her about Bob or failed to take a step that might have resulted in his freedom, such as releasing the Fellowship's report about what Ambassador Miraboutalebi had said.

21

The Twilight War

On most Wednesdays at 11:00 a.m., officials from the FBI, the CIA, and the State Department gathered at bureau headquarters to talk about Bob Levinson's case. By early 2015, such meetings had been going on for years and there wasn't much left to discuss.

Back in 2012, after the last two American hikers were released from Evin Prison, U.S. officials had quietly taken several steps to encourage prisoner swaps with Iran, hoping one might include Bob. An Iranian woman, Shahrazad Mir Gholikhan, had spent nearly five years in a federal prison following her conviction in 2008 for conspiring to export three thousand military-grade night vision goggles to Iran. Rather than requiring her to spend more time in a halfway facility, American officials allowed the government of Oman to negotiate her departure from the United States. Around that same time, the Justice Department dropped its effort to extradite to the United States a former Iranian diplomat living in London to face charges of trying to ship American-made military equipment to Iran.

Iranian officials hadn't responded to those gestures and the FBI decided in 2015 that a larger reward for news about Bob might bring in new information. That March, on the eighth anniversary of his disappearance, the bureau increased the reward from $1 million to $5 million. The lure of big money attracted plenty of people, all claiming to know something about the missing man's whereabouts. Agents chased down promising leads and, at the urging of Bob's old friend Larry Sweeney, traveled to Beirut to see an associate of the late arms dealer Sarkis Soghanalian. The man had insisted for years that he had connections who could help free Bob. When he was polygraphed, FBI agents found his answers to be so deceptive that they packed up their equipment after thirty minutes and left to fly home.

By then, some FBI officials thought the only way to try to break the logjam with Iran over Bob was to publicly admit the obvious— that he had gone to Kish as a "rogue" spy. Officially confirming Bob's CIA connection would hardly have surprised anyone. His agency ties had received extensive media publicity, and many FBI officials felt certain his captors knew about them. Chris and Dave were also urging the State Department to bring in an outside negotiator to restart talks with Tehran about Bob. For an intermediary to have credibility in such negotiations, he would need to be forthright about Bob.

But many U.S. officials still had an autoimmune response when it came to revealing Bob's CIA connection. Some FBI supervisors clung to the notion that officially confirming it would remove any last doubts in the minds of his captors, further jeopardizing his safety. By 2015, bureau officials had manufactured so many different stories about Bob they couldn't keep them straight. For years, they had said he went to Kish to investigate cigarette smuggling. In announcing the new $5 million reward, however, an FBI press release declared that Bob had gone there on "behalf of several large corporations." The claim was so unhinged from reality that it might have sprung from the fertile imagination of Dawud Salahuddin.

CIA officials were dead set against disclosing the nature of Bob's relationship; their collective DNA recoiled at the prospect. It's natural for an intelligence agency to go into disavowal mode when one of its operatives or assets is captured or disappears; such denials are so commonplace they serve as plot devices in espionage movies. The

CIA's desire to suppress the facts about Bob's case was especially strong because agency officials had lied not only to the outside world about him but also to their own government. White House officials had no way of knowing how Iran would react to an acknowledgment of Bob's agency ties. Iranian leaders might greet the concession as a signal to start negotiations or seize on it as a vehicle to whip up a public frenzy against the "Great Satan" and arrest other Americans on bogus spying charges.

In the spring of 2015, Bob and the three Americans held in Evin Prison—Saeed Abedini, Amir Hekmati, and Jason Rezaian—became front-page news again, this time as part of the political debate that erupted after the United States and Iran announced a preliminary nuclear deal. Republican lawmakers mounted a furious campaign to derail the plan, inviting the prime minister of Israel, Benjamin Netanyahu, to speak about it before Congress, where he denounced the proposal as a disaster. Soon afterward, forty-seven Republican senators wrote a joint letter to Ayatollah Khamenei warning him that a nuclear agreement signed by President Obama could be annulled by his successor. Opponents also argued that the Obama administration had forsaken Bob and the three imprisoned men to score a foreign policy victory. Some in the American public were outraged that the U.S. government had negotiated with a country holding their fellow citizens hostage.

Amid the maneuvering, Dan Levinson, Bob's oldest son, spoke before a congressional hearing. A year earlier, Dan had seriously considered traveling to Kish. The way he imagined it, he would arrive on the island and get arrested by Iranian authorities, an event that would give him a stage from which to declare that his father had gone to Iran at the urging of the CIA. He saw the action as a way to refocus attention on his family's plight and force a public confrontation between the United States and Iran that would finally provide answers about his father. Dan's sisters convinced him to drop the plan, arguing that their mother would be unable to bear the prospect of his imprisonment in Tehran.

Dan had come to believe, based on his talks with Ira Silverman and Dave McGee, that Iran's former president, Ali Akbar Hashemi Rafsanjani, might be behind his father's detention, a possibility at which he hinted during his comments to Congress. "It is true that those involved in the talks may not know where my father is or what happened to him," Dan told a congressional committee. "But we are certain that there are people in Iran who do."

In July, soon after Dan's testimony, negotiators reached agreement on the terms of a final nuclear control deal between Iran and the West. Iran agreed to keep its atomic energy program peaceful by reducing stockpiles of uranium, dismantling some equipment used to make nuclear weapons, and allowing inspectors to review its compliance with the agreement. In return, the United States and other nations involved in the plan said they would lift economic embargoes and release billions of dollars in Iranian funds that had been frozen in banks outside that country.

Chris and her children believed that the deal between the United States and Iran was Bob's best and possibly last hope for freedom. "We believe that right now is the time that my father's case can be prioritized, resolved and he can be brought home," Dave Levinson told *People* in 2015. Bob's daughter Sarah woke up one morning with a premonition that her father's story was about to have a happy ending.

The political fight over the nuclear plan continued, with opponents arguing that Iran shouldn't be trusted and would resume its pursuit of an atomic bomb. By the late summer of 2015, it became apparent that President Obama had secured enough support in Congress to get the agreement passed. Its adoption marked a new chapter in the twilight war, and a possible end to decades of distorted relations between the United States and Iran.

A wave of news reports appeared about possible prisoner swaps between the two countries, many mentioning Jason Rezaian, the *Washington Post* reporter. One Iranian official claimed the United States was illegally detaining nineteen of Iran's citizens in American prisons on embargo violations charges. Leaders in both Washington and Tehran disputed suggestions that an exchange was in the works, but it seemed inevitable that such a deal would take place.

White House officials assured Chris that American diplomats had continued to press Iran about her husband. Bob was mentioned in every newspaper account about Americans detained or unaccounted for in Iran. His place among that group, however, had begun to fade. His name was always there, but typically at the end of an article, almost as an afterthought. It was understandable. The three Americans held in Evin Prison were tangible and alive. Bob existed apart from them, in the realm of memory. The last image of him alive was five years old. His family had taken to calling him the "longest-held hostage" in American history, but his fate had long been unclear.

Most of the people involved in his case had moved on. Anne Jablonski still worked for investigative firms doing reports about Russian businessmen and taught yoga to injured U.S. soldiers returning from Iraq and Afghanistan. Along with her website devoted to healthy living for cats, she had created a new one called Yoga Set Free, on which she posted her spiritual musings. "The yogi sages say that your divine teacher is your deepest self," she wrote in one of them. "But at first it feels like *it's not you*, it's something 'other'—it's fine if it feels like that. So chill. And just ask it, like you're asking someone else, a good friend: *'Are you there?'* "

Dave, Ira, Larry Sweeney, and Jeff Katz, the private detective in London, continued to try to find out what had happened to Bob. Dave concentrated on his law practice, though he still provided Chris with legal advice when she needed it. Ira had gone back to writing movie scripts as a way of occupying his time and to avoid obsessing about Bob. He wasn't very successful. He continued to speak regularly with FBI agents, including some who told him they were outraged that the Justice Department hadn't pursued its investigation into the CIA's handling of Bob's case. Ira had also resumed his telephone talks with Dawud. The fugitive told him that he suspected Bob's captors had taken him out of Iran, possibly across the border into Afghanistan. Those conversations came to an abrupt end amid the intense media publicity about Bob's CIA ties. The Levinson family had provided CNN with one of the proposals Bob wrote in late 2005 to the CIA suggesting the possibility of recruiting Dawud as an agency informant. In it, Bob had described Ira as his "source" who would connect him with the fugitive. After CNN aired the segment, Dawud sent Ira an angry email, saying that he couldn't believe that the retired journalist would ever imagine he would agree to become a "snitch." Ira didn't hear from him again.

The Levinson children, despite the anguish of their father's absence, managed to thrive. Dan worked for a government contractor that put together briefing reports for the Treasury Department about overnight news developments affecting economic issues. Because of the job's nature, Dan could do it from wherever he chose, and stung by his father's wanderlust, he traveled widely. During his campaign to keep his father's name in the news, he had met many politicians, and Dan began to think about a career in politics, possibly as a congressman from Florida. Sue, the oldest of the Levinson daughters, had given birth to a child, Bob and Chris's fourth grandchild. Dave got married in the fall of 2015, and Samantha, the youngest Levinson daughter, had moved to New York and was working at the new Freedom Tower, the soaring building in lower Manhattan erected at the site of the Twin Towers, as a manager on its 102nd-floor observation deck. The youngest of the family's children, Doug, was on track to graduate from Florida State University in 2016.

The big new house that Bob and Chris had purchased in the 1990s to celebrate the start of a new and better life together was now an empty nest. Chris traveled a lot to be with her children, and under normal circumstances she might have sold the house and bought a smaller one. But as with much else in her life, that option was stuck in limbo. To do so, she would have to file legal papers declaring Bob dead, a step she had no interest in taking. Dave had given thought to ways to work around that roadblock, such as getting a sympathetic judge to hold that Bob was too incapacitated to consent to a sale. Whatever the case, the sale of the house was a symbolic step that Chris was not yet prepared to take.

Over time, hundreds of senators and representatives had signed on to congressional declarations demanding answers from Iran about Bob. Their anger was understandable; the idea that political and reli-

gious power brokers within Iran, one of the most repressive countries in the world, didn't know about the fate of a captured American
spy was absurd. But American leaders and lawmakers had also ut-
terly failed to give Chris and her children what they deserved most—
the truth about Bob. The CIA had never been forced to publicly
explain why it suddenly found $10,000 extra for Bob when it heard
about his Dubai "side trip," nor had the agency divulged the names of
those officials who misled the FBI and Congress.

The Senate intelligence panel allowed the CIA to cast Bob's case
as the fault of a few renegade analysts. Former spy agency officials say
that explanation doesn't ring true to them. They believe that many
CIA staffers and managers, even if they weren't aware of Bob's role
with the agency prior to his disappearance, learned of it in the days
and weeks after he vanished. Then each day, while Chris waited for
news about her missing husband, those CIA officials went home to
their spouses and children.

One day, well before the Iranian nuclear deal was struck, Chris
got a phone call from James McJunkin, one of the FBI agents who had
been involved in the search for Bob. In 2011, McJunkin had pushed
for talks with the Iranians following the arrival of the video showing
Bob as a hostage. Since then, he had retired from the FBI and gone to
work for Discover, the credit card company headquartered in Chicago. While in Florida on business, McJunkin suggested to Chris that
they get together, and she agreed to meet him at the place where she
saw most visitors, the Panera Bread restaurant in Coral Springs.

FBI officials had continued to assure Chris they believed Bob was
alive. The bureau's stance wasn't the result of any new evidence gathered by agents so much as a reflection of FBI policy, which considers
a person to be alive absent proof of his or her death. Since leaving the
FBI, McJunkin had begun to wonder whether such proof about Bob
would ever be found. He and other agents suspected that Bob's value
to his Iranian captors might have expired after they had used the
video to lure the FBI into talks about him. It was hard to imagine
another reason for his captors to devote the resources needed to keep
him alive for another five years.

McJunkin wasn't certain about what had happened to Bob, but he knew his captors had chosen the cruelest outcome for Chris and his children. Without finality, his family was trapped in a cycle of hope and despair, one that might never end. The kids would be okay, but McJunkin worried about Chris. He wanted to gently prod her into moving on with her life. As they sat together, he tried to talk to her about the future and the types of things she might like to do. Chris sensed where the conversation was headed. Years earlier, not long after Bob disappeared, she had sat down with her children. Their futures, she told them, lay ahead. They would marry, have children, and raise families. But Bob, she told her children, was the love of her life.

Chris looked across the table at McJunkin and said, "I want to be there for Bob."

On January 16, 2016, the day the nuclear deal between the United States and Iran went into effect, the two countries exchanged prisoners. Those released by Tehran included Jason Rezaian, the *Washington Post* reporter; Saeed Abedini, the pastor; and Amir Hekmati, the ex-marine. There was no mention of Bob Levinson.

Chris and her children learned about the exchange in the same way other Americans did: by hearing the news on television. They were devastated and appalled that the Obama administration had not alerted them beforehand.

"I thought that after nine years they would have enough respect for our family to at least tell us in advance that this is happening," Chris said in one interview. "I am very disappointed. I feel extremely betrayed."

The White House, the State Department, and the FBI put out statements saying they would continue searching for Bob, adding that Iran had agreed to assist in that effort, the same promise Tehran had made many times before.

When a reporter asked Secretary of State John Kerry if he knew whether the missing man was alive or dead, Kerry's reply was brief. "We have no idea," he said.

Notes

This book was based on interviews with many of the people portrayed in it. They include Christine Levinson and several of her children, including Dan, Dave, Stephanie, Sarah, and Samantha Levinson. In this account, I took the liberty of referring to Stephanie and Sarah by their maiden names, though they use their married names, Stephanie Curry and Sarah Moriarty. Susan Levinson now uses her married name, Susan Boothe. Chris's sister Suzi Halpin and Bob's sister, Judy Levinson, were also interviewed. Over the course of several years, I spoke regularly with David McGee, Ira Silverman, Sonya Dobbs, Jeffrey Katz, Boris Birshtein, and Madzhit Mamoyan. Several former and current FBI agents involved in the search for Bob also spoke with me, though in most cases they did so on the condition that they would not be identified by name. In reconstructing Bob's work and travels before his disappearance on Kish, I spoke with, among others, Houshang Bouzari, the Iranian-born oil consultant; Philip Séchaud, the Swiss detective; officials of Global Witness; and Hezi Leder, a former Israeli law enforcement officer. To my surprise, when I initially spoke with many of these people, they had not yet been contacted by the FBI. I also interviewed several private investigators who worked with Bob, as well as journalists who knew him. They included Brian Ross, Joe Trento, Linden MacIntyre, Neil Docherty, and Chris Isham. In late 2007, I exchanged several emails with Dawud about Bob's case. Dawud replied that he did not want to discuss the matter, and my subsequent efforts to contact him were unsuccessful.

This book also draws on a wealth of material written by Bob Levinson: reports to the CIA, memos about proposed assignments, emails with agency officials and private clients. Wherever possible, those reports and emails, or extracts from them, are reproduced verbatim. In a few cases, I corrected the types of common mistakes in spelling or punctuation that are typical of email correspondence. Those minor fixes were made for the purposes of clarity and did not alter the language's meaning. In those instances where exchanges of emails between two people are juxtaposed conversationally, the exchanges were part of an email thread or represent exchanges that took place within a short period of time, often minutes. I tried not to draw unwarranted inferences from documents or emails.

The decision by some key actors and organizations central to this book not to cooperate in it was disappointing, though not surprising. The Central Intelligence Agency refused to participate in any way with this project, even denying my request to visit Langley. The Federal Bureau of Investigation responded to a few written questions, but officials there would not address some central ones.

I interviewed Anne Jablonski on several occasions, the first time in 2009, not long after her dismissal by the CIA. My impression of her was similar to the ones given to me by her friends and acquaintances; she was bright, funny, and, yes, goofy. She spoke at length to me and was very eager to present her side of the story. During that time, she also spoke with reporters with the Associated Press and gave her friends permission to do so. However, after her role in the Levinson case became public in late 2013 when the AP published its article, she shut down and refused to speak to me. I contacted her on several occasions while writing this book, and some of Anne's friends encouraged her to participate in it. Her position, according to a note she sent me, was that she did not believe that any good would come from discussing Bob's case and that she viewed the episode as behind her. Both she and her husband, Robert Otto, did not respond to written questions sent to them. A lawyer for Timothy Sampson, Anne's boss at the Illicit Finance Group, said the former CIA official had prepared a response to written questions sent to him and submitted it in the spring of 2015 to the CIA for approval. The agency did not clear his response for release.

One of the first steps I took in 2014 when starting work on this book was to visit the Iranian mission to the United Nations and apply for a visa. In discussions with the mission's press attaché, I made it clear that while I was writing a book about Bob Levinson, I did not want to go to Iran to investigate his case but to gain a better sense of that country and its people. Over the course of one year, I repeatedly contacted the Iranian mission to get an update about the status of my visa request and was told each time that officials in Tehran were still reviewing it. In light of the Iranian government's unconscionable treatment of journalists such as *The Washington Post*'s Jason Rezaian, I suppose I should consider myself lucky.

Prologue

5   *"This is a serious message"*: Email from Osman.Muhamad@gmail.com to Ira Silverman, November 13, 2010.

6   *"For my beau— my beautiful"*: Transcript of videotape attached to email from Osman.Muhamad@gmail.com to Ira Silverman, November 13, 2010.

1. The House on Ninety-Second Street

10   *"If you do this right"*: "Managing Danger," *Florida Trend* magazine, September 1, 1999.

10   *his own one-man shop*: R. A. Levinson & Associates was formed on April 23, 2001. State of Florida corporate records.

10   *another large investigations firm, SafirRosetti, hired him*: SafirRosetti press release, March 26, 2004.

11   *teach seminars for young agents*: The presentation that Bob gave to FBI agents about identifying and developing informants was titled "Source Development and Penetration of Targeted Organizations."

12   *The DEA agent, who did undercover buys*: David Samuels, a former undercover agent for the DEA and a friend of Bob's, told me this story.

13   The House on 92nd Street: This film, which was released in 1945, starred William Eythe and Lloyd Nolan. It might have inspired a very young Bob Levinson, but I would not recommend it.

13   *City College of New York*: Bob attended Yeshiva University in New York on a scholarship for two years before transferring to CCNY, according to Dan Levinson.

13   *TGI Friday's*: Chris Levinson described her chance encounter with her future husband at this iconic Manhattan singles bar.

14   *Raymond Donovan*: My description of the long-running controversy involving the onetime labor secretary was drawn from accounts in *The Washington Post*, *The New York Times*, and *Newsday*.

14   *Michael Orlando*: The FBI investigation for which Michael Orlando served as an informant was called "Operation Tumcon" and named after its initial target, Angelo Tuminaro, the suspected head of a major heroin trafficking ring.

15   *"This kid Mike"*: William Masselli's allusion to Orlando's role as a Mafia contract killer proved accurate. FBI records show he later acknowledged carrying out at least one gangland murder.

15   *A subsequent internal FBI review*: The results of the internal bureau inquiry into the handling of Michael Orlando by Bob and Larry Sweeney are contained in an FBI report dated February 16, 1981.

15   *too much bad blood*: Larry Sweeney told me about the decision by supervisors in the FBI's New York office to take Bob off the organized crime task force.

16   *Baruch Vega*: Baruch Vega's career as a photographer and career as an

informant with the CIA, FBI, and DEA are described in reports in the *St. Petersburg Times* and other publications.

16   *"Bob Roberts"*: Baruch Vega told me about the scheme developed by Bob and him that involved a fictional FBI agent. Vega used a similar stratagem when he later became a DEA informant and was subsequently arrested and charged with taking bribes from cartel members. During a DEA investigation, Bob Levinson and other former FBI agents confirmed the "Bob Roberts" scheme. As a result, charges against Vega were dropped.

16   *Alexander Volkov*: His role in Summit International and its description as a Ponzi scheme is contained in Robert I. Friedman's book *Red Mafiya: How the Russian Mob Has Invaded America* (Boston: Little, Brown, 2000).

17   *Vyacheslav Ivankov*: The description of the FBI's sting operation against him is drawn from court filings and newspaper accounts.

17   *at a conference in New Mexico*: Anne Jablonski described her meeting with Bob.

17   *"Toots"*: In nearly all his emails to Anne, Bob addressed her as "Toots" and signed them as "Buck."

18   *The informant said his sources had spotted an executive*: The claim that a mole within Philip Morris was selling its technology to product counterfeiters is contained in a SafirRosetti report dated July 8, 2004.

18   *James Giffen*: Bribery charges against James Giffen were dropped after a judge allowed him to mount the defense that federal officials knew of his actions in Kazakhstan and that they had benefited U.S. policy.

19   *the Kazakh president was willing to help the U.S. government*: Bob detailed the president of Kazakhstan's offer of help to the United States on terrorism-related issues in a "briefing paper" dated October 23, 2004.

20   *The DEA already knew*: Interview with Philip Scott Forbes, who described the arrest of Leonid Venjik in Austria on drug and contraband trafficking charges.

20   *gave Austrian authorities a sworn affidavit*: Bob swore out a statement attesting to the honesty of Leonid Venjik on December 20, 2004.

20   *"I'm going to get eaten alive"*: Letter from Bob to Dave McGee, April 26, 2005.

21   *Bob sent a letter to Joseph Cooley*: Bob sent his letter to Cooley on April 26, 2005.

21   *Explaining to Philip Morris*: Officials of the cigarette company did not respond to inquiries about its decision to stop using SafirRosetti, but Philip Scott Forbes, the DEA agent, said the cigarette company was aware of the Venjik case.

22   *a "success fee"*: A private investigator, Jim Mintz, provided me with an explanation of how this form of payment works.

23   *Every month, Anne told him about a hang-up*: The hang-ups involved in getting Bob's contract approved by the CIA's bureaucracy are detailed in several emails written by Anne to Bob.

2. Toots

26   *"Meow . . . And welcome"*: Anne's account of her experiment that restored her cat, Duke, to health was recounted in a post on her website CatNutrition .org.

26   *"Anne-ski"*: Anne told me that her colleagues called her this.

27   *Robert Otto*: Emails show that Otto asked Bob for information about Russian politicians or businessmen in which he, apparently as a State Department official, had an interest.

28   *Anne met her at Union Station*: Sarah Levinson described to me her day in Washington with Anne.

28   *Jonathan Winer*: Winer acknowledged to me several years ago that he was a consultant with the Illicit Finance Group. He declined to be interviewed for this book.

29   *"Ugh . . . Pay NO attention to Bonnie"*: Email from Anne to Bob, August 29, 2005.

30   *Olga Vega*: The role of Baruch Vega's sister as a possible source of information about the three Defense Department contractors held hostage in Colombia is outlined in an email sent by Baruch Vega to Bob, October 11, 2005.

30   *"I'll pass it along"*: Email from Anne to Bob, October 12, 2005.

31   *"I'll try and get a debrief"*: Email from Anne to Bob, October 22, 2005.

31   *"I am sure you're weary"*: Email from Anne to Bob, May 2, 2006.

31   *Brian O'Toole*: He is described in Bob's contract as its administrator.

31   *The contract's language was vague*: The effective date of Bob's CIA consulting contract was June 15, 2006.

32   *Peter F. Paul*: Bob visited Paul in August 2006 at a federal prison and sent several reports to Anne about information Paul provided.

33   *"And for heaven's sake"*: Email from Anne to Bob, August 11, 2006.

33   *"We teeter on the edge"*: Email from Anne to Bob, August 15, 2006.

33   *The solution presented to Bob was simple*: The directions given to Bob about how he should prepare future reports for the Illicit Finance Group and send them to Anne at her home are contained in a note titled "Instructions pursuant to meeting of 22 August 2006." The same memo contains a list of "Principal Interests," such as Iran and Hugo Chávez.

35   *"Iran is the flavor of the day"*: Interview with Ira Silverman.

3. The Fugitive

36   *"In the past, I was Teddy"*: The documentary in which Dawud speaks these words is called *American Fugitive: The Truth About Hassan*, by Jean-Daniel Lafond, a Canadian filmmaker. Dawud also used the name Hassan Abdulrahman.

38   *Dawud drove to Tabatabai's home*: The account of Dawud's assassination of

Ali Akbar Tabatabei is drawn from accounts in *The Washington Post* and *The New York Times*.

40   *"Who am I, who grew up privileged and white"*: The writer who made these comments was Christopher de Bellaigue, a journalist living in Iran. He painted a sympathetic portrait of Dawud in the memoir *In the Rose Garden of the Martyrs* (New York: HarperCollins, 2006).

41   *Grady had never met the detective*: Interview with James Grady.

42   *"This country, this regime"*: Dawud made these comments in a tape-recorded conversation with Carl Shoffler.

42   *"I believe that I am in a position"*: While Dawud drafted this letter to Janet Reno, the then attorney general of the United States, it is not clear that he sent it.

43   *"I don't need a notch"*: Shoffler made these comments in a tape-recorded conversation with Dawud.

43   *Joseph Trento*: The freelance writer included an account of Dawud's recruitment as an assassin for the Iranian Revolution as a chapter in his book *Prelude to Terror: The Rogue CIA and the Legacy of America's Private Intelligence Network* (New York: Carroll & Graf, 2005).

44   *Ira wrote a eulogy*: His tribute to Carl Shoffler, "Capital Cop," appeared in *The New Yorker*, July 29, 1996.

46   *his relationship with Brian Ross*: Interview with Brian Ross and others who worked with Ira and Ross at NBC News.

46   *a critically acclaimed Iranian film*, Kandahar: Dawud's acting in this extraordinary film seems wooden, but the scene in which he examines its female protagonist from behind a curtain is memorable.

47   *a piece about Russian organized crime*: The *Fifth Estate* segment in which Bob appeared, "Power Play," examined the involvement of Russian organized crime in professional ice hockey.

47   *a twilight war*: I borrowed this phrase from *The Twilight War: The Secret History of America's Thirty-Year Conflict with Iran*, by David Crist (New York: Penguin, 2012). Crist's book is an arresting and authoritative account of the decades-long war between the United States and Iran fought through proxies.

48   *"The Iranians of my immediate association"*: Dawud's comments are drawn from Ira Silverman's profile "An American Terrorist," which appeared in *The New Yorker*, August 5, 2002.

51   *"The link below"*: Email from Ira to Bob, July 11, 2006.

52   *"It turns out that our friend"*: Email from Bob to Ira, August 3, 2006.

4. Boris

53   *Bouzari was among Tehran's best and brightest*: The description of Houshang Bouzari's career and harrowing experiences in Evin Prison is based on court filings in Canada and the article "Escape from Iran" in *The Atlantic*,

March 20, 2012. Bouzari was awarded damages in his lawsuit against Mehdi Rafsanjani, but a higher court determined that Canada was not the proper venue for the action. Separately, an Iranian court in 2015 upheld Mehdi Rafsanjani's conviction on corruption charges, and he was sentenced to a lengthy prison term.

54   *Bob learned about him because of a lawsuit*: Bob first contacted Bouzari by email on August 18, 2006—of interest because it was the same time a memo following a CIA meeting described Iran as a key target for the Illicit Finance Group.

55   *He said the family owned condominiums*: Houshang Bouzari described in an interview the assets the Rafsanjani family was suspected of controlling in Canada.

55   *"Just so you know"*: Email from Bob to Ira, August 26, 2006.

56   *"Have an op going"*: Email from Bob to Gazman Xhudo, State Department Bureau of Diplomatic Security, August 26, 2006.

56   *"Please tell our friend"*: Email from Bob to Ira, August 28, 2006.

57   *tying Mogilevich to the firm*: The focus of Global Witness's interest in Semion Mogilevich is described in a series of emails and memos.

58   *"You need to leave right now"*: Interview with a former FBI official based in Moscow who spoke on the condition of anonymity.

59   *Mogilevich had met with federal prosecutors*: Mogilevich's allegations against Boris Birshtein and others were made during meetings in October 1997 with federal prosecutors. Anne Jablonski said she believed Bob attended them. In 2006, he sent her several analytical reports about what Mogilevich said. In the memos, Birshtein's name is spelled phonetically as "Birshteyn."

60   *"I'd take whatever bullshit they give you"*: Email from Bob to Boris, September 8, 2006.

60   *Sisoev described Riza*: Analytical report from Bob to Anne, August 25, 2006.

60   *"definitely" interested in the subject*: Email from Bob to Anne, August 25, 2006.

61   *"Wow!!!!!!"*: Email from Anne to Bob, August 25, 2006.

5. A Gold Mine

62   *"This guy is a damn GOLD MINE!"*: Email from Anne to Bob, September 28, 2006.

62   *"Toots, say no more"*: Email from Bob to Anne, September 29, 2006.

63   *Robert Seldon Lady*: The friend of Bob's and former CIA Milan station chief declined to be interviewed for this book.

63   *$20,000 in travel money*: Bob's contract was supplemented in September 2006 with extra travel money, apparently because he exhausted the original amount.

64   *life aboard Hugo Chávez's presidential jet*: Analytical report from Bob to the Illicit Finance Group, September 22, 2006.

64   *Iranian engineers had arrived*: Bob sent several reports about possible Iranian

involvement in uranium mining in Venezuela to the Illicit Finance Group, including one on December 1, 2006.

64   *"Yup! The 9th is definitely a go"*: Email from Anne to Bob, October 31, 2006. Other emails and reports indicate the meeting occurred on November 9, 2006.

64   *Bob had also prepared a memo*: Bob wrote a memorandum for the Illicit Finance Group dated November 9, 2006, titled "Summary of On-Going Projects." In it, he described several potential operations involving Iran.

66   *"I'm attaching a document"*: Email from Bob to William McCausland, an FBI agent then stationed in Budapest, October 28, 2006.

67   *Bob walked into the lobby*: Interview with Philip Scott Forbes, DEA agent.

69   *Bob described the two Iranians*: Bob's reports to the Illicit Finance Group about his meetings in Istanbul with the two Iranians are dated December 8, 2006.

71   *"This has got to be the REAL 'welcome back' message"*: Email from Bob to Anne, December 12, 2006.

71   *"Our friend, together with his wife"*: Email from Bob to FBI agent Timothy Chapman, December 9, 2006.

6. Christmas

73   *"Sorry to have inundated your front yard"*: Email and memo from Bob to Anne, December 11, 2006.

74   *"Minor problem. We're OUT"*: Email from Anne to Bob, December 13, 2006.

75   *"Wanted to make sure"*: Email from Bob to Anne, December 14, 2006.

75   *"Oh, Bobby"*: Email from Anne to Bob, December 14, 2006.

75   *"T is losing faith"*: Email from Ken Rijock to Bob, January 14, 2007.

75   *"I too am pissed off"*: Email from Bob to Ken Rijock, January 14, 2007.

75   *"Enroute to your house"*: Email and memo from Bob to Anne, December 28, 2006.

77   *"Manhunter"*: Dan Levinson told me about Tom Mangold's interest in writing a book about his father's career with that title.

77   The Litvinenko Mystery: Both the transcript of Tom Mangold's interview with Yuri Shvets and Bob and Shvets's report about Viktor Ivankov were filed as exhibits during the inquest in 2014 into Alexander Litvinenko's death. By the fall of 2015, that inquest had yet to issue a report. Andrei Lugovoi has denied any role in Litvinenko's murder.

78   *"Can you give me any guidance"*: Memo from Bob to Anne, January 2, 2007.

79   *"Brian and Tim?"*: Email from Anne to Bob, January 4, 2007.

79   *"Thanks for the update"*: Email from Bob to Anne, January 4, 2007.

79   *"Hey Toots"*: Email from Bob to Anne, January 10, 2007.

80   *"Hope they find YOU some travel money"*: Email from Bob to Anne, January 10, 2007.

80   *"Look out!"*: Email from Bob to Anne, January 13, 2007.

80   *"Planning now to fly into DC"*: Email from Bob to Anne, January 14, 2007.

81   *"You've got to stop this shit"*: Interview with Anne Jablonski.

81   *"The first package came"*: Email from Anne to Bob, January 27, 2006.

81   *"Greetings from Paris"*: Email from Bob to Anne, January 29, 2007.

82   *"We don't have much money left"*: Email from Global Witness to Bob, January 29, 2007.

83   *"I know the pressure is on"*: Email from Bob to Global Witness, January 29, 2007.

84   *"I don't know if our friend has changed his mind"*: Email from Bob to Ira, January 31, 2007.

84   *"Whatever works for you"*: Email from Ira to Bob, January 31, 2007.

7. The Black Dahlia

85   *Bob and Chris rarely fought*: Chris described how Bob told her he needed to take a "side trip" for Uncle Sam while in Dubai.

86   *"TO: Tim"*: Bob's memo addressed to Tim Sampson was sent as an attachment in an email to Anne, February 5, 2007. It was the only document in Bob's files I saw that was addressed directly to Sampson.

87   *he and Chris drove to a Best Buy*: Chris described shopping with Bob for gifts for a source.

87   *"I wish I were hitting the stores"*: Email from Ira to Bob, February 7, 2007.

88   *"Dear Mr. Levinson"*: A copy of the fake BAT letter was among the documents contained in Bob's files. When I contacted officials of the company about it, they pointed out its mistakes.

89   *"When I speak with him next"*: Email from Ira to Bob, February 13, 2007.

89   *"Leaving tomorrow for Geneva and Dubai"*: Email from Bob to Anne, February 12, 2007.

89   *"The contracts people are NOT yet looped in"*: Email from Anne to Bob, February 12, 2007.

90   *"Hey, sorry about that"*: Email from Bob to Anne, February 12, 2007.

90   *"NO problem"*: Email from Anne to Bob, February 12, 2007.

90   *D'Arcy Quinn*: Quinn declined to be interviewed for this book. His departure from Philip Morris is described in a lawsuit he filed in New York against the tobacco company. It was settled out of court.

90   *Bob's former FBI supervisor*: James Moody, who clashed with Bob and Larry Sweeney over the informant Michael Orlando, apparently harbored a long-running grudge against him. Moody made his remarks about Bob's performance in the Mikhailov case in Robert I. Friedman's book *Red Mafiya*.

91   *"Uncle Ira"*: Email from Bob to Ira, February 16, 2007.

93   *"Not easy to assess this one"*: Email from Ira to Bob, February 17, 2007.

93   *"Our guy just called"*: Email from Ira to Bob, February 17, 2007.

94   *"Thanks so much"*: Email from Bob to Ira, February 18, 2007.

95   *"Have been concentrating"*: Email from Dawud to Ira, February 18, 2007.

96   *"Hey hey!!"*: Email from Anne to Bob, February 20, 2007.

96 *"A lot of what we discussed"*: Dawud's article, "An Expat's Letter from Iran: A Super Cop, a Revolutionary Prosecutor and Dumb Diplomacy," was published on Joe Trento's website on February 9, 2007.

96 *"He's obviously a brilliant guy"*: Email from Bob to Ira, February 25, 2007.

97 *"OOH! Excellent"*: Email from Anne to Bob, March 2, 2007.

97 *"My guys are very, very close"*: Email from Bob to Anne, March 2, 2007.

97 *"You hit a home run"*: Email from Anne to Bob, March 2, 2007.

97 *"Message received"*: Email from Bob to Anne, March 2, 2007.

8. An Appointment on Kish

98 *He filled a small roll-on bag*: A U.S. official who requested anonymity described Bob's departure from his Dubai hotel.

98 *Dubai proved to be a bust*: Interview with the Global Witness official who requested anonymity.

99 *"I've been a good, quiet boy"*: Email from Bob to John Moscow, March 6, 2007.

100 *"Off today for that place"*: Email from Bob to Ira, March 8, 2007.

100 *"Bob, so good to have your words"*: Email from Ira to Bob, March 8, 2007.

100 *Upon landing, his plane taxied*: I was unable to visit Kish, so my description of it and its airport is based on information provided by a fellow journalist.

102 *"Bob, how are you doing?"*: Email from Ira to Bob, March 9, 2007.

9. The Missing Man

103 *On Saturday, March 10*: The description of the day when Bob's family and others became aware of his disappearance is based on interviews with Chris Levinson, several of her children, Dave McGee, Ira Silverman, and others.

107 *Paul Myers*: Myers, the first agent on the Levinson case, did not respond to repeated efforts to interview him for this book. His comments and the actions attributed to him are based on interviews with people to whom he spoke.

108 *the closest FBI official*: The closest FBI official near Dubai at the time of Bob's disappearance was Daniel Roggenbach, who was the bureau's attaché at the U.S. embassy in Abu Dhabi. After *The New York Times* in December 2013 ran a lengthy article I wrote about Bob's case, Roggenbach posted a comment in a law enforcement chat room taking strong exception with the article's implication that the FBI's initial investigation had lagged. Roggenbach, who has since left the FBI, refused to be interviewed for this book or respond to written questions about what actions, if any, he took.

108 *Two of the investigators went to the Dubai Marriott*: A former U.S. official who requested anonymity described how investigators broke into Bob's bag.

110 *she walked into a Langley bathroom*: Interview with Anne Jablonski.

111 *Moody called Larry Sweeney*: Interview with Larry Sweeney.

114 *When Chris told Myers*: Interview with Chris Levinson.

114 *"I'm looking at tasking memos"*: Interview with a former FBI official who spoke on the condition of anonymity.

114 *"Those sons of bitches have lied to us"*: Ibid.

10. One of Their Own

116 *"I don't think he is missing"*: "Fugitive Says He Met Missing Ex–FBI Agent in Iran," *Financial Times*, April 13, 2007.

116 Frontline *refused to air*: Interview with Neil Docherty. The *Fifth Estate* documentary about Iran aired in Canada with Dawud in it.

116–117 *"Do you know about Highway 407?"*: Interview with Linden MacIntyre.

117 *"To the best of my knowledge"*: Email from Dawud to Thomas Cauffiel, April 19, 2007.

118 *Trento considered Ira's omission intentional*: Interview with Joe Trento. Despite his antagonism toward Ira, Trento urged Dawud to lobby Iranian officials to release Bob and offered to come to Iran to get him.

118 *"Iran is dissembling"*: Joe Trento's article about Bob's reason for going to Kish was published on his website on April 20, 2007.

119 *"One acquaintance of both Levinson and Silverman"*: Michael Isikoff and Mark Hosenball, "Terror Watch: The Case of the Missing Agent," *Newsweek*, April 25, 2007; updated on April 26 to include Ira's comments.

120 *many former FBI agents*: A number of former FBI agents interviewed for this book were appalled by the bureau's lack of initiative in the early part of the Levinson investigation.

120 *Good called Paul Myers*: Interview with John Good.

121 *Myers told Ira his supervisors had denied*: Interview with Ira Silverman.

121 *The FBI would not send agents*: Interview with a former U.S. official based in Dubai who requested anonymity.

121 *"I was told this morning"*: Email from Dawud to Joe Trento, April 30, 2007.

121 *"My CIA sources"*: Email from Joe Trento to Dawud, April 30, 2007.

122 *"People can think what they like"*: Email from Dawud to Joe Trento, May 2, 2008.

11. The Merchant of Death

125 *"He did it for the oldest"*: Ira Silverman and Fredric Dannen wrote about Dave's prosecution of F. Lee Bailey in a *New Yorker* article, "A Complicated Life," March 11, 1996.

126 *Her first interview*: Chris's interview with Diane Sawyer was broadcast on *Good Morning America*, August 6, 2007.

128 *"Perhaps the one good point"*: Email from Dawud to Chris, August 29, 2007.

129 *the bureau sent Scotland Yard a copy*: Interview with officials of British American Tobacco.

129   *"Mila"*: Jamie Smith devoted a chapter of his autobiography, *Gray Work: Confessions of an American Paramilitary Spy* (William Morrow, 2015), to SCG International's work on the Levinson case. In the book, he called the female operative who visited the Maryam hotel "Mila."

129   *She spoke with the hotel's manager*: The report written by Mila about her visit to Kish and the Maryam is dated September 23, 2007.

131   *In his heyday, Soghanalian*: My description of Sarkis Soghanalian is based on several sources, including *The New York Times*, *The Washington Post*, and television documents. Lowell Bergman, a former *60 Minutes* producer and *Times* reporter, introduced me to Soghanalian. I met with him in early 2008 at his home in Miami and spoke with him on numerous occasions. He was an engaging storyteller, though I believed he was spinning tales about Bob for his own purposes.

131   *"You need that comfort"*: Soghanalian made this comment in a documentary I found on YouTube called *Merchants of War*.

131   *the "Supernote"*: Richard Gregorie described Soghanalian's role in identifying the source of the near-perfect counterfeit.

133   *"My dear wife and friends"*: Email from "Osman.Muhamad" to Chris, Ira, and other recipients, August 6, 2007.

134   *"Some input my colleagues gave me"*: Email from Jonathan Beery to Suzanne Halpin, August 31, 2007.

135   *Her father raised her*: Interview with Sarah Levinson.

136   *Myers showed Ira and Wickham*: Interview with Ira Silverman.

137   *"I wouldn't push it"*: Interview with Ira Silverman.

12. Passwords

139   *Sonya logged into it*: Interview with Sonya Dobbs.

140   *Several folders were marked* GLOBAL WITNESS: I reviewed these and other folders from Bob's files.

142   *Stephen Kappes*: His appearance before the Senate Select Committee on Intelligence was described to me by people present.

142   *It was early December*: Chris, Dan, and Suzi Halpin described their visit to Tehran and Kish and Chris and Dan's meeting with Dawud.

145   *The call was from Jonathan Winer*: Interview with Dave McGee.

145   *"a pure cockroach"*: R. Allen Stanford's campaign to try to discredit Jonathan Winer was first reported by McClatchy newspapers, November, 29, 2012. In the article, Winer called the characterization of his ex-wife's sexual preferences "patently absurd."

13. The Nuclear Option

147   *"This is an odd and painful 'anniversary'"*: Email from Dawud to Chris, March 8, 2007.

149   *But the firm never paid*: Interviews with Dave McGee and John Moscow. Both

the law firm as well as lawyers involved with the Bank of Cyprus case who no longer work for Reed Smith did not respond to emails or phone calls.

150 *she agreed to be interviewed*: Anne's comment about homemade cat food appeared in a *Wall Street Journal* article, "How Do Cats Like Rabbits? Very Much and Preferably Raw," on July 30, 2007.

151 *"You were angry with your friend"*: Interview with Anne Jablonski.

151 *"What about those hostages in Colombia"*: Ibid.

153 *One of Anne's CIA mentors*: Paul Redmond, a former CIA official who argued on Anne's behalf, declined to be interviewed for this book.

154 *Richard Clarke*: He did not respond to an email.

154 *Janine Brookner*: My description of Janine Brookner's career is based on accounts that appeared in *The New York Times*, the *Chicago Tribune*, and other publications.

155 *Sampson and Clement had told her*: I sent Timothy Sampson a list of questions containing statements made by Anne about his actions in the aftermath of Bob's disappearance. After a long period, Mark Zaif, a lawyer for Sampson, contacted me and said his client had drafted a statement in response to my inquiries and submitted it to the CIA for clearance. The CIA refused to allow its release, Zaif said. I also sent Peter Clement a list of questions containing statements that Anne had made about his actions in the aftermath of Bob's disappearance. Clement, who now teaches at Columbia University, told me he would need the CIA's permission to be interviewed. He never received it.

156 *he sent her a lengthy memo*: Memo from Bob to Anne describing possible operation to recruit Dawud as an agency source, December 12, 2005.

156 *"Attached is something I would like you to review"*: Email from Bob to Robert Seldon Lady, December 23, 2005.

157 *"I will personally push them"*: Email from Robert Seldon Lady to Bob, February 13, 2006. Lady declined to be interviewed for this book.

14. "Heloo Cheristi"

159 *the subject line "Heloo Cheristi"*: The woman describing herself as a hospital technician sent her emails to Chris in April 2008.

161 *Soghanalian told Dave*: Sarkis Soghanalian also told me that the Iranians had given Bob to Hezbollah.

162 *They were greeted affably*: My description of Fouad al-Zayat's career is based on descriptions of it in several publications, including *The Observer*, *The Times* of London, and *The Guardian*.

164 *He summoned the NBC News anchor*: Brian Williams's interview with the Iranian president Mahmoud Ahmadinejad was broadcast on July 28, 2008.

166 *Years later,* Outside *magazine*: The magazine's piece about Jamie Smith, "The Spy Who Scammed Us?," was published October 10, 2014. As of September 2015, Smith's libel lawsuit against the magazine was pending.

166 *he wrote that he had warned Dave*: Both Dave and Ira said that Jamie Smith

was not present during their interactions with the person who said he represented Hezbollah.

166 *Mila might have told the story to Smith*: Jamie Smith said through his lawyer that Mila probably told him about the hair incident at the Maryam hotel but that he didn't have a specific recollection.

15. The Hikers

169 *"If we had him, we would announce it"*: My description of the 2009 meeting between Chris and her family and Mohammad Khazaee, Iran's ambassador to the United Nations, is based on contemporaneous notes taken by Sarah Levinson.

171 *a twenty-seven-year-old computer engineering student*: U.S. embassy officials in Istanbul reported the visit by an Iranian student who claimed to see Bob's name carved in a jail cell in a cable sent to the State Department. It was among the trove of State Department records released by the group WikiLeaks.

171 *In 2009, three young Americans became the newest political pawns*: The hikers— Sarah Shourd, Joshua Fattal, and Shane Bauer—provided an account of their capture and captivity in *Outside* magazine in April 2014 and in a book, *A Sliver of Light: Three Americans Imprisoned in Iran* (Boston: Eamon Dolan Books/Houghton Mifflin Harcourt, 2014).

172 *The Iranian judge was coming*: I was told by an FBI source about the Iranian judge's brief visit to Washington. It was confirmed by another bureau official. It is not clear whether any of the judge's statements about Bob were accurate.

173 *"The mullahs have industrialized the religion"*: Dawud's comments to Jon Lee Anderson appeared in *The New Yorker*, "A Fugitive in Iran," September 30, 2009.

16. The Young Man

174 *Oleg Deripaska*: My description of Oleg Deripaska, his career, and his lobbying efforts to get a U.S. visa is based on accounts in several publications, including *Bloomberg Markets* magazine, *Newsweek*, *The Guardian*, and *The Wall Street Journal*. He did not respond to inquiries seeking to interview him for this book.

175 *One of the lawmaker's advisors, Rick Davis*: The Washington Post broke the story of Deripaska's efforts to court Senator John McCain of Arizona on January 25, 2008.

176 *Madzhit Mamoyan*: I interviewed Madzhit on several occasions for this book and he told me about his relationship with Abdullah Öcalan, the imprisoned head of the Kurdistan Workers' Party.

177 *"I know that people are sucking your blood"*: Interview with Boris Birshtein.

180 *His most high-profile case at Kroll*: Jeff Katz recounted his work examining

the circumstances of Roberto Calvi's death in an article for *The Sunday Telegraph Magazine*, "Dead Men Talking," October 26, 2003.

181 *The consultant, Xavier Houzel*: Interview with Xavier Houzel.

181 *"getting results from other irons"*: Interview with Jeff Katz.

182 *the Fars News Agency*: The government news service's attack on Ali Akbar Hashemi Rafsanjani was published in 2009.

183 *it was Anne Jablonski's husband, Robert Otto*: Several FBI officials confirmed Otto's presence at meetings about Oleg Deripaska. Neither Otto nor the State Department responded to inquiries about it.

185 *reporters at* The Wall Street Journal *got a tip*: The newspaper's front-page article about Deripaska's visits to the United States, "FBI Lets Barred Tycoon Visit U.S.," appeared on October 30, 2009.

185 *"That's just a fancy name for gruel"*: The account of Deripaska's meal and the oligarch's comment was provided by a person present.

17. Proof of Life

187 *Amir Farshad Ebrahimi*: Jeff Katz and Dan Levinson described their meeting with Ebrahimi in a memo Katz sent to Chris on May 24, 2010.

187 *"Our Nation is Proud to Be the Student"*: The general consensus of intelligence and law enforcement officials was that these documents were forgeries. However, significant effort went into producing them.

190 *Chris received a phone call*: Interview with Chris.

190–191 *"I hope this message finds you in good health"*: Email from Chris to Dawud, April 20, 2010.

191 *"Forgive this tardy reply"*: Email from Dawud to Chris, April 26, 2010.

191 *"This report is completely fictitious"*: Email from Larry Sweeney to multiple recipients, including me, April 19, 2010.

191 *Seyed Mir Hejazi, the reputed son*: An FBI official told me that he was identified by the CIA as the son of Ayatollah Khameini's intelligence chief.

192 *he told Madzhit*: Interviews with Madzhit and Boris Birshtein.

192 *Hejazi, who was thirty-nine years old*: My description of Seyed Mir Hejazi is based on his passport photograph.

192 *"Martin finally called tonight"*: Email from Larry Sweeney to Dave and Ira, February 1, 2010.

195 *The similarities weren't coincidences*: Two federal officials who spoke on the condition of anonymity acknowledged the FBI had mistakenly ignored the first email from "Osman.Muhamad."

18. Tradecraft

200 *He told Chris something she never expected to hear*: Robert Mueller, who resigned as FBI director in 2013, declined to be interviewed for this book.

200 *Sean Joyce*: Joyce, who retired from the FBI in 2013, declined to be interviewed for this book.

201 *Whenever Joyce posed a question*: Interview with a former FBI official who spoke on the condition of anonymity.

201 *They suggested President Obama*: Interview with a former State Department official who spoke on the condition of anonymity.

202 *"As we approach the fourth anniversary"*: Secretary of State Hillary Clinton issued this statement on March 3, 2011. She declined to be interviewed for this book.

205 *"HE IS 99% SURE"*: Email from Madzhit to Boris, March 18, 2011.

206 *"These fucking people"*: Boris Birshtein made this comment to me.

207 *"My name is David Levinson"*: The CDs containing Bob's hostage video and Dave's and Chris's pleas for information about him were released on December 5, 2011.

19. Breaking News

209 *Linda Fiorentino*: I spoke with Linda Fiorentino on several occasions. When I informed her that her name would appear in this book, she did not respond to subsequent messages.

211 *Prosecutors said they had found an internal CIA email*: Interview with Dave McGee.

211 *"I have thought about your disclosure"*: Email from Dave McGee to Michael Mullaney, March 20, 2013.

212 *"You mentioned a person"*: Hassan Rouhani, president of Iran, made those comments to Christiane Amanpour on CNN on September 25, 2013.

213 *a reporter for* The New York Times: I was that reporter.

213 *Matt Apuzzo and Adam Goldman*: Interviews with Matt Apuzzo and Adam Goldman. Matt Apuzzo left the AP and now works for *The New York Times*. The book they coauthored is *Enemies Within: Inside the NYPD's Secret Spying Unit and bin Laden's Final Plot Against America* (New York: Touchstone, 2013).

215 *editors at the AP contacted Chris's sister*: Interview with Suzi Halpin.

215 *he didn't need those notes*: Interview with Adam Goldman.

216 *Senator Bill Nelson was irate*: Interview with Senator Bill Nelson.

218 *"The CIA sent Bob Levinson on a mission"*: Dave's comments were made on NBC Nightly News, December 13, 2007.

218 *"There hasn't been progress"*: John Kerry made this comment or similar ones to several news outlets, including ABC News.

218 *He told* The Christian Science Monitor: Dawud's interview with the newspaper, "Iran Nabbed CIA Asset Levinson, Says Witness," appeared on December 16, 2013.

20. The Fellowship

220 *"Today, again, we call on the Iranian government"*: President Obama spoke before the National Prayer Breakfast on February 6, 2014.

221   *Haleh Esfandiari*: Her book about her captivity in Iran is *My Prison, My Home: One Woman's Story of Captivity in Iran* (New York: Ecco, 2009).

222   *Terri Schiavo*: My description of that high-profile case and Robert Destro's role is drawn from accounts in several publications.

222   *Seyed Mehdi Miraboutalebi*: He was Iran's ambassador in France from 2008 to 2012.

222   *"As a believer and a follower of Jesus"*: This extract from Douglas Coe's letter to Ayatollah Khamenei is contained in a memo Robert Destro sent to the FBI agent Dean Harp on October 28, 2011. The memo is titled "Background Information on Putative 'Religious Channel' to the Office of Iran's Supreme Leader, and Robert Levinson" and lays out the Fellowship's involvement in the case.

223   *"I called Doug Coe"*: Ibid.

224   *Eshel told the Iranian official*: Madzhit Mamoyan and Ory Eshel met with Ambassador Miraboutalebi on October 30, 2011. Eshel subsequently sent an extensive memo about the meeting to Robert Destro.

225   *"The Ambassador added"*: The conditions for Bob's release put forward by Ambassador Miraboutalebi were outlined in a memo sent by Ory Eshel to Robert Destro following the meeting on October 30, 2011. Destro subsequently sent a memo containing that information to the FBI agents Dean Harp and Don Voiret on October 31, 2011.

227   *But Destro never heard another word about them*: Interview with Robert Destro.

21. The Twilight War

230   *Shahrazad Mir Gholikhan*: The circumstances of her release were described by a former State Department official who spoke on the condition of anonymity.

230   *a former Iranian diplomat living in London*: The name of that former Iranian diplomat was Nosratollah Tajik.

235   *Ira didn't hear from him again*: Interview with Ira Silverman.

237   *"I thought that after nine years"*: Chris's comments were made to ABC News and the Associated Press, January 18, 2016.

237   *"We have no idea"*: John Kerry's comment was reported by the Associated Press on January 19, 2016.

Acknowledgments

Every journalist hopes to find a rich, engaging story. No one expects seven years will pass before it sees the light of day. At times, I thought this book would never be written. Having made it this far, I thought readers might like to know how it came to be.

The story traces back to the fall of 2007, when I happened across a *Financial Times* article about the disappearance of a former FBI agent on Kish Island while investigating a case involving counterfeit cigarettes. I was interested in the account and the involvement of a fugitive, American-born assassin—Dawud Salahuddin. The story became more intriguing when private investigators involved with counterfeit cigarettes cases told me they never would have gone to Iran and were at a loss to understand why the former agent, Bob Levinson—a big white guy with a Jewish name—would take such a risk.

Before long, things took a turn toward the strange. I met Ira Silverman and Dave McGee at a New York hotel and both men insisted that Bob had gone to Kish on a mission for the CIA. They were dismayed by the FBI's lack of interest in the case and showed me Bob's CIA consulting contract. They hoped attention to his story from a publication such as *The New York Times* might force the FBI and CIA into action. It was impossible, I told them, to know what was going on without seeing Bob's records. I flew to Florida and had lunch with Chris Levinson. She agreed to allow me to review her husband's work files and emails. At Dave's offices in Pensacola, a journalistic fantasy awaited—about ten file boxes were piled high on a conference room table. The CIA-related documents and many of the emails cited in this book were a part of that trove.

I spent months reconstructing the path that Bob took to Kish, and by mid-2008, the *Times* could have published an account about his CIA relationship and ill-fated Kish trip. But Dave, as a condition to giving me access to the material, had insisted on one ground rule to which I had readily agreed—I could use the information as the basis for reporting, but I wouldn't write anything that jeopardized Bob's safety. Over the years that followed, there were times when I was certain that Bob was dead. On one weekend in 2010, I told my wife I was convinced he was no longer alive—absolutely nothing had been heard from him since 2007—and that I planned to go into the office on Monday and argue we should publish our story. That same evening, I was forwarded the email containing the hostage video in which he made his plea for help. Among other things I learned while working on this story is that the assumptions we make as journalists are sometimes wrong.

The *Times* published my account of Bob's story after the Associated Press released its story in late 2013. Critics contended that the newspaper had bowed to requests from the U.S. government to conceal what it knew about Bob's case. There is no truth to that. The simple fact is that we didn't want to do anything to jeopardize Bob or complicate efforts to free him. Perhaps that was naïve. But it was a decision that my editors at the *Times* and I never regretted or second-guessed. That said, when the AP published its article I felt a sense of relief; keeping a secret for seven years was a burden.

This book was made possible because of the help and participation of a large number of people. I especially want to thank Christine Levinson, Dave McGee, Ira Silverman, and members of the Levinson family, including Stephanie, Sarah, Samantha, Daniel, and David, for putting their trust in me. They may find parts of this book difficult to read, but my goal was to provide a clear understanding of why Bob Levinson would risk going to Kish and the events that transpired afterward.

Sonya Dobbs deserves a special shout-out for helping me with documents and sending me Sarah Palin's autobiography—which I never read. I want to thank Robert Amsterdam, Matt Apuzzo, Boris Birshtein, Houshang Bouzari, Kathleen Carroll, Robert Destro, Neil Docherty, Linda Fiorentino, Philip Scott Forbes, Adam Goldman, John Good, James Grady, Richard Gregorie, Suzi Halpin, Margaret Henoch, Xavier Houzel, Chris Isham, Michael Isikoff, Ron Jordison, Jeff Katz, Mark Lowenthal, Linden MacIntyre, Madzhit Mamoyan, Joyce McGee, James McJunkin, Jim Mintz, John Moscow, Senator Bill Nelson, Kenneth Rijock, Brian Ross, Philippe Séchaud, Betsy Silverman, Peter Smolyanski, Larry Sweeney, and Joe Trento.

Some U.S. officials who once worked or are still working for the FBI or other parts of the government provided information to me but requested anonymity in doing so. They know who they are.

I can't say enough about my colleagues at the *Times*, who allowed my reporting on the Levinson case to go on for so long. Matt Purdy and Paul Fishleder deserve special thanks. Several *Times* reporters, past and present, including David Johnson, Mark Mazzetti, Eric Schmidt, Mike Schmidt, Scott Shane, and Willie Rashbaum, provided valuable advice. Three executive editors at the *Times*—Bill Keller, Jill Abramson, and Dean Baquet—knew about this project and were supportive of it. Nazila Fathi, a former *Times* reporter in Iran who was forced to flee her homeland, sent me notes from her visit to Kish Island. David McCraw, as he has always done, provided sound advice. Dean Murphy kindly allowed me to take a leave of absence to work on this book.

A very special tip of the hat goes to my desk mates and friends, particularly Jad Mouawad and Andy Martin, who managed to maintain their senses of humor (and mine) despite hearing hours of strange conversations emanating from my direction. Other friends both inside and outside the *Times*, including Michael Moss, Richard Einhorn, and Amy Singer, knew about Bob's story for years and urged me to keep the faith. Peter Eavis, Sam Grobart, and Nathaniel Popper lent their support. Henry Griggs, Susan Bernfield, Claude Millman, Linda Gottesfeld, Phil Parker, Alice Blank, David Udell, Eric Abouf, Morgan Brill, and Cheryl Whaley were among those who kept my family fed and entertained. Catha and Viggo Rambusch, our summer neighbors, have been a constant source of delight, flowers, and inspiration.

My sincerest thanks go to Andrew Wylie, my agent, and Eric Chinski of Farrar, Straus and Giroux, who decided to take a chance on publishing a book despite knowing beforehand that its ending, at least in a traditional sense, might never be known. Eric did precisely what a writer hopes an editor will do, make his work better, a job he managed to do with grace and humor. I am also grateful to everyone else at FSG who helped turn a manuscript into a book, especially Laird Gallagher. Lisa Silverman smoothed rough spots and straightened out miscues. Elizabeth McNamara scoured the results.

Writing this book would have been impossible without the love and understanding of my wife, Ellen, and our daughter, Lily. When Lily was about twelve, I told her about Bob Levinson's story, explaining that she shouldn't say anything about it to anyone. I now realize that was way too much to ask, but Lily kept Bob's secret vouchsafed. I take great joy in her compassionate nature. As for Ellen, what can I say? Her endurance, her fortitude, her understanding, far outstrip my capacities in all these arenas. So do her capabilities as a writer and journalist. She was the guiding force behind this book and applied her talents as an editor to its structure and flow. Every husband and every author should be so lucky.

New York, 2015

Index

A Note About the Author

Barry Meier, a reporter for *The New York Times*, has been a finalist for the Pulitzer Prize and is a two-time winner of the George Polk Award. He is the author of *Pain Killer: A "Wonder" Drug's Trail of Addiction and Death* and *A World of Hurt: Fixing Pain Medicine's Biggest Mistake.*